The First Birmingham Battalion in the Great War

1914-1919

Being a history of the 14th (Service) Battalion of the Royal Warwickshire Regiment

BY

J. E. B. FAIRCLOUGH

with Forewords by
GENERAL SIR R. B. STEPHENS, K.C.B., C.M.G.
and
COLONEL G. WHITE LEWIS

The Naval & Military Press Ltd

Published by

The Naval & Military Press Ltd
Unit 5 Riverside, Brambleside
Bellbrook Industrial Estate
Uckfield, East Sussex
TN22 1QQ England

Tel: +44 (0)1825 749494

www.naval-military-press.com
www.nmarchive.com

In reprinting in facsimile from the original, any imperfections are inevitably reproduced and the quality may fall short of modern type and cartographic standards.

LIEUT.-COLONEL L. MURRAY, D.S.O.

THE FIRST
BIRMINGHAM BATTALION
IN THE GREAT WAR

DEDICATION.

THIS BOOK IS DEDICATED IN GRATEFUL MEMORY TO ALL MEN WHO SERVED WITH THE FIRST BIRMINGHAM BATTALION, TO THOSE WHO MADE THE GREATER SACRIFICE, AND TO THOSE WHO CAME HOME.

> "We have given all things that were ours,
> So that our weeds might yet be flowers:
> We have covered half the earth with gore
> That our houses might be homes once more:
> The sword thou hast demanded, Lord:
> And, now, behold the sword!"
>
> Geoffrey Howard.

CONTENTS

CHAP.		PAGE
	FOREWORD	viii
	PREFACE	xi
	CHRONOLOGICAL TABLE	xiv
I.	ENLISTMENT AND FORMATION, 1914	1
II.	TRAINING AT SUTTON COLDFIELD, 1914–15	8
III.	WENSLEYDALE AND CODFORD, 1915	21
IV.	THE BRAY FRONT, 1915–16	31
V.	ARRAS, 1916	45
VI.	THE SOMME, 1916	55
VII.	BETHUNE AND FESTUBERT, 1916–17	77
VIII.	VIMY RIDGE AND ARRAS, 1917	89
IX.	YPRES, 1917	109
X.	ITALY, 1917–18	127
XI.	FORÊT DE NIEPPE, 1918	143
XII.	THE FINAL ADVANCE, 1918	160
	FINALE	181
	DISTINCTIONS CONFERRED	188
	ROLL OF HONOUR AND CASUALTIES	191

LIST OF MAPS

SOMME, 1915–16	page 32
ARRAS, 1916	,, 44
SOMME, 1916	,, 56
FALFEMONT AND MORVAL, 1916	,, 66
LE BASSÉE FRONT, 1916–17	,, 78
VIMY FRONT, 1917	,, 88
YPRES, 1917	,, 110
BOIS DE NIEPPE, 1918	,, 144

LIST OF ILLUSTRATIONS

LIEUTENANT-COLONEL L. MURRAY, D.S.O.	Frontispiece
COLONEL G. WHITE LEWIS AND SIR WILLIAM H. BOWATER (HON. COL.)	facing page 2
THE FIRST CHURCH PARADE	,, ,, 4
THE MARCH THROUGH BIRMINGHAM, MARCH 13TH, 1915	,, ,, 20
A TYPICAL TRENCH SCENE	,, ,, 36
VAUX-SUR-SOMME	,, ,, 52
CARNOY	,, ,, 68
LEUZE WOOD	,, ,, 84
THE BATTALION ADVANCING ON MORVAL, SEPTEMBER 25TH, 1916	,, ,, 100
GORRE CHÂTEAU	,, ,, 116
POLDERHOEK CHÂTEAU	,, ,, 148
TRENCHES ON VIMY RIDGE TO-DAY	,, ,, 164

FOREWORD
by
GENERAL R. B. STEPHENS.

IT gives me the greatest pleasure to write an introduction to the history of the 14th Battalion Royal Warwickshire Regiment in the Great War. It is the least I can do to show my gratitude to them for the magnificent work they did in the Fifth Division. I think the great interest of the book lies in the fact that the 14th Warwicks were a battalion of a New Army Brigade which was incorporated into one of the old Regular Divisions. This, for a newly-formed unit, was a high trial. The Infantry of the Fifth Division consisted almost entirely of English County Regiments. These, to my mind, are the best infantry in the world, and not enough credit has been given to them. They may not be as spectacular as some, but they are absolutely reliable. You may be certain that whatever orders are given to them and however impossible the conditions are, those orders will be carried out if there is anyone left alive to do so! Also you cannot destroy their spirit; time and again the battalions of the Fifth Division were practically wiped out, but the spirit lived and in a few weeks with reinforcements, which were often their own returning wounded, they were ready to fight again. This was the standard set to the new army battalions who joined the Fifth Division. This history shows how the 14th Warwicks attained it. In the Battle of the Somme, and in the third Battle of Ypres, they had more than their share of the fighting, and suffered accordingly. Yet we find them in the successful operations in the Forest of Nieppe and in the final advance in 1918, in the forefront of the attack. The regular battalions knew this and treated them as one of themselves. The more honour to the men — civilian citizens of Birmingham — who raised, trained, and fought in this splendid battalion.

R. B. STEPHENS,
General.

31*st August*, 1933.

FOREWORD
by
COLONEL G. W. LEWIS.

THIS book will receive a hearty welcome from all who have served in the 1st Birmingham Battalion. The need of a permanent record of the deeds of the Battalion in the Great War has been felt for some time, and our thanks are due to the author for the time and trouble he has given to the work. He has obtained his information from many sources, official and otherwise, and, aided by the kindness of those who so generously placed their diaries and private papers at his disposal, he has given us an almost complete picture of the many phases of the Battalion's life.

In this book we read of the formation of the Battalion; its training; the positions it held in the front line; the rest camps, with the amusements and comforts provided in them; and the various attacks on the German lines, in which the Battalion took so prominent a part and suffered such terrible losses. It records the honours and distinctions won, and the places and actions for which they were conferred.

The Battalion is fortunate in having for its historian one who served in it from its formation till October, 1917, and who, thus, is able from personal recollection to recall at first hand the feelings and thoughts of the men. It was, in many respects, a remarkable battalion; remarkable for the high physical standard of the men and for the spirit of loyalty, patriotism, and civic pride which animated them. Birmingham gave of the best of her sons, and they, on their part, were determined to maintain and augment the fame of their native city.

The losses sustained by the Battalion were very severe, and of that fine body of gallant young men who assembled in the Park, Sutton Coldfield, in October, 1914, few returned at the end of the war. The loss of many valuable lives is to be deplored. Their bodies lie in foreign soil; but they are not forgotten; they still live in the thoughts and hearts of their comrades, and their heroic deeds, their courage in the midst of terrible dangers, and their cheerful endurance of almost unbearable hardships will ever be remembered with pride by their fellow citizens, and will serve as an example and incentive to future generations.

For myself, I feel proud to have commanded so distinguished a battalion, and thus been enabled to associate my name with it.

G. W. LEWIS,
Colonel.

PREFACE.

The History of the Great War has been written from so many different angles that another book to swell the stream may seem superfluous. As time slips by and the fateful years 1914-1918 gradually recede into the mists of history, it is a matter for regret that so many fine friendships and so many memories of common hardships should become merely ancient stories inaccurately remembered.

Every battalion has its own particular character, and that of the 1st Birmingham Battalion was tinged with local associations to an unusual extent. The men were all recruited from one city. Companies were formed of men who had been together at the same school, or of men who followed the same vocation; and although the experience of the 1st City Battalion overseas was similar to that of many another infantry regiment, yet what might be called the Birmingham spirit was never lost. After every expensive attack — and the Battalion had its full share of these — there were always sufficient of the originals left to keep alive the traditions engendered in the old days at Sutton.

Fourteen years have passed since the battalion ceased to exist as a unit of His Majesty's Army, but the spirit remains to-day to be revivified each year at the annual re-union, to the continued success of which we owe so much to Captain David Neal. Over a thousand individuals were assembled together in September, 1914, to constitute the Battalion, and these units were welded together to make as fine a body of men as could be found in the whole length and breadth of the British Isles. The fortunes of war were soon to break up this happy combination, but the memories of days spent with sterling comrades will remain with the survivors as long as life shall last.

War is a futile thing, but in its hideousness it brought out the best in men, courage in adversity, unselfishness, and a magnificent comradeship which has, unfortunately, been allowed to lapse with the War years. Could we but see more of that comradeship in these times the sacrifices made and sufferings endured would not have been made in vain.

The compiling of this history has been a work of very great interest and pleasure. Worthier hands would have achieved a work of literary merit, and one more readable. I have no claims to literary ability, but what is written is written with a fervent desire that the activities and achievements of a fine battalion shall not go unrecorded.

The reader may find that many incidents well worthy of inclusion have been omitted. For this I must claim indulgence in that these incidents have not been brought to my notice. It is the aim of this book to recall generally the main features of the Battalion's history and the reader is invited to fill in any blanks for himself. That this book may recall fully the incidents of the past and serve as a fitting memorial to the 1st Birmingham Battalion is my earnest hope.

I have been exceptionally fortunate in the assistance I have received in gathering material for the history. Many people have allowed me access to private papers from which I have been able to take extracts, and to them I record my grateful thanks. Major R. H. Baily and Mr. E. A. Stocks have allowed me to go through their extensive diaries, written on the spot, and I have found these of the greatest help in amplifying the somewhat matter-of-fact official War diaries. I wish to express my thanks to the Director of the Historical Section (Military Branch) Committee of Imperial Defence for permission to inspect the official War diaries, and to the staff of the Depôt at Warwick for the valuable assistance they have given me in going through these documents. To Major D. S. Inman, the surviving part-author of the *History of the Fifth Division*, which I have found of great help in compiling this history, I am indebted for permission to reproduce certain maps. For permission to reproduce photographs, I am indebted to the authorities of the Imperial War Museum, to Captain H. A. Taylor, and to Messrs. Stanley Paul & Co. (1928) Ltd., the author and publishers of *Goodbye to the Battlefields*.

Mr. H. E. Wasser has been good enough to prepare the maps for publication, and for this I am very grateful. To Mr. H. F. Knight I am indebted for much help in gathering material, which has saved a great deal of time in searching official documents. As my personal recollections of the

Battalion ceased in October, 1917, the history from that date is written largely from notes supplied by him. The old members who remained with the Battalion always had a very great friend in " Tiny," who always looked after their interests. He was a keen rugger man, and as secretary of the Battalion team overseas, he was, in a very great measure, responsible for its success. I pay my tribute here and express to him my deepest thanks for his collaboration, interest, and help in writing this book.

My thanks are also due to two other original members of the Battalion; to Mr. F. J. Patrick for help in going through the proofs, and to Mr. Geoffrey Dams for his invaluable help and interest in producing the book.

Finally, I owe a big debt of gratitude to another original member of the 1st Birmingham Battalion, Mr. T. C. Kemp, the author of *Supremacy*, who has been good enough to go through the written matter and round off the ugly corners. His help and advice have been of the greatest possible assistance, and to him I offer my heartfelt thanks. He has spent much time in going through the writings, and the book has benefited enormously by his experience.

General Sir R. B. Stephens, K.C.B., C.M.G., and Colonel G. White Lewis delighted the author's heart when they consented to write the forewords to this history, and the reader will agree that these add greatly to the value of the book.

With such willing help, any author should be more than content, and if the reading of this book gives as much pleasure as it has given me to write it, then I shall be amply repaid for my labours.

J. E. B. FAIRCLOUGH.

CHRONOLOGICAL TABLE OF EVENTS OF THE 14TH ROYAL WARWICKSHIRE REGIMENT.

1914.
Sept. 7.   Commencement of enlisting.
,, 19.   Parade at Thorp Street to receive button-hole badges.
Oct. 4.   Church Parade at St. Martin's Church, Birmingham.
,, 5.   Battalion goes into billets at Sutton Coldfield.

1915.
Mar. 13.   Inspection of battalion at Calthorpe Park, and march through the City.
,, 19.   "B" Company goes to Coleshill and "D" Company to Henley-in-Arden for company training.
,, 20.   "A," "C," and "E" Companies inspected by Earl Kitchener at Lichfield.
April 9.   "C" Company goes to Coleshill and "A" Company to Henley-in-Arden for training.
,, 13.   Battalion moves into huts.
June 25.   Battalion leaves Sutton Coldfield to go under canvas near Leyburn in Wensleydale.
July 28.   Battalion leaves Wensleydale for musketry at Hornsea.
Aug. 5.   Battalion leaves Hornsea for Salisbury Plain.
Oct. 6.   Colonel G. White Lewis leaves battalion.
,, 14.   Rifles arrive.
,, 18.   Musketry course commences.
Nov. 12.   Lieut.-Colonel L. Murray assumes command of battalion.
,, 21.   Battalion leaves Codford for France.
,, 23.   The Longpré march.
Dec. 3.   "A" and "B" Companies go into front line at Carnoy.
,, 8.   "C," "D," and H.Q. Companies go into front line at Carnoy.
,, 15.   Battalion takes over a sector of the front line.
,, 25.   Christmas Day spent in huts at Froissy.

1916.
Jan. 8.   5th Division leaves Carnoy Front.
,, 9.   Battalion arrives at Vaux-sur-Somme.   Measles.
Mar. 10.   Battalion leaves Vaux to join the 5th Division at Arras.
Mar. 15 to June 21.   Arras Front.
June 26.   Battalion takes over line at Wailly.
July 3.   Battalion moves back to Magnicourt. 5th Division as G.H.Q. reserve.

1916.
July 13 to July 15. — March down to Somme area.
,, 19. — Battalion takes over line near High Wood.
July 22/23. (night) — Attack near High Wood.
July 30. — Attack on Longueval.
Aug. 4 to Aug. 24. — Battalion at rest at Etrejust.
Sept. 3. — Attack on Falfemont Farm.
Sept. 10 to Sept. 14. — Leuze Wood.
,, 16. — In rest at Mericourt.
,, 18. — Waterlot Farm in support.
,, 25. — Attack on Morval.
,, 28. — 5th Division leaves the Somme area.
Oct. 1. — Move to Bethune.
Oct. 5 to Dec. 29. — Givenchy and Festubert Front.

1917.
Jan. 1. — Battalion at rest in Tobacco Factory, Bethune.
Jan. 14 to Mar. 15. — Festubert Front.
,, 17. — Rest and training at Marles-les-Mines.
April 2. — Move to Bois d'Ohlain and join Canadian Corps.
,, 9. — Battle of Vimy Ridge.
,, 14. — Bivouacs near Carency.
,, 20. — In support at Angres.
,, 23. — Battalion in front line at Lievin.
,, 24. — In rest at Guoy Servins.
May 2. — Move to Roclincourt.
May 3 to May 25. — Oppy and Arleux Front.
May 25. — Rest at Camblain Chatelain.
June 1. — Move back to Roclincourt under canvas and supply fatigue parties for the 13th Corps.
June 13 to Sept. 4. — Arleux and Oppy Front.
Sept. 5. — March to Magnicourt for rest and training.
,, 10. — Move to Le Souich.
,, 25. — Move to Wizernes near St. Omer.
,, 26. — Battalion as part of 13th Brigade go under canvas at Vlamertinghe.

1917.
Oct. 4. First attack on Polderhoek Château.
Oct. 8. Second attack on Polderhoek Château.
,, 26. Third attack on Polderhoek Château.
Nov. 5. Battalion in support for last attack on Polderhoek Château.
,, 11. 5th Division leaves the Ypres Front.
,, 15. At rest near St. Omer.
,, 29. Entrain at St. Pol for Italy.
Dec. 6. Arrival in Italy.
,, 19. Battalion goes into billets at St. Giorgio di Brenta.

1918.
Jan. 25. Front line on Piave River taken over by battalion.
April 1. Entrain for return journey to France.
,, 6. Billets near Doullens.
,, 12. Position taken up at Forêt de Nieppe.
April 13 to April 14. } German attacks beaten off.
April 15 to Aug. 1. } Nieppe Front.
,, 4. 5th Division relieved.
Aug. 21 to Aug. 31. } Battle of Bapaume.
Sept. 18. First attack at Gouzeaucourt.
Sept. 27 to Sept. 28. } Second attacks at Gouzeaucourt.
Oct. 5. Battalion become divisional pioneers.
Nov. 11. Armistice signed.
Dec. 9. March into Belgium begun.
,, 18. Arrival at Meux.

1919.
Jan. 4. Move to Eghezee.
Feb. 4. The Battalion's first colour — the King's Silk Union — presented at Leuze.
April 17. Battalion cadre embark at Antwerp for England.

Buttonhole Badge.

CHAPTER I.

ENLISTMENT AND FORMATION.

On Monday, 5th October, 1914, two special trains containing the full strength of the 1st Birmingham Battalion of the Royal Warwickshire Regiment left New Street Station for Sutton Coldfield, the first stage in the training of the battalion for active service. During the month of September much preparatory work had to be done before this entraining could take place, and Birmingham had taken steps to prove that it lived up to its motto "Forward," by providing its own battalions to take their place in the ranks of "Kitchener's Army," then in process of formation.

Towards the end of August, 1914, an idea had been mooted that special battalions, known as "pals" battalions, should be recruited from non-manual workers. This idea had been put forward simultaneously in Liverpool and Manchester, and the scheme was introduced to Birmingham on 28th August by a leading article in the *Birmingham Daily Post*. The following morning a telegram was sent from the Lord Mayor's parlour to the Secretary of State for War as follows:—

"Lord Kitchener of Khartoum, War Office, Whitehall, London. In the absence of the Lord Mayor, who is on military duty, I offer on behalf of the City of Birmingham to raise and equip a battalion of young business men for service in His Majesty's Army to be called the Birmingham

The First Birmingham Battalion in the Great War

Battalion. This is in addition to the ordinary recruits who have been enlisted in this city to the number of 8,000. W. H. Bowater, Deputy Mayor."

The following reply was received on 30th August, 1914:

"Deputy Mayor, Birmingham. The battalion you offer would be most acceptable and a valuable addition to His Majesty's forces. I presume you mean a regular battalion on the usual terms of service. If so, it might form a battalion of the Royal Warwickshire Regiment, to be designated the Birmingham Battalion, with a number. Kitchener."

The *Birmingham Daily Post* followed up their article of 28th August by opening a register at their office where volunteers could give in their names. A ready response to this gesture was soon forthcoming : it was just the thing wanted. The prospect of joining the army and serving with one's friends held out many advantages, and the list of names soon reached large figures. These names were published daily in this paper, and by Monday, 31st August, 1,293 names had been registered ; while in eight days the numbers reached 4,500, allowing for three City Battalions to be formed. Every effort was made by the authorities to allow friends to serve together, and lists were compiled of members of old boy and kindred associations to assist the officials sending out the calling-up notices. In most cases the men received two days' notice to attend at the special recruiting office which had been opened in the Art Gallery extension in Great Charles Street, where Colonel Sir John Barnsley was in command, and Major Hall Edwards in charge of the medical examinations.

The actual recruiting work commenced on 7th September and the first battalion was completed in a week ; the list of the men accepted being published in the *Birmingham Daily Post* on 14th September. The Art Gallery extension was a hive of industry, the recruiting clerks were members of corporation departments who had first been sworn in themselves, and the rooms were full of men in various stages of undress, undergoing the somewhat severe medical

Colonel G. W. Lewis and
Sir Wm. H. Bowater (Hon. Colonel).

Enlistment and Formation

examination. The physical standard set for the battalion was a very high one, but so keen were volunteers to join the battalion that many dodges were resorted to, to overcome the medical examination. Great anxiety was felt by individuals as to whether they would pass the physical tests, and in one or two cases little whispers outside the door during the eyesight test enabled the volunteers to pass the examination, and it was not discovered till four years afterwards that two brothers had given their ages with only one month between the dates of their births. It was stated at the time by the examining medical officer that men rejected as not being up to the City Battalion physical standard would be accepted for other units of Kitchener's Army.

When the recruits had passed the medical examination, they were sworn in and then received their first day's pay of 1/9 as soldiers. Subsistence allowance at the rate of 3/6 per day was paid at a later date for the period of waiting before the battalion went into billets. During this time men returned to carry on with their ordinary civilian work, and waited impatiently for the notices which would inform them of the date when they would commence training.

The original idea being that the City Battalions were to be equipped by the citizens at their own expense, thousands of pounds were immediately subscribed in response to a joint appeal by the Deputy Mayor and the *Birmingham Daily Post*. However, the War Office allotted to the battalions the normal allowance for equipment, so that the citizens' contributions were used to provide better clothing, and extra articles not included in the official kit and accoutrements. In consequence, the battalions were much more fortunate than the bulk of Kitchener's Army. The better quality clothing was a vast improvement on the ordinary blue serge issued, and the blue service caps with the red band were distinctly superior to the " Gorblimey " worn by the rest of the New Armies. These service caps created quite a sensation in some parts of the country : there was nothing like them in the whole of the New Armies, and they must have appeared very strange to the newly enlisted soldiers of other units who looked on them as representing something very special in the military line. Many cases were reported of City Battalion men receiving salutes and, in some cases, even guards turned out when the red banded cap was sighted. The huts at Sutton, erected with the aid of this fund, were almost luxurious : they were furnished with real beds, in marked contrast to those in the huts to be encountered later at Codford, which consisted of boards and straw palliasses.

The raiser of the City Battalions was directly responsible to the Army Council for housing and equipping them until they were taken over by the War Office in June, 1915, but in the administration of the Equipment Fund he was advised and assisted by the following committee of subscribers :—Mr. F. Dudley Docker C.B., Colonel C. J. Hart C.B., Alderman Neville Chamberlain, Captain Kenneth Davis, Mr. Charles Hyde, Mr. A. J. Keen, and Alderman Sir Hallewell Rogers J.P., while Captain R. S. Hilton acted as Honorary Secretary with Mr. A. Holland as Assistant Secretary. In addition, the officers commanding the City Battalions assisted in an advisory capacity. Many rumours concerning the destination of the battalion were afloat, forerunners of many such in the years to come, and interest was maintained by sundry news paragraphs appearing in the press from time to time. Sutton Coldfield, Castle Bromwich, Rhyl and Weston-super-Mare were mentioned as likely training centres, and articles were published in the *Birmingham Daily Post* on the probable lines of training for the battalions. Parties would meet to discuss these very important matters, for the whole future of the war seemed to depend on how soon the battalions could go into training. The great fear in everybody's mind seemed to be that the war would be over before we could take our share in the conflict.

The first parade for the City Battalions was at the Drill Hall, Thorp Street, on Saturday afternoon, 19th September, when buttonhole badges were issued to all members. The floor of the Drill Hall was filled with the members of the First and Second City Battalions, full of enthusiasm, and feeling that a further step nearer the commencement of

The First Church Parade, October 4th, 1914.

Enlistment and Formation

training days had been reached. It was a very eager crowd and opportunity was taken to look round and see what our future comrades would be like. The Lord Mayor (Sir William Bowater), who was later appointed Honorary Colonel of the 1st Birmingham Battalion, in the course of a lively speech, described the battalions as "the pets of the city," and he warned them that as Birmingham Battalions they had a big reputation to live up to, and that their doings would be watched very carefully. He emphasized the need for patience in view of the tremendous amount of work required to equip the huge citizen armies in course of formation. Colonel Sir John Barnsley, who had been appointed temporary commander of the 1st battalion, spoke on the future training of the battalions. He emphasized that they were regular troops, and that he was sure that his confidence in putting them into billets would be justified by their behaviour. He also informed the recruits that special pay, at the rate of 3/- per day, would be paid from 12th September until the day they went into training quarters. At the close of the parade, the buttonhole badges were distributed by the Lord Mayor and Lady Mayoress.

During the period of waiting, Mr. Reay-Nadin was busy arranging billets for the Battalion at Sutton Coldfield; this work, which allowed for friends to be billeted together, was carried out in a very efficient manner. On Sunday, 4th October, the battalion paraded at the Drill Hall, Thorp Street, for its first Church Parade. The recruits assembled in the companies to which they had been posted, and platoons were made up. Before moving off, they were put through a short drill in making turns and forming fours by the instructors attached to the platoons. This drill finished, the order was given to move off, the band struck up, and in good style the battalion moved out into the streets to meet the critical eyes of the spectators who lined the route to St. Martin's Church. It was the first opportunity the citizens of Birmingham had of seeing their own first battalion on parade, and appreciative remarks were passed on the physique and bearing of the new troops. A special service, in a crowded church, was held at which the address was

The First Birmingham Battalion in the Great War

given by the Bishop of Carlisle, a former Rector of Birmingham. A souvenir order of service was presented to each man, and on this the battalion was described as the 11th battalion, but at a later date the designation was changed to the 14th battalion. At the conclusion of the service the battalion marched back to Thorp Street, there to be dismissed.

Next morning, at 8.30 a.m., the battalion entrained for Sutton Coldfield. The drive dividing New Street Station appeared to be full of men wearing the buttonhole badge and carrying suitcases. A large crowd of spectators assembled to witness the departure, but only relations were allowed on the platform. Looking round one began to realize dimly that we were saying " goodbye " to our civilian life and entering on some new existence with promise of unknown adventure. We could not look far ahead for we had very little idea of what war entailed. Most of us had only very hazy memories of the Boer War and it was very difficult to imagine what this new life would mean. But whatever the future had in store for us we were prepared to meet it, and the sooner we could see active service the better we should be pleased. The enthusiasm of the battalion was manifest. It was evident from the labels on the carriages — " Berlin via Sutton," and " Tipperary via Sutton Coldfield," that our new training quarters were not the be-all and end-all of our service. Sir John Barnsley witnessed the departure of the trains and then motored to Sutton Coldfield to meet the companies on arrival. The senior officers associated with him at the commencement of training were Major Charles Playfair (second-in-command), Captain Harding (adjutant), Major Fleming, Captains Hilton, Robinson, Cooke, and Dimmock, and many time-expired N.C.O.'s were re-enlisted as instructors.

And so, after many rumours and much impatience, the battalion had arrived at the beginning of its first stage of preparation for active service. From the very commencement of training the battalion suffered " casualties," many members being given commissions in other units, and scarcely a day went past without losses from this cause.

Enlistment and Formation

As a result, recruits had constantly to be absorbed into the battalion with consequent interference and delay in training. In those enthusiastic days the battalion chafed at anything that seemed to put back, even for an hour, the day of our departure for France.

Chapter II.

TRAINING AT SUTTON COLDFIELD.

"BATTALION, sit down!" This was the first command given to the battalion on its first appearance on the parade ground outside the battalion headquarters at the Crystal Palace, and indicated the commencement of training.

On arrival at Sutton Coldfield, members made their own way to the park, and after assembly and an address by the Commanding Officer billets were allotted in parties. Here the author would pause to pay, on behalf of the battalion, a tribute to the people of Sutton Coldfield for the very cordial welcome they gave to the battalion and for the generous hospitality accorded during the battalion's training period at Sutton. We were treated as honoured guests, and for the most part billets were homes from home. Looking back after 18 years, Sutton days stand out as Golden Letter days, and for this we have to thank the inhabitants of the Royal Borough.

After billets had been allotted and the troops had settled down, we had our first parade in the afternoon. This took the form of squad drill, under instructors, a body of old regular N.C.O.'s who helped us over many difficulties and were full of useful knowledge. We assumed that they knew everything about the conduct of the war, and, in addition

Training at Sutton Coldfield

to the usual questions about training, many anxious enquiries were made concerning the destination of the battalion and the probable date of going overseas. The first day ended with the majority of members back in the city they had left earlier in the morning. Work commenced in earnest next day at 7 a.m. with physical jerks, followed by parades in the morning and afternoon for instruction in squad drill. For the first parades the battalion assembled in companies formed in order of enlistment, but during the first week arrangements were put into force so that the full spirit of the "pals" battalion could be perpetuated, and sections of friends were formed and necessary transfers arranged. After this the battalion trained in section, platoon, and company formations. N.C.O.'s were selected, and, as there were many members who had had previous experience in the Services and O.T.C.'s, there was no dearth of necessary material. For the first few months training was carried out in civilian clothes, the only item of equipment being the buttonhole badge issued at Thorp Street, but in the third week of October, 200 long rifles were received, and these were used by companies in turn, for rifle drill. On 17th October, Colonel Sir John Barnsley handed over command of the battalion to Colonel G. White Lewis, who remained in command until very shortly before the battalion left Codford for France. One remembers seeing a gentleman in civilian clothes, wearing a trilby hat tipped well over his eyes, and carrying a cane, critically examining our work, and many were the conjectures as to his identity. One individual, bolder than the rest, approached him one day and asked him what he was doing always messing about the parade ground. To this individual's astonishment he received the reply, " I happen to be your future commanding officer."

The training was carried out in ideal conditions — a beautiful park, well wooded, giving all types of country needed for company and battalion training, which became more intense as the days passed by. We were very anxious to get through training as soon as possible. Squad drill seemed to be a necessary evil, but too much of it became burdensome. Besides, the park was large and as yet unexplored, and we wanted to spread our wings, get further afield on manœuvres and be more like real soldiers. The woods and moors constituted ideal training grounds for tactical exercises, and it was surprising how many schemes contained an attack on Rowton Cottage : its tactical value was enhanced by the fact that light refreshments could be obtained there. Rapid progress was made and it was not long before companies forsook the formation known as " column of lumps " and moved more in the manner of soldiers. The battalion in training proved a constant source of interest to spectators who came from Sutton and Birmingham to see the " pets " performing. On wet days, training was carried out in the big hall of the Crystal Palace, in the basement of which we had our first lessons in musketry on a miniature rifle range. Early morning parade was devoted to " physical jerks," and the tale runs that on one of these occasions a certain sergeant, known as " Streaky," thus addressed his squad, " When I say ' Jump ! ' jump, and don't come down till I tell you." Those uncertain mornings upon which the weather could not make up its mind to be fair or foul were a constant source of anxiety. Wet weather meant that the " No Parade " would be blown by the Orderly Bugler at the Crystal Palace : and on those doubtful mornings many a straining ear would pop up out of the bed clothes hopefully listening for the bugle notes that would mean an extra hour in bed. The safety margin which one could allow was brought to an irreducible minimum, and constituted a fine exercise in " judging the time ! "

Route marches were started early, and the country round Sutton Coldfield soon came to know the battalion band. A favourite march towards Canwell would take us down a road on the right-hand side of the Sutton-Lichfield Road, and every time the battalion passed this way the following solemn ritual was enacted. A dear old lady on hearing the band would come to her front door and wave her handkerchief to the boys, and the boys would wave their handkerchiefs as well. Consequently the rear companies would see

Training at Sutton Coldfield

down the hill in front of them hundreds and hundreds of handkerchiefs being waved, and they, in their turn, would share in the waving. Two hundred yards of handkerchiefs in rows of four, is rather an unusual sight. Our little outings provided plenty of amusement, and the vocal efforts of the battalion were distinctly good. Many songs were sung — some proper and many decidedly improper, one in particular, a parody of " Gilbert the Filbert," being a special favourite of No. 6 platoon. We had a big drummer, one " Fatty," who objected to carrying the big drum on wet or windy days, and, strangely enough, on these occasions one of the skins of the drum would burst a short way out from the parade ground, and the big drum would have to return to headquarters. This happened only a few times, for orders were received that, although the drum might burst it had to be carried for the whole of the route march. On one route march a complete section of "A" company disappeared at the first fall-out in the park through the back door of a house in Four Oaks, and they were not seen again until 7 p.m. in the evening when they reappeared at the Royal Oak. In the early days we carried very little for these marches, but when rifles arrived a few were allotted to each platoon and carried in turn. Later on when equipment was issued the amount to be carried was increased gradually until we were marching in full equipment.

Night operations provided amusing incidents, and great was the delight of No. 5 platoon on one occasion when the subaltern in command (at a later date commander of " C " Company) fell down a gravel pit near Blackroot Pool. Night concentration marches were undertaken and the woods were used for night operations. In the early days, before uniforms were issued, civilians using the park at night would be disturbed by hoarse challenges and would have some difficulty in proving their identity before they were allowed to resume their journey. Training in passing messages down a line provided many amusing incidents. A message which would commence as " Enemy seen on left Flank " would end up as something about the German fleet being sunk in Keeper's Pool. Another pleasant form of exercise was indulged in at Westwood Coppice, when troops would parade in blue overalls and "Gorblimeys," carry picks and shovels to the coppice there to dig up earth, make holes, and pretend they were digging trenches. A light lunch would be taken out, and adjournments would be made to the "Parson and Clerk" to obtain necessary liquid refreshment. The photographers found plenty of scope for their activities at Westwood Coppice, and many groups were posed for the cameramen near the excavations. An excellent business was done during our training by these photographers, who wandered all over the park taking photographs of the various platoons at work. These were sold as postcards and very many of these photographs exist to-day as souvenirs of happy training days.

Our training period at Sutton gave us plenty of hard work, but week-end leave was plentiful and Birmingham was very near. In addition to ordinary week-end leave, members were allowed to go home for the week-end on pass, but had to come back to Sutton for church parade on Sunday morning. As the result, the parade ground on Sundays was surrounded by motor cars which had brought in those attending the parade from Birmingham. Sunday nights proved a time of great anxiety for the railway station staff. The men on week-end leave invariably returned to camp in a body, on the train leaving New Street at 9.15 on Sunday evening. On arrival at Sutton everybody seemed anxious to get out of the station as soon as possible without bothering the station people. This involved continual warfare between the railway authorities and the battalion, for it proved no joke trying to stop a concerted rush by a heaving mass of soldiery who did not want to give up tickets. Some had railway tickets, some had railway tickets a month old, some had railway tickets issued by other lines, but ticket or no ticket, everyone was cheerful, and there was usually a sprinkling of those, who, in the words of Will Kings, " had looked upon the vintage when 'twas crimson." One Sunday, soon after Christmas, Jimmy ——, a well-known connoiseur of "D" Company, had dined well, and wined better. For the first part of the journey Jimmy entertained the carriage

Training at Sutton Coldfield

with song and story, but after the train left Erdington he gradually became quieter, and as Wylde Green was left behind he grew silent and pale. When the train reached Sutton, Jimmy spent a short but busy time with his head thrust out of the off-side carriage window, and, after a reasonable period, he was helped out of the carriage. Immediately on stepping on to the platform he turned about and leaped down on to the railway lines, alongside the stationary train. Falling on to his knees, he began to peer among the sleepers and hunt among the stones of the permanent way.

"What's wrong, Jim ? " someone asked, " Why are you saying your prayers there ? "

" Prayers be damned ! " snapped Jimmy, " I'm looking for my teeth ! "

During the stay of the battalion, no opportunity was lost by the good people of Sutton to provide for our entertainment and Saturday evening concerts were very popular functions. On one weeknight, a misguided individual, wishing to provide light fare for the battalion, decided to give a lecture on Russia. This was treated as a parade, much to the battalion's disgust, and there were soon signs of irritation which the R.S.M. tried to quell. The only response he received from the audience was shouts of " Sit down," and the R.S.M., too astonished to speak, sat down.

Boxing tournaments were also arranged and, in addition to contests between our own men, well-known champions boxed for our edification. A battalion display was given in the Crystal Palace, Sutton Coldfield, on 16th February, 1915, under the personal supervision of Mr. Dick Swan, which produced a number of excellent bouts. A month later, on 16th March, 1915, a Boxing Tournament was held in the Crystal Palace, Sutton Coldfield, between the 1st City Battalion and the 2nd City Battalion, again under the supervision of Mr. Dick Swan. This proved a great success. The contests were keenly fought and provoked the utmost enthusiasm.

Company smoking concerts, and pantomime nights in Birmingham proved very pleasant functions ; even a special

The First Birmingham Battalion in the Great War

battalion pantomime was staged in the Sutton Coldfield Town Hall, in which Will Kings and Phil Brown, featuring " Mary Magee," played principal parts. In fact one would imagine that the battalion was being spoilt and treated as " City pets," but " on parade, on parade." Nor were we allowed to forget this, for as time progressed longer hours and harder work were the order of the day, and very soon a twelve-hour-day was the usual programme. But we were fit !

Sport was encouraged and proved a very useful part of the training ; the battalion contained many men who had played regularly in local rugby football, with a strong contingent from the Old Edwardian teams. In fact the battalion could field a number of strong fifteens, and the company rugger matches in the park on Saturday afternoons drew big crowds and provided keen games. Fixtures were arranged with Leicester and Coventry, then, as now, names to be respected in the rugby world : the games with both these teams were keenly contested and, although the battalion was beaten on each occasion, the margins were small. Games were also played against the second and third battalions, and these were won fairly easily. H. L. Higgins was an outstanding player in the back division, and he had the honour of being selected to play for the Barbarians on 10th April v. the R.A.M.C., and on the 17th April against Wales, at Cardiff. In the latter match the Barbarians were billed as an England side, and E. H. D. Sewell comments in his book on Higgins' wonderful play in this match. Higgins appeared again for the Barbarians, on 20th November, 1915, against a South African service side. But for a serious wound, sustained at Longueval on 30th July, 1916, there is little doubt that this very promising player would have gained the highest honours in the game. Games were also played at association football, and for hockey the battalion numbered amongst its ranks one international player, Lance-Corporal E. B. Crockford ("A" Company), and several players who had represented Warwickshire. It was, however, difficult to arrange fixtures, and only two matches were played, both of which the battalion won.

Training at Sutton Coldfield

Since October, sundry articles of equipment had been issued from time to time, and we had been measured for our blue uniforms. These, together with the leather equipment, were received in December, so that, except for a few outsize members, the battalion could go home on Christmas leave in uniform. When the battalion assembled again, it was learned that in many cases the red banded service cap had received salutes and caused guards to be turned out.

The battalion had been considerably depleted by members leaving with commissions, until on 9th January, 1915, an appeal was made for 250 recruits to form a reserve " E " Company. When this company had finished recruit training, the members were drafted into the regular companies of the battalion. Volunteers were called for to undertake specialist duties; the band under Drum-Major Gould had been formed in the very early days; signallers under Colour-Sergeant Whitaker were soon observed waving flags; and machine gunners under Lieutenant Peyton were equipped for training purposes with a German machine gun, captured by the Indian Corps. To produce the effect of machine gun fire on manœuvres, a weird and awful noise was made with a large and heavy rattle.

Brigadier-General F. W. Evatt took up residence at Sutton early in the New Year as commander of a brigade containing the three Birmingham battalions and the Bristol City battalion (12th Gloucesters), and he was favourably impressed by the battalions who were engaged on advanced military work.

In the next three months the battalion was inoculated several times as a precaution against various diseases. After each inoculation two days' leave was given to recover and opportunity was taken to return home. Birmingham always knew when the battalion had been inoculated, for in town would be seen blue uniformed men displaying a red ribbon tied round the left arm.

On Saturday, 13th March, 1915, the battalion returned to Birmingham for the inspection in Calthorpe Park by General Pitcairn Campbell (G.O.C. Southern Command) of the three Birmingham battalions. The battalion marched into Birmingham via Erdington and Aston, being received enthusiastically by the crowds *en route*. On arrival at Calthorpe Park, refreshments were provided by the Lord Mayor. At 2 p.m., the General Salute announced the arrival of General Pitcairn Campbell who, for the next half hour, critically inspected the troops on parade. Following this, the battalion marched via Five Ways and Broad Street, to the saluting point in Victoria Square. The parade was favoured with fine weather. All along the route the streets were thronged with enthusiastic citizens, and at Victoria Square the battalion was played past the saluting base by the City Police Band, to the tune of the regimental march-past, " The Warwickshire Lads and Lassies." No arms were carried by the battalion, the only armed forces on parade being the boys of King Edward's High School O.T.C. The battalion put up a good show ; march discipline was excellent ; and it was evident that the six months training had converted a collection of individuals into a battalion of soldiers in which dwelt a magnificent esprit de corps. Birmingham had reason to be proud of its battalions, and the battalions knew they had Birmingham's affection by the whole-hearted enthusiasm with which they were received. The G.O.C. in Chief Southern Command expressed his pleasure with the smartness and general appearance of the battalions, and with the marching and bearing of the troops. He congratulated Brigadier-General Evatt, the commanding officers, the Lord Mayor of Birmingham, and all those concerned in the welfare of the battalions, for the work they had done in making these battalions efficient.

Shortly after this, events moved quickly, for on 19th March " B " and " D " Companies moved out from Sutton for company training. So much time had been spent in the park that every part of it had been worked over, and it was decided that a change of training ground would be beneficial. Consequently " B " Company moved to Coleshill, and " D " Company marched to Henley-in-Arden. In these two places, a very pleasant week was spent in exercises over new country and the work was thoroughly enjoyed. At Coleshill " B " Company learned that the girls of the village had been

Training at Sutton Coldfield

warned of the evils of speaking to the brutal licentious soldiery billeted in their midst: but the charm of "B" Company soon created an impression, and later on "C" Company reaped the advantage of the good pioneer work done by "B" Company.

On 20th March, Earl Kitchener inspected some New Army troops at Lichfield, and the companies remaining at Sutton ("A," "C," and "E") marched to Lichfield to take part in the inspection. It proved a very arduous day's work, as the battalion left Sutton at 9 a.m. in the morning and did not return until 9 p.m., having taken part in the parade and marched 21 miles on very meagre rations. In the battalion orders it was notified that the General Officer commanding had the pleasure to announce that Field-Marshal Earl Kitchener expressed himself as being pleased and satisfied with the serviceable appearance of the Birmingham battalions.

On 9th April, the two remaining regular companies went away for a week's company training — "C" Company to Coleshill, and "A" Company to Henley-in-Arden. "A" Company were warned that one night there would be a night alarm for operations. Each night passed with undisturbed rest until Thursday night (the last at Henley). By a process of elimination it was evident to everyone in the company that this must be the fateful night; no one went to bed, but sat up in billets and other places waiting for the "Surprise" alarm, which duly sounded: the company arose as one man and comic night operations ensued.

The huts were completed by the end of March, and on 13th April the battalion moved into them. The huts were very comfortable and situated in picturesque surroundings. They had been well built and excellent recreation rooms were provided: the baths were good, and after a route march in the warm spring weather there was a concerted rush for the shower baths. With a battalion in billets, it was not an easy matter to maintain the corporate spirit of the regiment, but this move into huts proved very beneficial, and very soon one realized that here at Sutton was a grown-up boarding school. The sections and platoons, which off parade had been separated in billets, now messed and slept together: this was all to the good in producing a more homogeneous body. Life in huts proved very pleasant: acquaintances ripened and closer contact was made with one's companions. Keen rivalry existed between companies and between the various huts. When one company was practising fire drill, their own huts were never used for the purpose. The windows of the huts of another company might not be properly closed and if the interiors suffered damage by water, well! you could not blame the company practising. The move into huts involved many changes in our daily routine. New bugle calls were heard and, at first, each call caused many arguments as to its meaning. Orderly duties and sundry fatigues added to the day's work and week-end guard mounting was an evil to be shunned when possible. Later on, at Codford, the hut orderly's job was one much sought after, for the orderly for the day remained in camp when big schemes were undertaken.

In May and June, field training was eased down somewhat and other exercises took its place. Very fine spring weather made training pleasant and on many occasions cross-country runs in the park were substituted for ordinary parades. During the first winter of the war, the Army Council took every step to encourage cross-country running, having a high opinion of its usefulness in a soldier's training.

The battalion took to the sport kindly from the beginning, and runs in which platoons and whole companies took part proved very popular. After a time, a match was arranged over a stiff course in Sutton Coldfield Park against the Second Battalion, for which a silver cup was awarded as a prize. The match took place on the 20th day of May, 1915, the battalion team being composed of picked runners from the various companies, and the Second Battalion team being chosen in a similar manner. The battalion won very easily with a score of 732 points to the Second Battalion's score of 1,112. The battalion also furnished the first seven men home. The move to Wensleydale in June, 1915, and the subsequent moves to Hornsea and Codford put an end to

Training at Sutton Coldfield

all further cross-country running, though the sport was revived for a short time in France, when the battalion went into rest billets in January, 1916, at Vaux-sur-Somme. Then, however, no competitors could be found, and the conditions were generally adverse, so that little could be achieved.

Bathing parades were made up for Keeper's Pool: these were thoroughly enjoyed, and so were the open air concerts outside the canteen. Harris, of " B " Company, with " Otto of Roses," made a reputation which lives to this day, and no battalion dinner goes by, if Harris is present, without a rendering of that classical ditty.

The battalion had a sprinkling of good cricketers among its ranks, but did not run a Battalion XI as there was appreciable difficulty in arranging adequate fixtures and obtaining the use of a suitable ground. Cricket was played to a limited extent by company teams during the early part of the summer of 1915, until the battalion moved to Wensleydale. In particular, " B " Company ran a most successful team, captained by Lieutenant Spencer. They played a number of matches on Saturday afternoons against various local Birmingham elevens, such as Harborne, West Bromwich Dartmouth, and Aston Unity, and had the satisfaction of winning every match, thanks in a large measure to the excellence of their bowling and fielding. One of the best bowling feats was that of Private Fearn, who took 7 wickets for 20 runs in the match against West Bromwich Dartmouth. Several matches were won by narrow margins: West Bromwich Dartmouth were defeated by 10 runs; Aston Unity by 4 runs; but the record of the team was preserved unbeaten to the end.

As a result of appreciable work and organization on the part of a Special Committee, a Sports Meeting was held in Sutton Coldfield Park on Friday, 4th June, 1915, shortly before the battalion moved to Wensleydale. The programme consisted of Flat Races, an Inter-Company Relay Race, a Hurdle Race, a 3 Mile Inter-Company Race, a Tug-of-War, a Bayonet Fighting Competition, a V.C. Race, and an Obstacle Race. Two runners met with conspicuous success:

The First Birmingham Battalion in the Great War

Private F. Mantel ("B" Company) won the Mile and the Half-Mile, and was first in the Three-Mile Inter-Company Race; and Private Birch ("A" Company) won the 100 Yards, 220 Yards, and Quarter-Mile. The day was a typical June day, sunny and warm throughout, and the Park looked at its best. Many civilians were present as spectators, and the prizes were distributed by the Lady Mayoress of Birmingham. The event was a good and fitting conclusion to the period of the battalion's training at Sutton Coldfield. After the move to Wensleydale, there was neither time nor opportunity for athletic meetings.

On 19th May, General Pitcairn Campbell inspected the battalion at Sutton Coldfield, and in June the battalion was taken over officially by the War Office. A reserve company had to be raised, but recruits were not up to the physical standard of the original enlistments. The first phase of our training was drawing to a close, and our pleasant stay at Sutton was terminated on 25th June, when the battalion left Sutton Park Station for Wensleydale. The battalion had a very wonderful send-off from the people of Sutton, and our Honorary Colonel came to bid us "God Speed." During our nine months' stay at Sutton, over 200 members had left the battalion with commissions, and there had been 50 transfers to technical units, so that some of the recruits of the recently formed reserve company were drafted into the battalion just prior to the move. The remaining portion of this company stayed at Sutton with the reserve companies of the other two Birmingham battalions to form the 17th (Reserve) battalion, and the Adjutant (Major Harding), known familarly as "Gold Flake," or "Yellow Peril," was left behind to command these three companies.

The March through Birmingham, March 13th, 1915.

Badge of 32nd Division.

CHAPTER III.

WENSLEYDALE.

SITUATED amidst the lovely country of Wensleydale, with its wide expanses of field and moorland, is the park of Bolton Hall. This was to be the new camp of the battalion, which arrived to find tents pitched and various divisional troops already in occupation. In a short time the whole of the 32nd Division, with the exception of the artillery, had assembled in this beautiful Yorkshire dale, and preparations were soon in progress for brigade and divisional manœuvres. We soon made the acquaintance of the men from the other battalions of the division and were able to compare notes concerning the histories of their units and incidents in training. The infantry of the 32nd Division was composed of " pals " battalions. One brigade consisted of three Glasgow City Battalions of the Highland Light Infantry, and one battalion of the Border Regiment : the other brigade was made up of Lancashire Battalions. Only the 14th and 15th Battalions wore the blue uniform : the rest of the division was already in khaki. Conditions of life were very different from our Sutton experiences, and we soon had a foretaste of a harder and more concentrated life. Sixteen men in a tent with full equipment and kitbags took some getting used to, and many were the recriminations passed at times when everyone was dashing round getting ready for parade. Men who were heavy footed and awkward proved

The First Birmingham Battalion in the Great War

a constant source of annoyance to their comrades. The surroundings were beautiful and the air was wonderfully bracing, and on the wide moors there was plenty of room for military schemes, but camp life in the early days at Wensley seemed " 'ard — cruel 'ard ! " There was only a single line of rail to bring rations and other military requirements up to the camp, so that the sudden dumping of over 12,000 men in the midst of a peaceful and quiet dale meant a very heavy strain on the railway resources. Consequently rations were very meagre, and the canteen could do little to supplement them, but this matter, including the beer supply, occupied the very early attention of Colonel Lewis, and an improvement was soon effected.

The water supply was inadequate, and for washing purposes resort was made to a running stream in a small glade near the camp. For bathing we were able to use the River Ure at Wensley, and this was a very popular parade. Very shortly after our arrival we experienced severe rain-storms and large ditches had to be dug round tents and through the camp to take away the heavy rainfall, in fact, the camp might have served as a model for a Heath Robinson trench system. During the periods of leisure, excursions were made to the many beauty spots near the camp. Bolton Castle, Aysgarth, Penn Hill, Redmire, and Leyburn ; these names bring back many happy recollections of pleasant hours spent amongst delightful people, in gorgeous country. Very often in the fine summer evenings, with the setting sun outlining the mountains of the Lake District, a magnificent panorama would be gained of the dale looking towards Aysgarth.

At first the battalion manœuvres over the moors familiarized us with the country, and then progression was made via brigade and divisional schemes. Many of these operations involved whole-day absence from camp, and sometimes individual field cookery was practised. As only the cook had to eat the results of these culinary experiments, there was no room for grumbling at the meal, but it often occurred that just when the fire had been lit and the ingredients were nearly cooked, word would arrive that the

Wensleydale

foe was attacking, and cooking would have to be suspended to carry on with the battle. The operations involved exploration over much of the surrounding country, and even on long marches compensation would be afforded by some unexpected sweep of exquisite landscape. On 10th July, the sleep of the battalion was disturbed by a fire alarm, and the camp turned out in greatcoats and little else, only to be dismissed almost at once. Next morning it was discovered that a fire in the third battalion camp had been put out before we had assembled. Some verses appeared later concerning this episode, but as the author's identity is unknown, we are unable to make the usual acknowledgements. Should these lines meet his eye, we hope he will accept our tribute!

" T'was a bugle blown at 5 a.m.
    That woke me from my nap,
I couldn't find my button stick,
    My puttees, boots, or cap.

Then, as rememb'rance came to me,
    I sought a bugler small
And asked for some enlightenment
    On last night's bugle call.

He told me that we'd been called out,
    In last night's cold and damp,
To quell a conflagration
    In the third battalion camp.

Then, as if expecting trouble,
    He dodged within his tent
And told me that the fire was out
    Before the bugle went."

On 15th July, the battalion received a night alarm at 10.30 p.m., and after parading in full equipment, proceeded to join the rest of the brigade. A steady $3\frac{1}{2}$ hours' march followed, and then night operations by the whole division

The First Birmingham Battalion in the Great War

were undertaken. In the dawn light, the battalion found itself opposed by some Lancashire Fusiliers who informed us that, with our red banded caps, we had appeared to be a mass of brigade majors. When at about 5 a.m. the manœuvres finished, the journey was begun back to camp, and this was reached just in time for breakfast. Altogether it was reckoned that in addition to the manœuvres, the battalion had covered over 22 miles. As the operations had been carried out without any undue signs of fatigue, the Divisional General reported the battalion fit for service in France. Shortly after this, the battalion changed over to khaki uniforms, and cameramen started their work of taking photographs of all sections of the battalion. The Honorary Colonel (Sir William Bowater) visited the battalion in full kit, and we realized then why we had at last received our khaki uniforms — the Lord Mayor had been fitted out and now there was some cloth left for us. This was his own favourite joke. His visit was very cheering to the battalion ; his good humour and conversations with all ranks were very encouraging.

On 28th July, after a very happy month full of incident and hard work, we left Wensley for a firing course at Hornsea. Parading at an early hour and travelling via York, we reached Hornsea about 9 a.m. to find the camp was situated on a cliff, about 2 miles south of the town, with the butts just on the edge of the cliff, overlooking the grey North Sea. After settling into camp, an early start was made with the practices of the musketry course. At this time the battalion was only armed with a certain number of the old long rifles issued at Sutton, but for this firing a number of short Lee-Enfields were used. Every available minute of the daylight was utilized for firing, but when a company was not engaged on the range — either firing or marking — sea bathing was allowed, and this was very much appreciated by all ranks. We were favoured with fine summer weather which made all the difference when waiting on the range to shoot or in the very early morning when we had to parade for the range. Hornsea town also was an attraction, and the orchestral concerts at the Floral Hall

Wensleydale

were enthusiastically supported. As we were on the East Coast, we had to be careful with lights, but our nights were not disturbed with Zeppelin alarms.

On 5th August, the battalion left Hornsea for Codford, on Salisbury Plain, and the last stage of its training. "A" and "D" Companies left in the first train and were followed later in the day by "B" and "C" Companies. The long journey via Doncaster, the north of London and the Great Western main line, occupied 12 hours, and Wylie Station was reached late at night. Going round the north side of London caused great excitement, as we encountered many business trains taking people home. We were received very kindly, and with our usual discretion, and to mislead any foreign agents, on being asked our destination we cheerfully replied "Southampton and France."

"Hope deferred maketh the heart sick." Nearly twelve months had passed since we commenced training, and it seemed that we should never see active service. At this period of our training our first flush of enthusiasm had dwindled somewhat, and, although we still looked forward to the day when we should go overseas, we had learned to take each day's work as it came along. In many quarters we were being looked upon as England's last hope. We had seen and heard of other battalions embarking for active service, and it almost appeared as though a story then in circulation might prove true in our case. The story went that sometime in the future, when the war was finished, an official of the War Office would remark, " Birmingham, ah ! now didn't they raise three City Battalions there in the last war ? What happened to them ? " " Well, sir, the battalions were at Sutton and I believe they went up to Yorkshire, but then we lost all trace of them." However, the battalion had actually obtained a footing on Salisbury Plain, but after our late pleasant surroundings, the prospect was far from pleasing. On arrival that dark night, sundry fatigues were needed before the battalion was allotted to huts, to sleep in clothes on the floor. On awakening in the morning, it was found that the outgoing battalion had left the huts and utensils in a filthy condition and much hard work was necessary to make these respectable. Sutton hut comforts were things of the past, the beds here consisting of boards and straw palliasses. Altogether the surroundings seemed very depressing, but the battalion soon settled down and made itself at home.

Manœuvres were soon resumed, and much of the training centred round a big trench system, which had been commenced a considerable time before and then carried on by successive units. These trenches, dug in the white chalk so prevalent there, were on the plain some two or three miles from the camp, and the battalion did its share of extending the trenches, and spent night and day tours in them. Big training schemes involving several divisions were participated in, and gradually the length and severity of operations were increased. Shortly after arrival at Codford five days' leave was granted to the old members of the battalion and week-end leave was resumed. A special train for members of the three battalions left Wylie Station for Birmingham every Friday afternoon, and returned from Snow Hill late on Sunday evening. The train was always very full, and many people came down to Snow Hill on Sunday evening to witness the departure of the train, which arrived at Wylie in the early hours of Monday morning. Sometimes those returning were informed that as the battalion was out on a training scheme, they would have a slack day, but more often orders were received that the leave party was to start right away and join the battalion in the trenches. After a long railway journey and march up from Wylie, this seemed to be the last straw. Those unfortunates remaining in camp during the week-end consoled themselves by visits to Salisbury, Bath, and other places near by. Salisbury was always full of troops, and on Saturday nights the theatre was packed. Codford was quite a busy little wartime village : its many wooden shacks gave it the appearance of a country fair with the usual amusement and refreshment centres, and in addition to these, a music hall, known to the battalion as the " Codford low-down," provided light and varied fare for the evenings. This theatre was one of many dotted all over the

Wensleydale

plain and the artistes travelled by car from one theatre to the next. One cannot say that the turns were of a high order, but we were not over-critical ; while occasionally a member of one of the battalions would be invited to give a show. So, although training was heavy, there were compensations.

In September, long day and night manœuvres commenced, and from that time onward, the battalion was often away from huts for long periods. In addition to the days and nights spent in the area of the trenches, open warfare schemes, involving day and night operations were practised some distance away from camp. These were carried out on an active service basis with nights spent out in open fields.

On 6th October Colonel Lewis left the battalion after being with us practically twelve months, during which time he had endeared himself to all ranks. His soldierly qualities were pre-eminent and the welfare of the men under his command was always his first thought. He was quick at discovering where essential things were wrong, but he had no time for unnecessary trivialities. In his eyes one could always perceive a merry twinkle, and during his regime, he did all in his power to ameliorate any unpleasant conditions in our heavy training. We esteemed our commanding officer very highly, and regret that he could not take us overseas was felt both by him and by us. His going was sudden and unexpected : he left us in the evening, when the battalion was having tea ; but everyone turned out to give him a rousing send-off in an attempt to show him our regret at his departure. Major Playfair assumed temporary command of the battalion, and on 11th October, we were inspected by General Sir Arthur Paget. Rifles arrived on the 14th, and in consequence week-end leave was stopped so that the new best friends could be issued and our old comrades, the gas pipe affairs, returned to stores. The usual week-end leave parties from the other two Birmingham battalions passed the camp, on the way to Wylie Station, in great glee, but much to our annoyance ; and it was poor consolation to know that we were one up in having the new rifles first. Firing practices commenced on the 18th, and were continued until the 22nd in appalling weather, but despite the conditions of rain and mist, the standard of shooting for the battalion was very high. " C " Company won the cup for the best shooting company, and D. Northwood ("A" Company) proved the best shot of the battalion — the best shots subsequently became battalion snipers under Lieutenant H. L. Higgins. It was understood afterwards that the brigade made a divisional record in musketry, and very nearly a record in the New Armies.

With the beginning of November, the last and hardest period of training commenced with a three-day manœuvre centring on the trench system. The weather was very cold, and one of the neighbouring battalions lost one man by death from exposure. A day at Larkhill enabled the battalion to practice field firing with ball ammunition, in conjunction with the artillery firing shrapnel. Starting off in the dark, early morning, we continued marching for four hours before we reached our destination. Then came the order to load with ball ammunition, our first experience away from the ranges. To us it seemed a great step forward, and considerable anxiety was felt lest some careless individual should accidentally let off a round. The battalion extended into open order and advanced in rushes firing on targets, with the artillery firing with shrapnel over our heads. The practice concluded without casualties, and after a short rest we started back on the return journey, reaching camp late at night. Although we had marched 28 miles, in addition to the manœuvre, no ill effects were noticeable.

Colonel L. Murray took over command of the battalion on 12th November. On the first parade he informed the battalion that General Sir Arthur Paget had remarked that the Fourth Army, of which the 32nd Division formed part, was physically the finest body of men that had ever left the shores of England : this applied particularly to the 32nd Division. We were warned that any day we might move out of camp on a route march which might end in entraining for overseas, and consequently on all such marches a full overseas equipment must be carried. The closing stages of our training included a brigade route march in full overseas

Wensleydale

equipment, and an inspection by a Russian General: all this in pouring rain. Long after the other three battalions had arrived on the parade ground along came the 12th Gloucesters, headed by their band cheerfully playing "Keep the home fires burning."

Rumours played a big part in our life then, and all sorts of places, from the Riviera and Paris to the Hohenzollern Redoubt at Loos, were mentioned as probable destinations. A paragraph in battalion orders, asking for names of men who knew the countries in the Near East and any of their languages, strengthened the rumours which had been received " straight from the horse's mouth," that we were bound for Turkey. Shortly before our departure various transfers of specialists had to be made. Machine gunners were transferred to "A" Company, transport men to " B " Company, headquarter personnel to " C " Company, and signallers with some original members of "A" Company to " D." As this involved the splitting up of sections of friends who had wished to spend their service together, the transfers were not by any means popular. Stores and equipment were being issued, and in this connection one is reminded of " Skin " Newton's (C. Coy. Q.M.S.) famous dictum when dealing with an issue of boots, " them as 'as got boots and don't want 'em, give 'em to them as 'asn't and does." However, we struggled through, and preparations became more feverish; parcels of goods not required were dispatched homewards, and after many months, active service was in sight. The Lord Mayor of Birmingham (Alderman Neville Chamberlain), our Honorary Colonel (Sir William Bowater), and the Bishop of Birmingham, visited the battalion on 19th November to wish us " God Speed," and they addressed the battalion in a bright and optimistic manner.

Early in the morning of 20th November, an advance party consisting of transport, with a few signallers and machine gunners, left Codford under command of Captain T. P. Cooke and proceeded to Southampton for embarkation. On the night of 20th-21st November, after a short service, the battalion left the huts at 12.5 a.m. en route for Folkestone and Boulogne. Various details were left behind to clear up and hand over the camp, and we were particularly sorry to lose Major Fleming, who had commanded "B" Company since the commencement of training. It is interesting to recall that Major Fleming had commanded the service company of the Warwickshire Volunteers in the South African War. Second Lieutenant G. F. Bennett, who had only just come out of Salisbury Hospital and was not fit to proceed overseas with the battalion, was left behind in charge of the details to hand over the camp to the Barrack Warden, who tried to confiscate all the private property which had belonged to the battalion since Sutton days. This had been given us by the citizens of Birmingham, and we were free to dispose of it as we liked. With the aid of Drum-Major Gould, most of this stuff was sold to Salisbury tradesmen, and quietly carted away. Long and lengthy arguments took place concerning the battalion flag, which was kept flying till the last moment. The Barrack Warden wanted it, and Lieutenant Bennett wanted to keep it for the battalion. Somehow, it disappeared during the last night and found its way to Minehead, where it remained during the war: it has since been restored to its proper quarters and appears every year at the battalion dinner.

At last our turn had come to proceed on active service, and to take our part in the ranks overseas. The battalion had changed in character considerably since our first parade at Sutton: the ranks of the original battalion had been sadly depleted through the granting of over 400 commissions, but, one and all, we felt fit, and keen for any job which might lie before us. And so, in the early morning of 21st November, 1915, we left for France, with high hopes and many conjectures concerning the future.

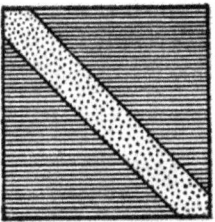

Badge of 5th Division.

Chapter IV.

THE BRAY FRONT.

On arrival at Folkestone, the battalion boarded the " Invicta " and sailed at 9 a.m., escorted across the channel by destroyers. Boulogne was reached about 11 a.m., and it was very apparent that the British Army had taken over this busy seaport, for everywhere could be seen khaki uniforms, and although the troops tried their French on the inhabitants, they found that the natives did not understand their own language, at least, not as it was spoken by the Birmingham Battalions. After disembarkation, the battalion trudged up the weary hill to St. Martin's Camp where the night was spent on these bleak windswept heights, in tents, with only one blanket per man. The cold was intense, and reveille was welcomed by the troops so that they could get about and warm themselves. The rest camps at Boulogne, situated high up above the town and involving long marches uphill were never comfortable at the best of times, but in the winter, exposed to all the winds that blew, they were a severe trial to the men whose fate took them there. In the afternoon, the battalion paraded in full marching order for a three-hour route march over the slippery pavé roads, and at 7 p.m. left camp for the railway station to entrain for Longpré. Condé, a station close to Longpré, was reached at 12.30 a.m. next morning, and then commenced a gruelling twelve-mile march in full marching order to the billeting village of Vauchelles-les-Quesnoy. Oh! that Longpré march!

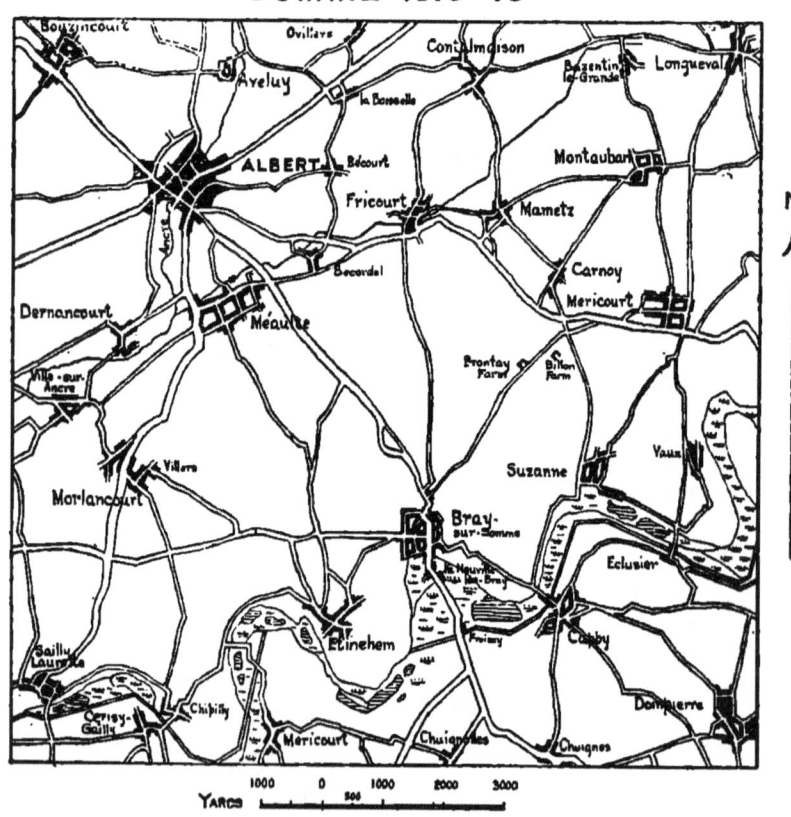

SOMME 1915-16

The Bray Front

Even to-day it has savours of nightmare for, coming on top of the route march in the previous afternoon and the five hours train journey, the strain was too heavy for many of the battalion. In addition to the ordinary equipment and ammunition, each man carried a blanket and a spare pair of boots.

To make matters worse, the roads were coated with sheets of ice, giving no grip on the surface for the troops, and men fell out through sheer exhaustion. The valiant hearts who stayed the course received a severe telling off from Colonel Murray on arrival at Vauchelles, but we have heard since that the C.O. apologized afterwards, although this apology did not reach the rank and file at that time. It was an unfortunate experience for a battalion new to active service, and the march, of short duration though it was, will always stand out as one of the most unhappy events in which the battalion took part.

In the meantime, the advance guard had settled down in the village. The journey from Southampton was undertaken in the night on the S.S. *Maidan*, and the loading of mules and transport for the brigade had been going on throughout the day. The *Mauretania*, which had recently arrived from Gallipoli, was in the same dock looking magnificent in the white livery of a hospital ship. Going down the Solent in the dark with no lights, seemed an eerie affair and destroyers were soon picked up. Morning saw them safely in the outer harbour of Havre, and then commenced a heavy day unloading mules and transport and entraining them. They stayed in Havre all day and left at night by troop train (40 hommes, 8 chevaux), arriving early next morning at Pont Remy where they had to unload our transport and march to Vauchelles to make preparations to receive the battalion.

The battalion remained five days in Vauchelles, so that we had an opportunity of acclimatizing ourselves to the new conditions and French billets. These latter were a new experience for us and, as we were destined to spend many periods in them, it will serve a useful purpose if we describe them now. When the battalion was moving to a village an advance party went on ahead to arrange billets, and they would divide up the village so that each company would have its own quarter. In most cases the houses in the village were inhabited by farmers, who owned or rented land outside the village. The general lay-out of the farm was in the shape of a square with the house on one side, and barns and stables occupying the other three. In the barns accommodation was found for the troops, and straw was provided for bedding — sometimes a thick layer, but very often very thinly spread. In every farm was found in the middle of the yard, and occupying most of it, a heap of farm refuse evidently years old, on which the farm hens would spend most of their days. However, we soon became accustomed to these billets and welcomed the news that we were going into them, for they were easily the best shelter. We were usually well received by the inhabitants and were often invited inside the farmhouse to partake of coffee and other refreshments.

There was much novelty in our new surroundings but we quickly settled down. Soon we made contact with the inhabitants and the cafés were filled with troops anxious to learn everything they could of the country. Liqueurs were being sold at one penny each, and at first a roaring trade was done; but in view of their rather poisonous nature, the Colonel very wisely forbade further purchases. Abbeville was very near, and opportunities were taken to visit this town. By easy stages, the battalion marched via Bouchon to Vignacourt, where we stayed for a few days and then moved on to Allonville. At one point on our journey, just before we turned off the main Amiens road, we had an excellent view of Amiens with its imposing cathedral standing out as a prominent feature in the landscape of the Somme Valley. After settling down in billets, it was discovered that the village was unsuitable, and we marched on to Pont Noyelles. Next day we marched through Corbie to Sailly Laurette, where we came under the orders of the 13th Brigade of the 5th Division and here final preparations were made for our first visit to the trenches for instruction. The sound of gunfire betokened our prox-

The Bray Front

imity to these, and at night, away to the east, we could see the Verey lights, indicating the position of the front line. It was in this village that Headquarters Company was formed, and the specialists, comprising machine gunners, signallers, and battalion headquarter personnel were transferred to it from their various companies. "A" and "B" Companies moved to Etinehem on 3rd December, and on the 5th they went into the front line trenches in front of Carnoy. H.Q., "C," and "D" Companies reached Etinehem on the 6th and went into the front line on the 8th, where they were attached to the K.O.S.B. in the right sector in front of Carnoy Village. "A" and "B" Companies were relieved on the same day and marched back to Chippilly.

During their tour in the front line, the battalion suffered its first casualty, when Private Hackett, of "B" Company, was killed.

The front line trenches were in a valley running from Maricourt to Fricourt and the German lines were on higher ground, rising to the ridge on which is Montauban. Rumour ran that the Germans used the advantage of the slope to drain their trenches into ours. Whether that was true or not, the fact remains that our front line trenches were in an appalling state, for the recent heavy rains following a hard frost had caused the soft earth to crumble. In many places, noticeably 47 trench, the mud was nearly waist high, and at least two instances occurred of men sinking up to their armpits where the mud was specially deep.

Our only experience of trenches had been those at Codford, cut in the firm chalky ground, and consequently deep and dry, and we had not imagined that such conditions could exist as those we found at Carnoy. Our march from Etinehem through Bray had been in the fast dwindling light of a winter evening, and when we had passed through the town of Bray, the place appeared quiet and deserted. At Bronfay Farm support troops seemed to be comfortably settled down and we could see braziers glowing and the lights of candles in the billets. This seemed to be quite a good position and we hopefully continued our march on to Carnoy and down the sloping road we were soon to know so well. On our journey up our minds were occupied as to what the new experiences would be like: we were soon to learn, and that without much delay, for on reaching the battalion headquarters we were met by guides who proceeded to lead us through a maze of trenches half-filled with mud and water. At length we reached what looked like an open drain full of mud. This, we were informed, was the front line. Sentries were posted and we began the night's vigil in surroundings completely strange, and with no idea of what might appear out of the darkness. The situation was very different from what we had imagined. We seemed to have reached the depth of misery. It was a cold, dark night, and there we were squatting on a wet fire step with no shelter of any description. Later on we treated such a case as all in the day's work, but as yet we knew nothing. However, the regular battalions to which we were attached for instruction, looked after the new soldiers very well and we owed them what little comfort we did obtain. The old hands realized our greenness, but they treated us as guests and by their unselfishness, advice, and help ungrudgingly given, taught us excellent lessons in the comradeship of the Western Front. Except for a few shells passing overhead and the whine of stray bullets, the night and subsequent period of the first tour passed off uneventfully, but the ration arrangements broke down completely, for practically no rations, at any rate no hot rations, came up for us during this time: so that with little food and in the appalling living conditions, our first visit to the trenches was not the soul-stirring adventure we had hoped for.

A vivid memory remains of the first ghastly march or straggle back from the trenches to the support position. The roads were thick with real Somme mud, with shell-holes full of water waiting for unwary footsteps, and the exhausted troops found these all too frequently. "C" Company, including H.Q. details, arrived in Billon Wood early in the morning of the 12th, very exhausted and played out. The men had been wearing greatcoats, and these had been saturated with mud and become very heavy. When all the companies had completed their first tours, the battalion

Capt. H. A. Taylor.

A TYPICAL TRENCH SCENE.

The Bray Front

was assembled in the support position as battalion in reserve, to supply working parties. This position consisted of dug-outs and canvas tents in Billon Wood, and billets in the ruined farm outbuildings at Bronfay. This farm, when visited in 1929, appeared very much as we had left it in 1916, and there seemed little or no improvement in the road surface. When we arrived back at the support position everything we had seemed to be soaked and plastered with mud. Clothing could be brushed when dry but equipment and rifles were a different proposition. There was a fairly deep pool of water in the courtyard of the farm and we adopted the simple method of cleaning them by plunging them in this water and scrubbing.

- In the history of the 5th Division the authors write of our first tours of the trenches :—

" The troops were sent up for training in the trenches, first by platoons and companies attached to the regular battalions holding the line, and later as complete battalions, holding sectors of the front under the guidance of officers of the old battalions. For new troops fresh out from home their ordeal was a severe one owing to the physical conditions prevailing, but they acquitted themselves well."

Very soon the battalion settled down to these appalling conditions : the spirit of the men was excellent, and on 15th December, we took over a sector at Carnoy from the 2nd Battalion, West Riding Regiment (Duke of Wellington's) and held the line as a battalion, under the guidance of officers and N.C.O.'s of the old battalion. Carnoy was a typical Picardy farming village, lying in a dip just in front of the main Albert-Peronne Road, and headquarters of both front line battalions of the brigade were in the village. Among the trench stores handed over at Battalion H.Q. was a cow ! No one knew how or when this animal had been added to the list of trench life amenities : but there the cow was, housed in an outbuilding, and the job of milking the animal fell upon the C.O.'s bugler. Another peculiar feature at Carnoy was in a communication trench leading to the left sub-sector of the battalion front. The body of a French soldier had been buried in the side of the trench in an erect position, but the earth had fallen away, leaving exposed the skeleton of a hand. It was part of the etiquette of the sector for passers-by to greet this corpse by shaking the hand and passing the time of day.

One of the main offensive weapons used in this sector was a catapult bomb-thrower, with a leather cup attached to strong elastic for sling; our instructors were very proud of this contraption, and soon the throwing of jam tin bombs with this projector absorbed the attentions of our own bombing section. This was one of the many examples in which ancient armoury was adapted for use in this modern war. On the 18th, we were relieved by the Royal West Kents, and marched back through Bray to huts at Froissy, on the banks of the Somme canal. Our march back this time was vastly different from our first experience, and very little sign of fatigue was noticeable. Christmas, 1915, was spent in these huts, which remain on the canal bank to this day, and every opportunity was taken to make the day a cheerful one. A Christmas dinner, with plum puddings sent from Birmingham, together with a pint of beer per man was served in the evening, and Phil Brown provided a gramophone concert for " B " Company in the huts. Now he provides whole bands! The bombing section conceived the idea of adding to their rations by catching fish, which were plentiful in the canal. A Mills bomb exploded in the water brought to the surface stunned fish, which were immediately landed.

On the 27th, we returned to the front line, and moved back to the support positions on New Year's Eve. The New Year was ushered in with a big artillery bombardment: as the guns were in and about the support position at the farm, the noise seemed to us then to be nerve racking.

In the New Year, the forces of the 5th and 32nd Divisions were reorganized, the 95th Brigade being transferred to the 5th Division; and the 14th Brigade Headquarters, the K.O.Y.L.I., the Duke of Wellington's, the Manchesters, and Dorsets were transferred to the 32nd Division; the 14th and 15th Royal Warwicks joining the 2nd Battalion

The Bray Front

King's Own Scottish Borderers and the 1st Battalion Royal West Kents in the 13th Brigade. Naturally, the move was not popular among the old battalions, but the splitting up of New Army troops among those more experienced in war was a very sound policy. The 5th Division had a wonderful fighting reputation. As one of the original divisions of the Expeditionary Force, it had seen service at Mons and was concerned in the immortal stand at Le Cateau. Since then it had been engaged continuously in heavy fighting round Ypres, and the present sector at Bray was its first taste of comparatively quiet trench warfare. We were very new to the war game, but we were fortunate to join this famous division and share in its further successes. The divisional tradition counted for much and proved an incentive for us to make ourselves the equals of the more war experienced regular battalions and maintain the high reputation of the division.

Trench reliefs and periods of duty with our new comrades of the brigade became a matter of routine. We were settling down to our new conditions: the trenches became more familiar and we began to take a more philosophic interest in our new life. The mud certainly was a serious matter and the companies in the front line were kept fully occupied in dealing with this big handicap to movement. Trench pumps, assisted by scoops, were used and hard work soon improved matters. Ration parties, however, encountered difficulty in getting the dixies of stew and tea up to the front line, so that often these did not reach their destination as hot as could be desired. The dixies were oblong shaped box affairs and needed two men to carry them, with a long pole thrust between the handles and supported on the shoulders with one man in front and one behind; none too easy a job on the best of surfaces, but when each man had to look to his own footsteps in the clinging mud, the job became one of extreme difficulty and it was not surprising that the dixies did not reach the front line as full as when they left the cookhouse. The heavy sticky mud made walking a matter of great exertion, and progress was much impeded by the fact that one had continually to drag each foot out of the mud to place it in front of the other. Placing two feet together meant sinking and disaster.

Brigade headquarters and rest billets were at Bray, and here also the divisional concert party, "The Whizz-Bangs," performed. At Christmas-time, they gave an excellent pantomime in which Will Kings made his debut with the party; this was a very clever and enjoyable show. When the Queen Victoria's Rifles left the division, many of its members had to leave "The Whizz-Bangs," and their places were taken by several Birmingham Battalion men.

On 8th January, the relief of the 5th Division by the 30th Division commenced, and the battalion was relieved at Carnoy by the 19th Manchesters. The trenches were left in good condition after very hard work, so that it was possible to walk along the front line without encountering mud more than ankle depth. We had learnt a great deal about active service conditions during our stay in this sector, and the general bearing of the battalion was improved by our experiences. We left behind in Carnoy cemetery four of our comrades, Sergeant-Major Kitchen, Privates Hackett, Hall, and Burnside; and they lie to-day, side by side, in the pretty little British cemetery near the ration dump of 1915.

We stayed for a night at Bray, and next day marched back ten miles to Vaux-sur-Somme, a delightful little village in which the battalion was destined to spend many happy days.

A thorough clean-up of clothing and equipment was undertaken; when we were reasonably clean, battalion training was commenced. The country round was typical Picardy upland, but in Vaux we were right down in the valley, and close to the river and canal of the Somme. Corbie was our nearest town (then very much alive with troops, but in 1932 very quiet and deserted), and passes were granted to go there in the afternoons. The walk either by road or along the river bank was very pretty, and a marked contrast to the scenery we had left behind. Route marches soon acquainted us with the surrounding country, and, from the high ground above the village, a vast area of

The Bray Front

country could be seen, stretching away on all sides and composed of the rolling Picardy downlands. On fine days, away to the east, we could see the observation balloons forming a long line and indicating the position of the trenches. The band, which up till now had confined its music to bugles, started practising with fifes, and soon gained proficiency. Route marches were soon enlivened with their music, and one of the most popular items in the repertoire was the " Lily of Laguna," which provided a fine lilting strain for marching. There were many concert parties in the district and at Mericourt we had opportunities of hearing Lieutenant Radford (R.F.C.), more familiarly known as Basil Hallam of " Gilbert the Filbert " fame. During our stay at Vaux, an exchange of officers and N.C.O.'s was made with the Royal West Kents, so that we could benefit by the experiences of the older troops. It was very interesting to hear the stories of Mons, Ypres, and Messines, and using a grain of salt, we were able to digest the main parts of the stories. The battalion was inspected at Vaux by Major-General Sir C. T. Kavanagh. Although much preparatory work had been done to present a smart appearance, the turnout was viewed with disapproval by the inspecting officer as not being in any way up to the 5th Division standard. Consequently a smartening up regime was instituted, weekly parades were held for the Colonel's inspection, until the battalion presented a really smart appearance. After this severe lesson, about which one must be candid and admit was needed, there was never further need to grumble at the turnout, and the battalion could compare favourably with any unit of the division.

An attack of German measles caused the battalion to be isolated in Vaux, and while the rest of the 5th Division marched away from the area, the battalion remained in the village and was attached in turn to various divisions. This caused some delay with the letters which, at ordinary times, were received daily. On one occasion, the officers' mess corporal came back from a town near with the news that the mail was waiting for us there. As we had received no letters or parcels for several days, this information was

The First Birmingham Battalion in the Great War

very welcome and with little delay the transport harnessed up a limber to fetch the mail. On their return, they announced that the battalion mail consisted of four letters! Contact cases were isolated in the château of the village, but the rest of the battalion carried out battalion training. Most of this training took place on high ground, close to the Bray-Corbie road, in full view of the winding valleys on the Somme and Ancre, and companies in turn provided parties for repairing the lower road through Vaux and digging sump holes to drain away the colossal quantities of mud. One incident in this connection is worthy of record. About this time, an order had appeared encouraging the troops to fraternize with the French soldiers, who were our near neighbours on the other side of the river. One day there appeared before the company on road work a French General and his staff. A well-known character of the company, a typical Brummie, bearing in mind the latest order, approached the General, saluted smartly and, in what he thought was good French, greeted the great man thus: " Bon sod, Manure." To the credit of the French General the salute was gravely returned and then he rode away. A detachment of French artillerymen was quartered in Vaire, a small village on the opposite bank of the river, and visits were interchanged. The men in horizon blue came over to sample English rations and English issue rum, then they in turn acted as hosts in their own village to small parties from the battalion. Very hospitable were these French soldiers : their cook was a veritable wonder-worker : he had been a chef in a large Parisian hotel before the war, and the astounding dishes he concocted from bully-beef and vegetables were awe-inspiring !

Recreation was provided for the battalion in all ways. Concerts were given in the schoolroom and much hidden talent was discovered in the battalion. Rugger and Soccer matches, keenly fought out, were plentiful. Inter-company matches vied for interest with inter-section matches and a soccer match between the officers and N.C.O.'s, ending in a draw (1 goal all), provided the battalion with much amusement. Private E. A. Stocks, who reported the match, in-

The Bray Front

cludes the following in his description: " the spectators were quite impartial and some of the remarks were quite amusing, such as ' Give the lads a chance ' (when the non-coms' line came bundling down the field), ' Stop his rations, Quarter,' when a Q.M.S. collided with a sergeant, and so on. Roars of merriment arose when a fat old quartermaster-sergeant tripped up a major ; this caused cries of ' are you getting your own back, Quarter ? ' " Rugger matches were played on a good field at the corner where the road to Vaux leaves the main Bray-Corbie road, and the villagers were often bewildered spectators of the games. Occasionally, companies of French infantry, who crossed the river to fire on a range behind the village, lined the field of play and applauded the amazing antics of the mad English Tommies. During all this period, the M.O. was busy isolating various sections, but on 10th March, after two months' stay, the battalion moved away from the pleasant village of Vaux to re-join the 5th Division, which had taken over the line at Arras from the French. We regretted very much our departure. We had made excellent friends with the inhabitants, and our stay had been thoroughly enjoyable. Visits to Vaux of recent years have confirmed our pleasant impressions, and our stay in 1916 is still remembered by the villagers.

The First Birmingham Battalion in the Great War

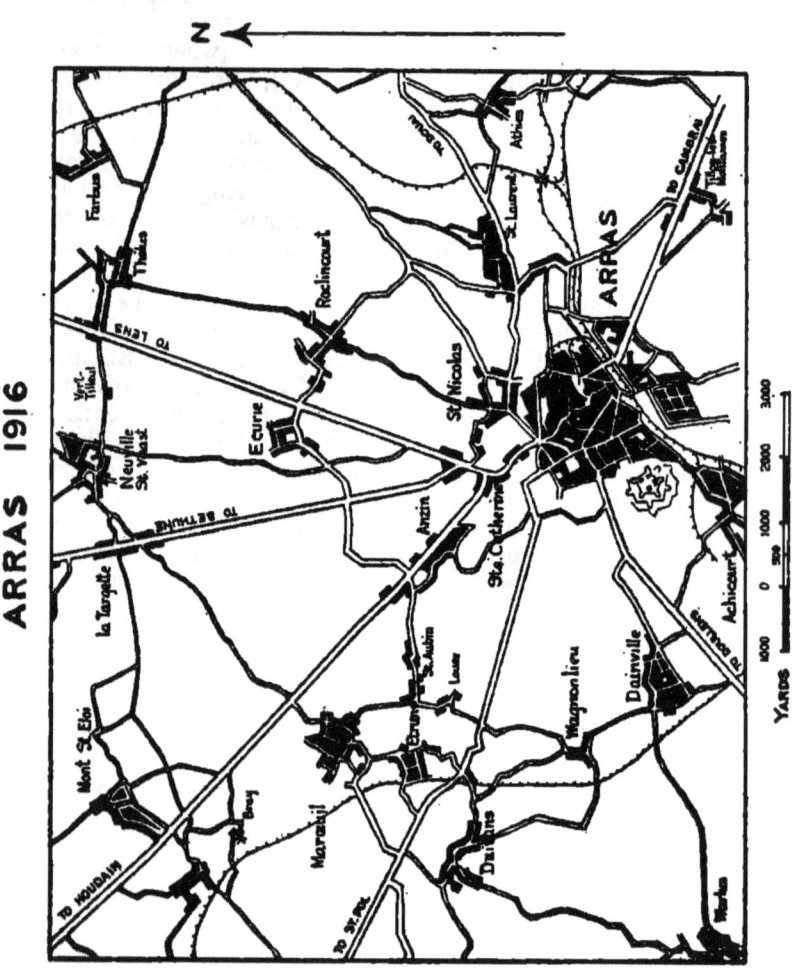

Chapter V.

ARRAS.

On a cold, frosty day, we marched from Vaux through Corbie to Villers Bocage, on the main Amiens-Doullens road, and next day we moved on to Doullens, a fine town with good buildings. A big change in the weather occurred next day for our march to Grand Rullecourt, and the unexpected heat made conditions none too pleasant. Grand Rullecourt was a dirty little village, and after two days there we were glad to be on the move again to Agnez-les-Duissans, where preparations were made to move up to the line at Arras.

On 15th March, we left Agnez, and marched via Duissans and the Arras-St. Pol road, to the trenches in front of St. Nicholas. The long, straight, poplar-lined main road ran parallel to the front line and was in full view of the Germans, so that only individual cyclists could use the road in daylight. From this road a wonderful view of the trenches could be obtained, with the ruins of Mont St. Eloi, a prominent feature, to the north, and in the evening gun flashes and Verey lights would indicate activity in the notorious Labyrinth sector. A few yards before entering Arras by the old arched gate, this road turns south, and the corner thus formed was one of the most unhealthy spots in the district. At intervals, the Germans would shell it fiercely for a few minutes, and so bad a reputation did it make for itself, that it became known as "Dead Man's Corner." On our first march into Arras, we reached "Dead Man's Corner" soon after dusk, and, all-ignorant of local topography, the battalion fell out here. We sat about the road laughing, talking, and smoking, for nearly half an hour, but ultimately moved on in blissful ignorance of the fact that we had been very lucky indeed. We very soon learned to give "Dead Man's Corner" a wide berth.

We took over support positions in front of St. Nicholas from the D.C.L.I. Companies manned Fort Thelus and the

The First Birmingham Battalion in the Great War

Observatoire and Bosky redoubts, with details at Chalk Farm : battalion headquarters were in St. Nicholas, a suburb of Arras, entirely deserted. There were some very fine houses here, with pretty gardens : and battalion headquarters was in a big house next to a mill, with a stream running through the garden. Brilliant moonlight nights were experienced during our first period at St. Nicholas and, as one looked back from the trenches towards the city, the gaunt buildings outlined against the moonlit sky gave an impression of a deserted, skeleton city, silent and grim.

Grey old Arras appeared a city of the dead and, although some inhabitants still remained and a few shops were open, signs of ruin and desolation were everywhere apparent. The Cathedral was a sad sight : as a prominent feature of the town, it had been used as a ranging mark for the enemy artillery. The roof had been knocked in and the walls were badly battered and scarred but there remained at the West End, on the highest point of the cathedral front, a stone cross, chipped slightly but still upright, a position which was maintained till the end of the war. The site of the Hôtel de Ville, which had been a magnificent edifice, richly decorated with stone carving of olden days, was nothing but a mass of ruins and broken stone blocks. Arras contained some fine specimens of old Spanish houses, and the deserted Grand and Petit Places contained rows of these fine old structures, some marked by shelling and others more severely damaged. In the main, the streets were narrow and in the side streets one came across glimpses of a 16th century town. Houses were deserted, and in many cases, where the walls had been removed by shell fire, furniture and all the intimacies of the deserted homes could be seen from the street. In the support positions, vacant furnished houses were used for billets and provided very comfortable accommodation. One seldom met any of the inhabitants, and at night this great town, with its old-world atmosphere, presented a strange and empty appearance. Under many of the important buildings, huge dug-outs had been excavated in the chalk, and these were of vital importance in 1917. The railway station had been frequently shelled,

Arras

and the Hôtel du Commerce, near by, was used as an Officers' club!

The town of Arras and our positions were in a salient overlooked from Vimy Ridge on the north and east, and from the high ground at Beaurains on the south. A good view of the German lines could be obtained at Chalk Farm, and looking back from our front line Arras and its prominent buildings were clearly seen. The trench system was a very complete one, cut out of the chalky ground, which is the main subsoil of the Arras area : trenches were dry and very different from those at Carnoy. The long communication trenches, essential in view of the excellent enemy observations, were named after the months and days of the week. Many fearsome and dangerous bombs had been left behind by the French, and one of our first jobs was to assemble these in dumps for safety. Other relics included French cartridges, the copper bullets of which were found very useful for making signal exchanges, or for filing into fancy articles. The brigade was disposed in a sound system of defence with two battalions in the front line, one in support at St. Nicholas, and one battalion in brigade reserve near Duissans. A full tour of the line consisted of three periods, each of eight days' duration, and the routine adopted consisted of a period in the front line followed by eight days in support, after which the battalion would return to the front line. On the conclusion of the second period in the front line, the battalion went back to rest for eight days. There was very little time for leisure, either in the front line or support : for in the front line sentry duties, work on the trenches, wiring, and patrol work at night kept all hands busy, while in support there were always continual demands for fatigue parties to work in the forward areas or to help the mining engineers. During our first tour of the front line, we were greeted from a German listening post with a shout of " Good old Brum." The tour passed off quietly and the battalion moved back to Habarcq for rest, arriving there in good spirits, after a ten-mile march. It is interesting to record that in 1931 a drawing of the battalion cap badge was found on a wall at Habarcq, under

The First Birmingham Battalion in the Great War

the limewash of an old barn that had been used as a billet in 1916. Habarcq was a long march back from the trenches, but the stay in the village was very restful in the good weather. Rugger and six-a-side soccer matches were played, and visits were made to the " Whizz-Bangs " at Agnez.

On 1st April, General Sir R. B. Stephens assumed command of the division. During his two years' command he was very popular with the rank and file. His courtly manner and care for his division made him greatly respected. The division experienced some very heavy fighting during his tenure of office, but even in the hottest places all ranks could be sure of a cheery greeting from their G.O.C.

We left Habarcq on 3rd April, and following the usual route along the St. Pol road we arrived in Arras to spend the night in the French cavalry barracks there. No lights could be shown, and the huge buildings were gaunt and bare with little accommodation for sleeping. Next day we relieved the D.C.L.I. in the candle factory sector and, as this regiment receives many recruits from Birmingham, we found many fellow citizens.

The candle factory sector has always been remembered as the ironical sector, for here, where candle fat and implements for making candles were found in abundance, all dug-outs, which were in excellent condition, were lit by electricity. The power was obtained from St. Nicholas and carried to the trenches by wires. Words fail us when we attempt to describe what the signal sergeant said when he found his telephone lines connected to the power cables. The dug-outs in the front line received their supply of light from the German side. The trenches had previously been in enemy possession and evidently someone had neglected to cut off the power when vacating the position. The candle factory had been a very big establishment, and it was appalling to see the fine machinery wrecked and candle fat and implements for manufacture scattered about in confusion. One member of the sanitary squad, who was in the oil trade, was especially horrified at the waste. While in support, a project was mooted by the signal officer that

Arras

when the battalion moved up to the front line, the signallers should provide a patrol and lay a cable parallel to the front line in order to tap German signals by induction. There was a certain signaller, known as Jumbo, who was not the most graceful of mortals, who, on hearing of the patrol, volunteered for duty. This caused many misgivings amongst the signal section and mutterings were heard, "Well, if Jumbo wants to go I shan't — he's sure to fall over something and give us away." Whether this had anything to do with the postponement or not, it is difficult to say, but the scheme did not materialize.

In the front line, on 17th April, "B" Company were wiring when Captain Erhardt and Private T. F. P. Sanders were seriously wounded. Private Sanders died of his wounds at Habarcq hospital. In connection with this incident, one is pleased to quote from the battalion war diary, "During this tour, the battalion had been heavily shelled and bombarded with trench mortars, aerial torpedoes, and rifle grenades. Captain Erhardt, Sergeant Weatherhead, and Private Sanders did excellent work and displayed great pluck when out wiring, and 2nd Lieut. Jacot considerable courage and energy in bringing in Captain Erhardt and Private Sanders." After eight days in the front line, the battalion moved back to Habarcq, which was reached in the early morning, and after the long spell in the line, this march of ten miles was a big achievement.

On 28th April, we relieved the 1st Devons in the support position for Roclincourt, and on 5th May we took over the left subsector in front of Roclincourt from the West Kents. The front line ran some way in front of Roclincourt, and the journey from St. Nicholas up the communication trench to the front line was a long and tedious trek. Our position was in a basin-shaped depression, for to the right and left of the battalion sector the line ran up to higher ground; and in front of us, the Germans had excellent observation from the village of Thelus, situated on the high ground of Vimy Ridge. The village of Roclincourt was a typical ruined one with trenches running by the sides of the roads which intersected it. Battalion headquarters, with its various attached units, occupied houses and dug-outs here: above the signal dug-out was the Calvary for the village, surrounded by a hedge and trees scarcely touched. On fine days it was possible to get on top and enjoy to the full the delightful sunny weather. The water squad was responsible for a well from which water was drawn by the agency of a specially-constructed chain of rings running round a windlass. Although we did eventually get water, it was a slow process, especially when the Germans decided to shell the locality. Another period in support, and one more in the front line followed and after twenty-five days in support and front lines, the battalion marched back to Duissans·full of life and vigour. During our periods in support, fatigue parties had to be provided for mining duties, and on one occasion, when the sergeants of " B " Company occupied an old French dug-out in St. Nicholas, one, " Dickie " Jenks, returned late from a fatigue party and thought that, before he retired, he would indulge in his favourite poached egg. Eggs and other food stuff to supplement the army rations could be purchased in the shops of Arras or from odd hawkers who made their way to St. Nicholas and found ready purchasers. Using Jimmie Weatherhead's primus stove, he duly prepared the meal and added what he thought was vinegar from a pickle jar. Loud shouts woke up the inhabitants of the dug-out to discover that the " vinegar " was only rifle oil, which had been placed in this jar as no other receptacle was available.

During the period in the front line just before we moved back to Duissans, the weather became very hot. Unfortunately, the wind was blowing from the east and a " gas alert " period was ordered. In those days we only had the gas helmets of the jelly-bag pattern, very uncomfortable and smelly, and during a " gas alert " period these had to be worn rolled up on the head under the steel helmet ready to be pulled down. It was not a comfortable form of headgear, while the perspiration caused the chemicals to run, and during a " gas alert " the battalion soon assumed the aspect of a party of coal heavers.

After the front line, Duissans appeared to us a very pretty

Arras

little village, well wooded and seemingly far away from all war. Here we had sports and cricket matches, and were able to visit the " Whizz-Bangs " and the Divisional Cinema. These entertainments were a great help to us, and the concert parties did good work by taking our minds away from war matters. After the shows, it was very pleasant to stroll back over the fields or along the country lanes in the fading evening light, with our heads full of the tuneful songs and happy jests. And so to bed, feeling that we had caught a glimpse — even if only a faint one — of a happier " Blighty " life.

After our rest at Duissans, we went back to the front line at Roclincourt for what turned out to be our last tour in this part of the line. On 4th June, the battalion was due for relief to move back into support at St. Nicholas, but at 9 p.m., the Germans blew three mines on our right under the front line of the 15th Royal Warwicks and raided them. The right flank of our battalion just escaped the attack, but the 15th battalion suffered heavy casualties. Down in St. Nicholas the shock was felt, and as far back as Arras the vibrations were distinctly perceptible. The artillery immediately opened out and for a time pandemonium reigned. The K.O.S.B., who were just moving up from Duissans to relieve the 15th, were caught on the Arras-St. Pol road at " Dead Man's Corner," and suffered casualties in the transport, while the whole brigade relief was very much delayed. As the battalion was on the left flank of the attack, the casualties, mainly in " D " Company, were comparatively light, but during our period in support much work was necessary, and parties were provided by the battalion to straighten out the front line trenches and to reconstruct the position round the craters, which came to be known as Clarence, Cuthbert, and Claud, after a famous " Whizz-Bang " song then in vogue. Dug-outs had been smashed in and many bodies of men of the 15th Royal Warwicks were recovered for burial, in many cases they were men who had enlisted together for the City Battalions.

During our next, and last period in the Roclincourt sector, two platoons of " B " Company took over part of the 15th battalion front to relieve the strain, as their casualties had been heavy. On 17th June, we said good-bye to the Roclincourt sector and marched back to Duissans over a new route, arriving about 4 a.m. on a delightful summer morning.

On arrival for the last time at Duissans, orders were received that the battalion was to hold itself in readiness for any eventuality, and on 21st June we moved back to Lattre, a village standing on high ground and commanding an excellent view of Arras and Vimy Ridge. Here all baggage was cut down, surplus stores were got rid of, and a period of intensive training commenced. On the 26th, the battalion relieved a territorial battalion of the King's (Liverpool) Regiment in front of Wailly, a village south of Arras, and lying in a dip east of the Arras-Doullens road. The trenches were found to be in a bad condition and wet weather did not improve matters. Preparations were being made for an attack with the 55th Division against the enemy positions south of Wailly, and the battalion did this tour to familiarize itself with the ground over which the attack was to be made. Very good patrol work was carried out on wire and trenches to be attacked, and on the afternoon of the 28th a big daylight raid with gas was carried out by parties from battalions of the King's (Liverpool) Regiment. There was very little enemy retaliation, so that we were able to stand up and get an interesting view of the raiding parties disappearing into the gas cloud. The battalion was relieved on the same evening and marched back towards Duissans; two companies were billeted in Agnez and two companies in Goures, with headquarters at Larassette. Training was carried out over marked tapes in the method of attack for the Wailly operations, but on 3rd July the division moved back to the Le Cauroy area, and although the Wailly stunt came on again, it was eventually cancelled.

Our stay in the Arras front had been interesting, and by comparison with what came after, enjoyable. We had been favoured with a fine spring and a warm summer, while casualties had been comparatively light. Many happy memories remain of the days spent in and about the quaint

Vaux-sur-Somme.

Canal, Vaux-sur-Somme.

Battalion Headquarters.

Arras

old town of Arras, with its interesting old Spanish houses, dignified even in ruin. The rest periods back in the peaceful countryside, behind the Arras-St. Pol road were days of sunshine and enjoyment. The Arras front, too, provided many humorous incidents, in the streets of Arras, in the country lanes, and in the trenches themselves. There comes to mind the incident of the listening post troubled by a sniper. A newly-joined subaltern was informed one night that a certain post was being continually troubled by a sniper. On hearing this, he hurriedly raised himself above the parapet, fired two shots from his revolver in the direction of the sniper, who was over 100 yards away, and then explained to the inhabitants of the listening post, " I don't think you'll have any more trouble with him, I've put him out of action." On another occasion a sentry's " Who goes there ? " produced the answer " Frank," to which the sentry replied, " And who the hell is Frank ? "

Aerial torpedoes and trench mortars were very troublesome in this sector, and owing to a shortage of ammunition, it was not always possible to obtain retaliation. Evidently shells were being accumulated for the approaching Somme attack, for there was a distinct shortage. Frequently requests were made to the artillery to fire on a certain point, but they would have to reply that as they had exhausted their weekly supply of ammunition, they could not comply with the request. But we were always very well supported by our divisional artillery, and the closest possible co-operation and confidence existed between the two arms. We had a taste of their quality on 4th June, when their work in opening out quickly and their sustained rate of fire were excellent.

Whilst in the Arras sector, the transport remained at Larassette and rations were taken from there to a dump, about a mile away. From here motor lorries conveyed them to the Quartermaster's Stores in Arras, an imposing building near Brigade Headquarters, with a nice courtyard, a garden, and big rooms. When the battalion was in the line, the section of transport stationed in Arras would take rations via Ecurie to the dump in Roclincourt, there to be met by the company ration parties. It was here that an acting orderly corporal of H.Q. Company smashed two jars of rum against the chalky side of the trench. Fortunately the rum was for garrison stores and not for immediate use, but the trench smelt of rum for days afterwards and the comments of passing troops are better imagined than written.

On the right of the divisional sector flowed the River Scarpe, running eastward through the German lines, and one day a barrel was noticed drifting with the stream away from Arras. When this was landed it was found to contain information concerning our dispositions, gained by enemy agents. After this a barrier was put across the river, and many floating bottles containing notes of use to the enemy were stopped. In fact, during our stay in Arras, the spy scare was always with us, and one spy dressed as a British officer was captured in the front line.

For the last two weeks in and around Arras there had been coming from the south rumours of the Big Push which was to be launched on the Somme. Day and night the incessant rumble had sounded in our ears, and we were by now sufficiently experienced soldiers to read the omen, and we knew that serious work was afoot. Also we knew that it was more than likely that we should be called upon to take part in it, and so the never-ending cannonade on our right was our background during those expectant days. It was certain that we had definitely said good-bye to the Arras front for 1916, and that we were preparing for sterner work farther south near the sector where we had received our baptism of fire.

CHAPTER VI.

THE SOMME.

The Battle of the Somme will always remain one of the outstanding features of the Great War, for in this battle Britain's citizen army attacked the trained forces of Germany. The original Regular Army had disappeared gallantly in its heroic efforts to hold the front, while the New Armies were being formed and trained. Now it was the turn of the New Armies to show their worth, for in every unit which took part in this great battle, the majority was composed of men who were not professional soldiers before the war broke out. Never before in history had Britain placed in the field so large a force as that which went to the attack on 1st July. In estimating the extent of this struggle, one is reminded of the words of the Prince of Wales at the unveiling of the Thiepval Memorial, when he pointed out that 90 per cent. of the million dead of the British Empire were untrained in arms prior to 1914.

At first, the role of the 5th Division was one of reserve to G.H.Q., ready to take up position in the line at any time. On 2nd July, the battalion was inspected by General Stephens, who, after the inspection, told us of the break through near our old sector at Carnoy. Later in the day the battalion marched back from Larassette through delightful, sylvan country to Magnicourt, where special training and musketry courses were carried out. Ten very pleasant days were spent in this delightful village; the weather was glorious, cricket matches were very popular, and in one game against the brigade machine gunners, Percy Jeeves of Warwickshire, and a potential England cricketer, appeared against us. Cheering news was reaching us from the Somme, and we knew that it would soon be our turn to take our share in this action. In order to reduce our baggage to its lowest limits, surplus canteen stores were sold by auction — one "Revilo," a well-known auctioneer, wielding a hammer

The First Birmingham Battalion in the Great War

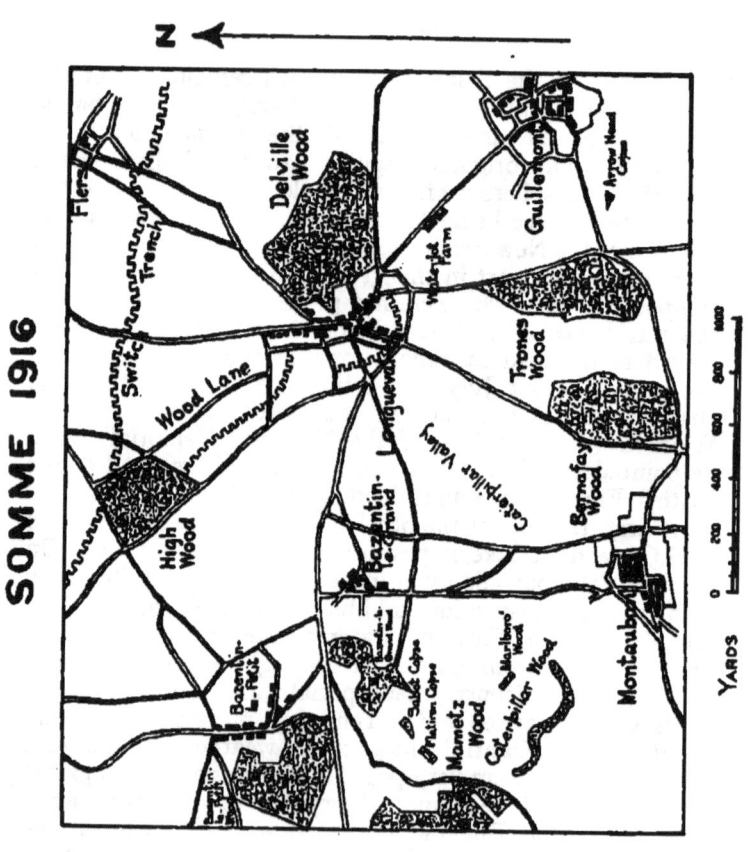

The Somme

in his best professional style. In the afternoon of 13th July, orders were received to leave at night, and the battalion moved by night marches, via Bois Bergues and Herrisart, to the divisional assembly point at Franvillers. The marching at night was very much appreciated for the days were hot and the roads dusty, and the night marches were much more pleasant. Altogether, 45 miles were covered in 45 consecutive hours and the battalion arrived at Franvillers in very good condition.

Here we found ourselves in the centre of bustle and excitement, units of all arms sharing our billets, and much aerial activity was noticeable. On the 17th we moved up with the brigade to Meaulte, passing on the way what appeared to be a huge camp, extending for miles on either side of the main Albert-Amiens road, and containing all arms of the service. Meaulte was very full of troops: the long straggling village was crowded to capacity with the overflow sleeping in fields, and canteen and Y.M.C.A. resources were strained to the utmost. All day long incessant streams of traffic passed both ways, and troops coming from the line tramped through the village in good spirits in anticipation of rest after work well done. Great excitement was aroused when news came down that the cavalry had been in action near High Wood; and, although it is difficult now, after so many years, to describe the feelings of the moment, the impression remains that we were anxious to take our part in this great battle.

Final preparations were made, packs and overcoats were dumped, and on the 19th the battalion marched up to the line through Fricourt, past Pommier Redoubt which had overlooked our lines at Carnoy in the previous December, to Montauban, where we halted on the side of the road until the evening. We had crossed over conquered territory and noted the signs of the advance. During our short stay at Montauban we were able to get some idea of the surrounding country and of the immensity of the battle. Everywhere seemed a hive of industry; bivouacs, tents, transport lines, and batteries of artillery vied for interest with gangs of men repairing roads, putting up light railways

The First Birmingham Battalion in the Great War

and laying signal wires. Villages were ruinous heaps and the souvenir hunters reaped quite a harvest in the recently abandoned trenches. All around us the artillery was continuously in action and the noise was deafening. Little did we realize what lay before us, and because we were new to this type of warfare, ignorance shielded us from too much anxiety.

The first rush of the advance had died down and efforts were now being concentrated on the capture of dominant features which impeded the move forward. High Wood, Longueval, and Delville Wood were proving very tough nuts to crack and the division was allotted a share in the task of capturing these strongholds. Many costly efforts had already been made and the fight was raging hotly to and fro round these points. The position allotted to the brigade was between High Wood and Longueval, with Caterpillar Valley in our rear. From Caterpillar Valley the ground rose to a ridge on which was the support line. In front of this the ground sloped down and then rose again, forming a valley. Along the opposite ridge, which was dominated by High Wood, the road ran from Longueval to Martinpuich.

In the evening the brigade moved forward into position. The 2nd K.O.S.B. occupied the front two lines, the 14th Royal Warwicks the third line, with the Royal West Kents in support, and the 15th Royal Warwicks in brigade reserve. The dressing station and field kitchens were in Caterpillar Valley, which seemed to house units of every kind. This valley was a trap for all kinds of shelling; the "Caterpillar Valley" barrage will always be remembered by those fortunate enough to survive; so will Longueval, as the place where there was a more intense and continuous shell fire than at any other place in the whole course of the war. The Germans had to a nicety the range of the road which led to the valley. One golfer described it as the action of a good player "mashieing" into a bottle-necked green. On our journey up through Caterpillar Valley we passed German railway trucks left behind, smashed limbers, and many dead horses, the results of previous bombardments.

The Somme

The roar of our own guns combined with the explosion of the enemy shells produced an indescribable inferno. We soon found that our position was in a salient; at our backs we had Guillemont and Leuze Wood, then in enemy hands. When we visited Leuze Wood in September, we found an observation post in a tree at the corner of the wood, and from here a good view was obtained of our position near Longueval; it was evident that this post had controlled the battery which caused so many front line casualties prior to the attack. Another unpleasant feature of the sector was the number of dead horses, killed in the cavalry attack, which called aloud for burial. The weather was hot and ultimately a party of the K.O.S.B., protected by gas masks, buried the horses and earned our gratitude.

On the 20th, the battalion took over the second line from the K.O.S.B., to enable them to push forward and consolidate a new line nearer the enemy trenches. Later in the day the battalion took over the right half of this new line, which ran along the near-side of the Longueval-Martinpuich road to the right of High Wood: the Royal West Kents were on the left with " A " and " B " Companies of the 14th Royal Warwicks, completing the brigade front line. This position was maintained for the 21st and 22nd : the trenches were continuously and heavily shelled, and casualties were being sent down all the time. Late, that evening an exciting aerial fight was witnessed. A British plane chased a German, and both 'planes came so low down that from the support line in front of Caterpillar Valley the spectators could look down on the 'planes. Cheers were raised when it was seen that the British airman was victorious. 2nd Lieutenant Turner carried out excellent patrol work and obtained very valuable information, while 2nd Lieut. E. W. Jacot, although wounded in several places, rendered very valuable aid in dressing and caring for the wounded in his platoon. His trench was being very heavily shelled, and when he was eventually taken down badly wounded, he gave Sergeant Davis morphia tablets to use if necessary. Eventually this trench had to be evacuated with five very badly wounded men, and morphia was administered to them with remarkable effect — one man started to sing comic songs, another began to deliver a speech, and the three others began to talk very loudly.

On the 22nd, as orders had been received that we were to attack the enemy trenches in front of our own line that night, 2nd Lieut. Turner and Sergeant Weatherhead carried out a very plucky and successful reconnaissance of the enemy's line in broad daylight, to supplement information gained overnight. The artillery bombarded the enemy position from 4.30 p.m. to 10 p.m., when the barrage was lifted from the objective, and between 8 p.m. and 10 p.m. the artillery concentrated on the enemy trenches in front of the battalion. At 9.50 p.m., in conjunction with the Royal West Kents, the attacking companies ("A" on right, " B " on left), advanced from the front line trenches in two waves, under cover of artillery fire; both waves were seen to extend from sections in file into line, perparatory to lying down close to the enemy trenches until the artillery fire lifted at 10 p.m. The advance was carried out under cover of the artillery barrage and without opposition of any description, until 9.55, when a sudden and very violent outburst of rifle and machine gun fire broke out along the whole length of the enemy's line opposite the battalion front. It was realized that the enemy trenches could not have come under direct artillery bombardment, and from the volume of fire it was apparent that the trenches must have been manned shoulder to shoulder along the whole front : it was certain that nothing could possibly live against such fire. The attacking companies were cut to pieces, and details who managed to get within bombing distance of the enemy were met with a regular curtain of bombs. " D " Company moved up to the original front line, with " C " Company in close support position. Supports were sent up to reinforce the front line companies and to carry on the attack, but as these two companies were met by the same withering fire, further efforts to reach the German line were obviously futile. It was evidently a question of reorganizing the original front line to meet possible counter-attacks, and Captain Bryson was instructed to collect all

The Somme

details and carry this out. The enemy fire was well directed, and it was evident that the attack had been undertaken against well trained troops. Colonel Murray felt more than justified in saying that, as our artillery barrage was so intense and included both shrapnel and high explosive, no troops could have stood up and opened such a concentrated fire had the artillery range been accurately gauged. The battalion behaved extremely well in the circumstances and when the German fire was opened the line moved forward with great determination and spirit. One feature of the landscape near our front line was a solitary tree standing out conspicuously, and Sergeant Davis of " B " Company had noticed this before starting in the attack. He was wounded early in the proceedings and dropped into a shell hole, from which he looked round to discover what was going on, but could see no one. Behind him, in the distance, he saw the lone tree, and began to crawl towards it. On his way he picked up various wounded men and arrived back at the tree with a party of twenty men, all wounded and crawling on all fours, because of the intensity of the German machine gun fire.

The action had cost the battalion the following casualties: Officers — killed 4, wounded 7, missing (believed killed) 3, missing (believed wounded) 2, total 16. Other ranks — killed 36, missing 195, wounded 238, total 469. The Royal West Kents and the K.O.S.B. had suffered equally and the day of 23rd July was occupied in consolidation of the front line and in patrol work to recover the dead and wounded. At night the battalion was relieved and marched back to Pommier Redoubt, the total remnant of the battalion being less than an ordinary company.

The first parade on Pommier Redoubt was a very sad one: a battalion had practically disappeared, leaving a mere handful to carry on its fine traditions. It is comforting to remember that the companies went to the charge in magnificent style, never faltering or hesitating, in face of a murderous fire, and Birmingham has reason to be proud of her sons and of the courage they displayed in the face of hopeless odds. Our first attack did not succeed, but

The First Birmingham Battalion in the Great War

in that magnificent effort and failure the City "pets" proved their worth and iron manner.

During the rest at Pommier Redoubt, visits were paid to the old familiar spots at Carnoy, just behind the bivouacs, and it was interesting to look down on our old lines from the old German position. The warm summer weather proved a boon for open air "bivvy" life, and here we were reinforced with two drafts totalling 240 men. The battalion was reorganized and refitted and the Divisional Commander paid a visit and thanked the battalion for their very gallant conduct in the recent fighting. We were very soon destined for another attack, and on the 29th orders were received to take over trenches on the right of our last positions. Moving up without a single casualty, we relieved the 15th Brigade in front of Longueval by 2 a.m. on the 30th. The attack was carried out by "C" Company on the right and "D" Company on the left, with the 51st Division on our left, and the K.O.S.B on our right. At 5.50 p.m., the attacking companies left their trenches and, under cover of the corn between the trenches, extended into line of attack within easy striking distance of the enemy, and with both flanks in close touch. Half an hour later a report was sent back that the attacking companies had come under a very heavy frontal and flank fire from machine guns and infantry. They had been badly cut up, and investigation showed that only odd details with big intervals between were left, and these were in shell holes about 50 yards in front of the German trench. Supports were sent up and the line was stabilized, but as so few had survived they could not do much good in the way of advancing, and orders were received to dig in. As neither the division on the left nor the K.O.S.B. had gained their objective, these were withdrawn to their original front line, and the battalion conformed to their movement. The original front line was reorganized and the few remaining details of "C" and "D" Companies were withdrawn to it. It appeared that the artillery preparation had been too short and, although the German trenches were reported to be badly smashed at one point, the remainder of the line had escaped artillery fire. Throughout

The Somme

the bombardment the heavies were dropping short and at times shells landed behind our front line : all through the operation the heavies were undoubtedly off their target and did little damage to the German trenches. The enemy had direct observation and could see companies assembling for the attack : they had their machine guns on a slope immediately behind their front line trenches commanding our line of advance. The behaviour of all ranks was excellent and the attack was carried out with the utmost dash and every effort was made to push it home in face of insuperable odds.

The battalion was relieved by the 15th Royal Warwicks and the 16th Royal Warwicks came up in support, so that all three Birmingham battalions were in the same trenches at the same time. The casualties for this action amounted to 6 officers and 165 other ranks, so that in the two attacks the battalion had lost 22 officers and 618 other ranks within eight days. A day was spent on Pommier redoubt, and the 5th Division, now only a skeleton and very exhausted, was relieved by the 17th Division. The battalion marched back to tents about 2 miles north-east of Dernacourt, and during this period of rest bathing parades in the Ancre at Buire were very much appreciated as the weather was blazing hot. It was possible to take stock of the position and realize how very few of the old battalion had survived the two ghastly attacks. The First Birmingham Battalion had practically ceased to exist, for very few of the original officers and men were left. When the division was relieved, 16 officers and 289 other ranks constituted the full strength of the battalion. Comrades of many months had disappeared, the fate of many was unknown, and many were gone beyond recall. It was a sad time : numerous old associations, formed in happier training days and strengthened by common hardship during the winter of 1915 were broken, and, although there was no parade of sentiment, the losses were keenly felt.

The battalion entrained on 4th August, and moved back to Airaines, for Etrejust, which was to be our resting place for three delightful weeks. Etrejust was a charming little

The First Birmingham Battalion in the Great War

village in a rich corn-producing district, well wooded, and above all peaceful, and we were the first British troops to be billeted in this area. For the first period of our stay the battalion bivouaced in the woods; and the quiet countryside, combined with the lovely summer weather, were in marked contrast to the incessant shelling and the continual din and hustle of the Somme. Drafts were arriving continually to make the battalion up to strength, and reorganization and full training — with extra attention to specialists — went on apace to prepare the battalion for a further share in the Somme battle. A draft of 195 men was received from the Hunts Cyclist Territorial Battalion, which had been engaged on East Coast Defence. These men were well set up and of excellent physique, and many of them stayed with the battalion to the end of the war. An order was received permitting all the old members of the battalion to go for a 48 hours' week-end leave to any place in France — Amiens and Paris being excepted. Full advantage was taken of this, and Abbeville and Le Treport were the two towns chosen by the majority. Le Treport proved the more popular and parties left camp on Friday morning for Airaines, where the hotel in the town had a rush lunch hour providing pork-chop-and-chip meals for the excursionists. No journey to the seaside was ever more eagerly anticipated than this. The amenities of hotel life at Mers were in marked contrast to life in Dead Horse Valley. Sea bathing; meals served on tables with white cloths; turning into a clean bed at night; all came as echoes of former days. We had had a real taste of civilized life, and succeeded for a short time in forgetting the army, and the Somme. The scene on Monday morning at Le Treport railway station was reminiscent of Sunday evenings at Sutton. Some delay occurred in admitting the troops to the platform, and the troops therefore took matters into their own hands and stormed the gates to get in the train, much to the consternation of the French railway staff. Walking back from Airaines to the camp at Etrejust one party met a group of four walking in the opposite direction. Enquiries were made, and the party returning to the battalion was informed " We are going home

The Somme

to England to become chaplains, you are going back to Delville Wood on Thursday!" The irony of this statement was justified, for back to the Somme we went on Thursday.

During the last few days of our stay at Etrejust, the weather broke and the battalion moved into billets in the village. The Divisional Band and the "Whizz-Bangs" paid us visits and provided an excellent entertainment to which the inhabitants of the village were invited. An interesting episode comes to mind at the mention of the "Whizz-Bangs." When we marched down to the Somme in July, the members of the "Whizz-Bangs" had been returned to their units, and the pianist, Private Turley, a member of the battalion, was wounded in the hand at Longueval. He feared that his wounds would result in losing his right hand, but as the result of a skilful operation he regained the use of it. He was so delighted that he composed a piece of music which had suggested itself to him during the period in hospital, and dedicated it to the surgeon who had performed the operation. It was entitled "Longueval," and the proceeds were devoted to the Ulster Volunteer Hospital, where the operation was performed.

On 24th August, the battalion left Etrejust, marched to Airaines, and entrained for Dernacourt, where the night was spent. Next day, a move was made to bivouacs near Bray, where we had had our first experience of trench warfare under the very worst conditions. On the 26th, the 5th Division relieved the 35th (Bantam) Division in the Falfemont area — the battalion going into support for the 13th Brigade, which occupied a position on the extreme right flank of the British Army. On the 29th, the Royal West Kents were relieved in the front line, and the battalion received orders to dig a forward assembly trench in view of the impending attack. The weather had completely broken up, and during this tour heavy rains created appalling conditions. The universal mud and the incessant rain made life miserable and movement difficult. As a result, the battalion was relieved by the 1st Cheshires and moved back to an open-air camp with no vestige of shelter; however, attempts at cleaning-up were made and general preparations

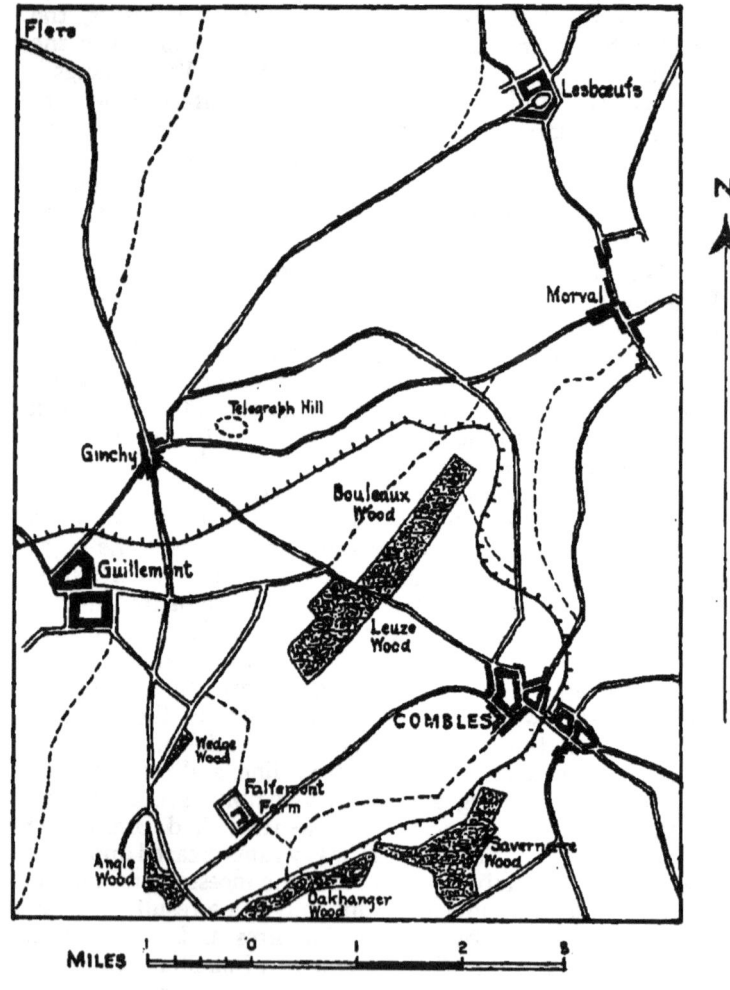

The Somme

made for the attack. It was with great pleasure that here we received the news that 2nd Lieut. J. T. Turner had been awarded the Military Cross. While in command of the bombing section, first as sergeant and later as officer, he had been a most capable and fearless leader. "Yank" was a fine soldier, popular with all ranks and it was a loss to the battalion when he left us, late in September, to join the Royal Flying Corps.

On 2nd September, the battalion moved up into position for the attack which was to take place next day. This attack was to be made by the British Army in conjunction with the French Army on the line High Wood-Guinchy-Guillemont-Wedge Wood-Le Forest. The objectives for the 13th Brigade were :— (1) the capture of Falfemont Farm, and the main trench line for about 400 yards to the right ; (2) the capture of the German main line trenches from the left of the farm up to and including Wedge Wood. The attack on the first objective had to be carried out prior to the main attack as the enemy in possession of the farm would be able to enfilade the French left flank. This attack was carried out by the K.O.S.B., and they were followed at noon by the 14th Royal Warwicks, who were entrusted with the attacks on the second objective. The position at Falfemont Farm consisted of a valley opening to the right and ending in high ground on our left at Leuze Wood, with the opposing lines of trenches on either side of the valley. As our position was overlooked from Leuze Wood and the high ground to the right, the battalion headquarters position, consisting of nothing more than two shelters above ground, came in for very heavy shelling. So fierce had been the bombardments in this region that the ground was churned up and broken until it was the consistency of sea-sand, piled into hillocks and sunk into pits. A detachment of signallers was sent to a post to assist the maintenance of communications between brigade and battalion. This point was under direct observation, for they were shelled heavily, and one large shell making a direct hit killed four men out of the six in the detachment.

The K.O.S.B. attacked at 9 a.m. and were seen to advance

The First Birmingham Battalion in the Great War

very gallantly and in splendid order, but they soon disappeared from sight over the ridge, and until 5 p.m. the situation remained obscure as no message came back from this battalion. At the time of the attack, not a shell was falling on Falfemont Farm, and the Germans were able to bring up machine guns from their deep dug-outs and pour a murderous fire into the advancing line.

* " Under this terrific deluge, the attacking columns melted away, further advance against the undisturbed aim of the enemy's gunners being a sheer impossibility. It subsequently transpired that the guns detailed for the attack had been switched to meet a German counter-attack farther south, although we had no notification of this at the time."

Deprived of the help of the French 75's, and with no covering fire whatever, the attack on the farm failed; consequently when the battalion advanced at 12.10 p.m. in conjunction with the 95th Brigade on the left, the right flank of the battalion was open to the concentrated fire from machine guns and rifles from Falfemont Farm. " C " Company attacked the first objective, which was the gunpits position in the valley running south-west from Wedge Wood, and came under very heavy artillery, machine gun, and rifle fire from the farm and gunpits, losing very heavily and being held up. The attack was resumed and after repeated attempts the gunpits came into our possession at 1.40 p.m., prisoners being taken. At 12.50 p.m., "A" and " B " Companies attacked the second objective, the enemy trenches from the left edge of the farm to the left of Wedge Wood. With the heavy fire from the right flank it seemed that the impossible was being asked, but both companies advanced in good spirits. The heavy flank fire, however, caused numerous casualties, and the ranks began to wither away. "A" Company on the right bore the full brunt and soon only a few remnants were left but they continued the advance and were finally held up a short distance from the

---

* *"The Fifth Division in the Great War,"* by Brig.-Gen. Hussey and Major Inman.

Carnoy Cemetery.

Bronfay Farm.

Billet Barn, Bronfay.

The Somme

enemy trenches. " B " Company on the left suffered almost as severely, but, struggling on, they managed to occupy and hold the front trench of the enemy position just south of Wedge Wood. Captain Addenbrooke displayed splendid bravery during this attack, and with seven men, only two of whom were unwounded, and he himself wounded in both feet, fought his way into an isolated gunpit, captured 17 prisoners and 2 machine guns, and held the post until relieved about 9 p.m. The battalion in its behaviour had lived up to tradition and it was no fault of theirs that the attack did not reach a fully successful conclusion. The lack of artillery fire for the attack of the Scottish Borderers and the consequent heavy enfilade fire on the battalion had made a successful advance impossible.

On the left, the attack had progressed much more smoothly, and with great dash the 12th Gloucesters and 1st D.C.L.I. captured all their objectives. The 13th Brigade was relieved at night by the 15th Brigade, and the battalion moved back to Dublin Trench on the Maricourt-Montauban road. The casualties for the attack were : officers—killed 2, wounded 7 ; other ranks—killed or missing 142, wounded 152, total 293.

The attack was resumed on the 5th September, and Falfemont Farm was captured after very heavy fighting together with Leuze Wood and valuable positions on the left.

* " The positions gained were held against all counter-attacks and the seal set on one of the finest efforts of the 5th Division during the war. In the attacks of the 3rd and 5th September, the 95th Brigade had advanced 3,500 yards without a set back of any kind, while the 13th and 15th Brigades had attacked and finally captured one of the strongest redoubts ever made by the engineering skill of the Germans."

At the conclusion of these operations, the battalion withdrew to the Citadel at Bray for rest and reorganization.

* " *The Fifth Division in the Great War,*" by Brig.-Gen. Hussey and Major Inman.

The First Birmingham Battalion in the Great War

In connection with the battalion attack, it is interesting to record that a battalion runner (one Hedley Vickers), was sent with a message to the front line company. He took with him the runners' mascot, a small dog, and when setting out on his return journey he got out of the trench and, mistaking his direction, walked towards the enemy lines. The Germans opened fire, killed the dog and slightly wounded the runner, who was taken into one of their dug-outs. Shortly afterwards the Cornwalls attacked and captured the line. Some of their men, seeing Vickers at the bottom of the dug-out, mistook him for a German spy and wished to shoot him. However, he was able to convince them of his identity and was soon back on his way to the battalion.

On 8th September, the 13th Brigade was inspected by Major-General Sir R. B. Stephens, G.O.C. 5th Division, and, after the inspection, he addressed the brigade. He commenced by reading a congratulatory message from the Commander-in-Chief in which Sir Douglas Haig said that he wished to thank all ranks of the 5th Division for the very successful part they had borne in the recent operations. The Divisional Commander went on to say that, although the brigade might think it had failed, it must be understood that they had been asked to attempt the impossible. The 2nd King's Own Scottish Borderers and the 14th Royal Warwickshire Regiment advanced gloriously and with the utmost gallantry, and their advance was witnessed by officers of the General Staff. He was sorry the brigade had failed to carry through its objectives through no fault of its own but owing entirely to some error in the matter of artillery preparation. Although there was practically no artillery support the advance was pushed on with the utmost determination and perseverance. He mentioned that the brigade had had bad luck in the last three shows, but he knew that whatever the 13th Brigade were asked to do in the future, they could be relied upon to carry it through as in the past and he could trust the brigade to do anything on earth.

During our stay at the Citadel, rumours reached us that peculiar new engines were to be seen in the vicinity, and

The Somme

investigation revealed to us our first view of the Tanks, which were preparing to go into action. They certainly looked monstrosities, and it seemed uncanny to see these huge machines with such names as "Creme de Menthe" and "Cherry Brandy," waddling round, climbing over trenches and negotiating huge shell holes with ease. Doubt has been cast on the wisdom of putting these tanks into action before we had large numbers of them, but it can be safely said that they gave confidence and put new spirit into the attacking troops. At this period, it appeared that every attack was bound to fail owing to the overwhelming enemy machine gun fire, but when it was seen that machine gun posts were flattened out and subdued, thus making the infantry advance much easier, the spirits of the attacking troops rose to a remarkable degree.

A composite brigade, consisting of the 13th Brigade, the Devons and East Surreys of the 95th Brigade, the 6th Argyll and Sutherland Highlanders, and the 15th M.G. Company was left behind in the area under command of Brigadier-General L. O. W. Jones, and on the 10th, the battalion relieved the Queen's Westminsters in front of Leuze Wood. This move was made in order to rest troops who were to attack on the 15th. Leuze Wood, better known as "Lousy" Wood because it was so lousy with 8in. shells, was heavily shelled all the time we were in occupation, and the battalion was very fortunate in having comparatively few casualties. In contrast, the Royal West Kents suffered very heavily and had to be relieved after 24 hours. After two days, the battalion moved back to trenches near Falfemont Farm, which had been attacked by the K.O.S.B. on the 3rd. Although the tour in the front line had been only of short duration, everyone was glad to get away from the constant heavy shelling. Leuze Wood was a wood no longer, but a churned up net-work of shell holes, with tree trunks partly standing, but more often broken and twisted masses, littering the ground. Enemy and our own dead lay everywhere, and although our men worked hard at burying them, much remained to be done when we left. Leuze Wood remains a memory of a nerve-racking nightmare, and

The First Birmingham Battalion in the Great War

Falfemont Farm was little better. The 2nd London Regiment relieved us, and we moved back to bivouacs near Billon Wood. Next day we marched back to Mericourt for rest, and at one halt by the side of the road, the Prince of Wales rode past us on a bicycle. We constantly had glimpses of His Royal Highness in the forward areas and in front of brigade headquarters, and we were impressed by his unassuming manner and his desire to be up in front with the troops.

As we were on the extreme right of the British line, we were often in contact with French troops, and near Maricourt on the Albert-Peronne road we were continually passing the Alpine Chasseurs and other French infantry, transport, and artillery.

At Mericourt, Colonel Murray commanded the brigade, and Major Playfair took over command of the battalion. Orders were issued to clean buttons and equipment buckles: previous to this all these had been left dull, but for the rest of our service bright buttons and brasswork remained. The " Whizz-Bangs " paid us a visit which was thoroughly enjoyed. Up-to-date as always, the concert party had evolved a parody on George Robey's " Another little drink won't do us any harm," of which the chorus ran :—

" There was a famous div. went to take a certain farm,
They put the wind up Fritz and caused him great alarm.
But the Corps Commander said,
When he heard what they had done,
Well ! another little stunt won't do 'em any harm."

The battalion now numbered a total strength of only 20 officers and 537 other ranks, and the commanding officer remarks in the war diary that even after the heavy strain, the spirit of the battalion was as good as ever. It was hoped that we had finished with the Somme, as we were led to understand that if a certain operation was successful, the Division would be released. Evidently matters did not go so smoothly as was expected for on 18th September, after a short rest, the battalion received orders to take up position

The Somme

at Waterlot Farm. The march commenced in pouring rain, which fell continuously throughout the day. As the roads were reserved for horse and motor traffic, the route had to be taken over field tracks, which in their slimy condition made marching very heavy work. Dinner was served at 5.30 at Billon Farm close to a 12in. gun on the railway; then the march was resumed and Waterlot Farm was reached late at night. The troops were wet to the skin, and the trenches and surroundings of the farm constituted a sea of mud. A party of signallers left the battalion at Billon Farm to go back to the transport lines at the Citadel to get further equipment. Night came on before they had gone far on their return journey. After leaving Trones Wood all landmarks disappeared, and in stygian darkness they floundered in shell holes, and dodged as best they could the batteries firing from every fold in the ground. Waterlot Farm seemed as far off as ever; so, tired out, the party laid out ground sheets on the mud and went to sleep in the pouring rain. On awakening in the morning, the ruins of the farm buildings were observed a very short distance ahead and a move was made to join the battalion and obtain much-needed breakfast.

The battalion remained in this position in reserve to the 20th Division and was then relieved by a brigade of the Guards Division, to go into trenches in Chimpanzee Valley. The next move was to support trenches north of the Quadrilateral, as part of a relief by the 13th Brigade to give the 15th and 95th Brigades a rest before their attack on the 25th. Immediately prior to this attack, the battalion moved back to assembly trenches near Guillemont, which village, together with Ginchy, was merely a name on the map; for they existed as masses of brick dust with scarcely two whole bricks remaining together.

In the Morval attack on 25th September, the 13th Brigade advanced in support of the 15th Brigade, with the 14th Royal Warwicks leading. The enemy front line was taken with little opposition, and the battalion advanced in four extended lines to a position where we were able to watch the advance on the second objective. This met with instant success and so effective was the creeping barrage that the attacking waves were able to enter the enemy trench only a few seconds after the artillery fire lifted. The battalion followed up this advance and occupied the original British front line trench, and half an hour later, when it was too late, the enemy opened out a very heavy barrage on either side of the sunken road and across the ground over which we had just advanced. At night we moved up still further, and dug in on the slope west of Morval, this change of positions being carried out in pitch darkness without hitch and with no casualties.

In this attack, tanks were allotted to the division for the first time, but they were not an unqualified success. The crews of the disabled tanks, however, dismounted their guns and joined in the infantry attack, rendering very valuable assistance. The day's operations on Morval formed part of a main scheme to encircle Combles, and at the end of the day this was achieved, for with the British at Morval and the French round on the right only a small gap remained to complete the circle, with the result that Combles was captured next day. The Morval attack was a huge success, and made a splendid conclusion to our share in the Battle of the Somme ; the whole scheme having been carried out exactly to plan and time table. The battalion share in the attack had not been a heavy one, and casualties were light, but all ranks, though sadly in need of a prolonged rest, acted splendidly and carried out orders as if on parade. The British artillery fire had been heavy ; the artillery stationary and creeping barrages appeared all that could be desired, and in one sunken road alone the enemy had suffered terrible casualties. From the position taken up by the battalion on the night of 25th-26th September, we could see Combles down below and behind us, and away to the east we had a wonderful panorama of the country behind the enemy lines.

News reached us next day that we were being relieved at night and were leaving the Somme area. A battalion of the 20th Division took over our positions in the evening, and we marched back to bivouacs at Oxford Copse near Maricourt.

The Somme

One remembers vividly the relief experienced when it was known that our share in the battle had concluded, and that we had finished with the Somme. All the way back from Morval to Maricourt, the feelings of relief were mixed with dread that a stray shell might come along before we had reached comparative safety. Fortunately very little shelling was encountered and the lights of the bivouacs and the fires of the field kitchens were a very welcome sight. The next morning we moved back to huts at the Citadel, passing the Prince of Wales standing at the side of the Albert-Peronne road. The railway was being pushed rapidly forward, and it was a strange sight to see British locomotives moving near our support positions of 1915. During our night at the Citadel we were visited by enemy airmen, who bombed the camp and killed some men of the Bedfords — rough luck, surely, after all their late experiences and within sight of safe areas behind.

The battalion had been through very hard times; we had seen some heavy fighting and suffered very heavy casualties, as the table at the end of the chapter will show. Nowhere before had we experienced such shelling, nor had we any idea that men could live under such conditions. Since July, the battalion had changed very much and very few of the men who came out in the previous November were left. Of the officers who landed at Boulogne with the battalion, there remained only Colonel L. Murray, Major C. Playfair, Captain D. Neal, and Lieutenants T. A. Furse and C. W. Hughes. Hard fighting and costly holding of the line had taken their toll, but the battalion could leave the Somme proud of its record and of its association with the 5th Division. In each of the three attacks undertaken by the 13th Brigade, the 14th Royal Warwicks had been in the front line and we considered that the position, although arduous and involving heavy casualties, had been an honour for the battalion. While at the Citadel, General Cavan, commanding the 14th Corps, congratulated the Brigade Commanders and Commanding Officers of the 5th Division on their successes, from 20th July to Morval, and thanked them for their most valuable assistance.

The First Birmingham Battalion in the Great War

General Lord Rawlinson, in bidding farewell to the Division, wrote that " the heavy fighting in Delville Wood and Longueval, the attack and capture of Falfemont Farm and Leuze Wood, and finally, the storming of Morval are feats of arms seldom equalled in the annals of the British Army. They constitute a record of unvarying success which it has been the lot of few divisions to attain : the gallantry, valour, and endurance of all ranks has been wholly admirable."

We entrained at Grove Town on the 28th and said goodbye to the Somme ; thankful that we were leaving behind us the incessant shelling, and the appalling living conditions.

Somme Casualties, 19th July to 25th September, 1916 :—

	Officers.	Other Ranks.
Killed ...	9	117
Wounded	21	600
Missing	3	312
Died of Wounds...	3	18
Total	36	1,047

Chapter VII.

BETHUNE AND FESTUBERT.

This time we were not going back for rest and reorganization: we were destined to take over a part of the line in front of Bethune — but we knew that this move would be a welcome relief after our strenuous months on the Somme. Our journey back from Grove Town was leisurely in the extreme. Many halts, some of long duration, hindered our progress, and it was not until 1 a.m. on the 29th September that we arrived at Longpré, after a ten-hour journey in the usual cattle trucks. Very few billets were obtainable, so that some sections had to sleep out in the road. Our second visit to Longpré certainly did nothing to compensate for our previous visit to that place, and the subsequent march over ice-bound roads carrying very heavy packs.

In the afternoon, we marched to Caubert, near Abbeville, along the Somme valley and found most comfortable billets. Headquarters was in a pleasant château on a hill overlooking Abbeville and commanding a lovely view of the Somme valley. In the grounds were some very excellent apple trees with windfalls lying on the ground — at least the wind had caused some of them to fall, and these were very popular with the troops. Two days' rest in this delightful spot did much to restore our balance, and on 1st October we entrained at Abbeville and journeyed through Frevent and St. Pol to Lillers. Tea and rations were waiting for us, and then we marched through Bethune to Les Choquaux, moving on next day to Essars.

The 5th Division had been in this area in October, 1914, when they moved up from the Aisne, but it was a fresh type of country to us of the New Army. It was flat with the exception of a slight rise at Givenchy, just north of the La Bassée Canal, and mostly arable land intersected with muddy dykes and rows of trees which screened movements and afforded excellent cover. The district was well populated and the villages three or four miles behind the front

LA BASSEE FRONT

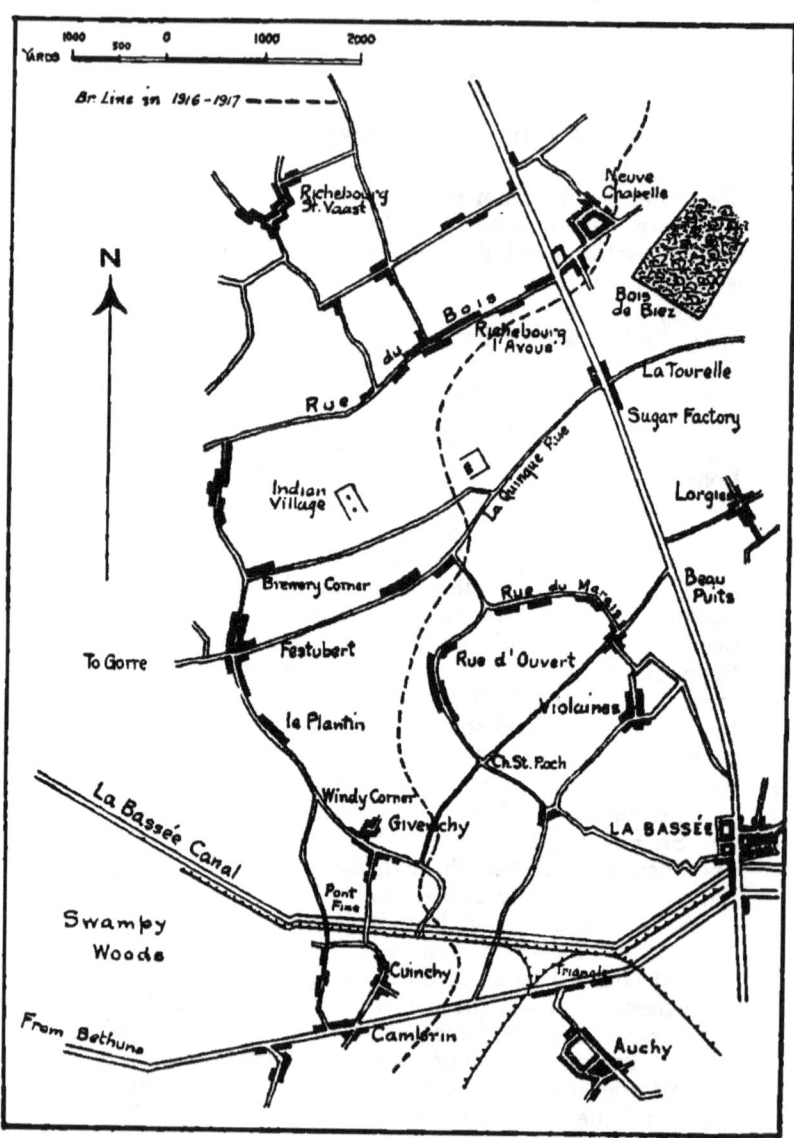

Bethune and Festubert

line were fully occupied. The inhabitants carried on their normal life and continued the farming of their holdings. They were quite reconciled to the British invasion : the British occupation was profitable. There were estaminets in abundance, and some of the artillery positions boasted estaminets of their own. Close liaison always existed between the different brigade, battalion, and artillery signal sections, and visits were exchanged at favourite rendezvous. When the artillery entertained, a feature of the visit would be an invitation to the guests to fire a gun, and this was done with much éclat. In the Givenchy sector, a trench wireless set was installed and the official communique sent out from the Eiffel Tower would be taken down for translation — a very fascinating study taking signals in a foreign language. So quiet was the war in this district when we arrived that small boys and girls would come up to the support line selling " Daily Mails " and chocolates, but this practice was soon stopped, much to the small people's disgust, and so annoyed was one little fellow that he turned round and cursed the Adjutant in good British, soldierly oaths.

On 5th October, the battalion took over the support position in the village line from the 11th East Lancs. of the 31st Division, and five days later relieved the 1st D.C.L.I. in Givenchy. The sector, known as Givenchy right subsector, being on high ground had ordinary trenches, dugouts, and communication trenches, and appeared to us a very " cushy " position. We had the canal on our right and away to the south we could see the slag heaps of Annequin and other mining villages. There were many craters in the front line, the result of incessant mining, but the trenches were in good condition and many of them were even floored with bricks. On our arrival, this sector was so quiet as to be almost uncanny : reliefs were carried out in broad daylight, and the only sign of war was the lazy whistle of a casual bullet or the drone of a rare shell.

The Division arrived in the area very much below strength and drafts for the battalion were infrequent and very few in numbers. This necessitated heavy work for everyone and all sections of the battalion had to do extra duty. In addition to ordinary garrison duties much work had to be done on the trenches, and after a relief in the morning the battalion would remain to do four hours' fatigue work in the line. When this was finished, the battalion marched back to rest billets at Gorre. During our six months' stay in this sector, the brigade had two battalions in the front line, one in support in the village line which ran through Windy Corner, Le Plantin and Festubert, and one battalion in reserve billets at Gorre.

Here, in Gorre, we found a French village carrying on almost as though life were normal. There were strangers in the village, but these strangers were good customers and made themselves very much at home. The whole of the battalion was billeted in the big château, which had tiers of wire mattressed beds in each of its many rooms. The building surrounded a large square court, which was convenient, and altogether the quarters were very comfortable. The villagers drove a thriving trade and every other house catered for the ever-hungry and ubiquitous Tommy. Eggs and chips, washed down with coffee, seemed to be the favourite dish of the district, and the inhabitants and their hens were kept busy providing this fare. Estaminets were there in number, and our favourite haunt, known as the Piano Shop, attracted large numbers for more or less musical evenings, which nevertheless proved very enjoyable. Bethune was not very far away and a short walk along the canal bank brought us to a moderately sized town with plenty of good shops and cafés and restaurants offering a pleasant change from ordinary army fare and the more plebian catering of the Gorre restaurateurs. When walking back to Gorre in the evening, along the canal bank, one felt that the world was not such a bad place after all. Bethune reminded one of civilization.

It was during our first stay in Gorre that the battalion was notified that the Military Medal had been awarded to Lance-Corporal J. A. Roberts, Privates W. E. Tongue, R. V. Sorge, and W. Poulton in recognition of gallant services and devotion to duty.

Bethune and Festubert

We returned to Givenchy, and on 26th October, a raid on the German lines was made by a party under 2nd Lieut. Hendy, their objective being to take a prisoner. They failed to get a prisoner, but Hendy secured a German rifle, by which the regiment in front of us was identified. The trenches were bombed in three of the four points selected, and it was estimated that about a dozen Germans were killed or wounded. At the fourth point, Hendy entered the sap and remained there for about fifteen minutes, but there were no signs of the enemy. After relief, and the usual four hours' trench fatigue, we went back to support in the village line. This village line consisted of more or less ruined houses with isolated strongholds, and artillery observation posts. The billets were in the houses of the villages and were comparatively comfortable, and while in this position the battalion was responsible for working parties for the line, fatigue, and carrying parties.

Our next tour in the front line was in the left sub-sector: an entirely different proposition from our previous front line experiences. The ground in the new sector was lower than that at Givenchy, and it was so waterlogged that continuous trenches were impossible. Parapets above ground, like grouse butts, were used for defences, and the front line consisted of a series of islands held by posts of eight or ten men, with machine guns and Stokes mortars. The islands could be visited only at night and the intervening ground was heavily wired. The support position was in the Old British Line, more familiarly known as the O.B.L. This consisted of a long continuous breastwork, with iron splinter-proof shelters, none too comfortable, and very low, with little room for moving round, but at any rate fairly dry and warm. Just behind this position were ruins of the line of 1915, and one often came across signs of the Indian Corps who had been in possession in those days. The Powers that prevailed were not satisfied with the quiet conditions, and orders were issued that the enemy was to be harrassed with artillery, and that raiding and patrol work were to be carried on each night. The wet ground made patrol work a misery, as No-Man's Land was intersected by ditches containing much water. The weather conditions were very bad ; the rain played havoc with the breastworks, and extra fatigue work was necessary to keep them in repair. As the battalion was so depleted, H.Q. Company provided all ration parties until reinforcements were sent. Rations were brought up from Gorre to the Tuning Fork dump, and there transferred to trucks, which were pushed along a light railway up to the O.B.L. The track was laid over muddy fields and the ditches were bridged to carry the track. A slip into a ditch produced mirth in the spectators and curses from the victim. When the rations had been delivered, the trucks had to be pushed back to the dump, and then, before returning to the line, a visit was usually made to an estaminet in close proximity to the dump in order to revive our energies for the return walk. In its six months' occupation of this sector the Division made two side slips, and in November, when the brigade gave up Givenchy to the 6th Division, we formed the right battalion and consequently Le Plantin took the place of Windy Corner as headquarters for the village line. It was about this time that authority was given for all the original men of the battalion to wear the two-year good conduct stripe.

Artillery fire was increasing weekly, and on 14th December, two officers were wounded by shell fire, one dying on the 20th, while two other ranks were wounded. Having regard to the usual quiet prevailing in the sector, these casualties call for comment. During the front line tour ending on 14th December, patrols were sent out every night, Mr. Hendy carrying out very useful work : raiding parties also were sent out, but owing to the thickness of the enemy wire, nothing noteworthy was achieved. After our usual term in support, which was enlivened by an eighteen-hour stand-to, owing to heavy bombardment of the front line, we relieved the 15th Royal Warwicks on 22nd December, and remained in the front line until relieved by the 95th Brigade on 29th December. As it was Christmas-time, it was feared that the enemy might attempt to fraternize and make a truce as he did in 1914. On the 24th, therefore, our artillery

Bethune and Festubert

commenced a steady bombardment of the German lines with frequent periods of intense fire. There was little or no reply from the Boche, and the bombardment continued until midnight of the 27th-28th, when normal conditions prevailed. During the three months of our stay, conditions had changed from peaceful to hostile warfare, and during November and December casualties increased. There was no opportunity for Christmas festivities in the line ; Christmas and Boxing days being days of ordinary routine with extra vigilance for fraternizing patrols. Weather conditions were of the worst ; rain fell heavily on Christmas Day and, although patrols were sent out each night, the heavy artillery bombardment interfered with free movement in No-Man's Land.

When the battalion was relieved on the 29th, the brigade went out for rest, and we marched back, via Gorre and Beuvry to Bethune, where the whole of the battalion was billeted in a large tobacco factory. On the march back a sergeant of H.Q. Company was feeling very concerned that he would not have a change of underwear at Bethune, but he was promised by a signaller that he could have one of the two sets he was carrying. Unfortunately, at one of the halts, Bob the signaller walked too far off the road, and fell into a deep ditch full of water, soaking his clothing and the contents of his pack. His first comment on emerging was, " Sorry, Tiny, I'm afraid those pants won't be any good to you now." Our quarters in Bethune were very comfortable, and from the factory we had good views of the German side of Vimy Ridge and the surrounding mines and slag heaps. We knew Bethune slightly from our occasional visits whilst at Gorre, but now we had time to explore it thoroughly and make full use of its amenities. The old square of the town, the centre for the market stalls in more peaceful times, contained some fine specimens of old Spanish houses, and in the centre was what remained of the town belfry. Here one could see the damage caused by shells, but except for an occasional house here and there in the town, very little other damage had been done. Occasionally a stray shell would land in the town, and when the smoke had

The First Birmingham Battalion in the Great War

cleared away it would be seen that some house had suffered; but we never experienced either continual or heavy shelling. The well-stocked shops and busy life so close to the front seemed remarkable. The inhabitants, now thoroughly accustomed to the British soldier, made every provision for our requirements, and we made full use of the opportunities offered. The " Whizz-Bangs " occupied the municipal theatre and provided excellent entertainment. In 1930, a party of the battalion survivors visited Bethune, where they met one of the inhabitants who had been scene shifter at the theatre, and remembered the " Whizz-Bangs " and Will Kings. The Fancies of the 6th Division were also in the town during our rest, and in addition we found one or two French cinemas. Altogether, our two weeks' stay was thoroughly enjoyed and time went all too quickly. On New Year's Day, the following members of the battalion appeared in the honours list : Colonel Murray was awarded the Distinguished Service Order, and Sergeant H. W. Perry the Distinguished Conduct Medal. Special mention in despatches was accorded to Major C. Playfair, Captain A. Addenbrooke, Captain D. Neal, Captain F. W. Richmond, Regimental Sergeant-Major G. F. Downes, Sergeant F. W. Dow, and Private A. L. Cooke. The same evening the battalion Christmas dinner took place, and this was a very happy function. Battalion training was carried out during our stay, and football matches in both codes were played.

On 14th January, 1917, the 13th Brigade went back to the old sector and, as it was our turn to be in reserve at Gorre, we enjoyed an extra few days' rest. During our next tour of the front line, a spell of very cold weather commenced and lasted for about a month. Severe frosts set in, reaching 22 degrees of frost ; the marshes and shell holes were completely frozen over and the breastworks and ground became iron hard. Water was very scarce in the front line and, although patrol work was made easier, wiring was an entirely different matter as the hard ground made the driving-in of pickets a very difficult job. At the beginning of February, the Royal West Kents carried out a very successful daylight raid in front of Givenchy, capturing one

LEUZE WOOD, 1916.

Imperial War Museum.

Bethune and Festubert

officer and 28 other ranks, and doing considerable damage to the enemy trenches. One feature of the raid was the plucky conduct of an airman on contact patrol work, for, although peppered by " Archies," he continued to fly low over the trenches and carry out his observation duties. Not long after this, the somewhat monotonous routine of the sector was enlivened by the capture of a party of Germans, who were taken by a patrol which went out into No-Man's Land as a covering party for wiring operations. Later in the night, a lance-corporal went out in search of the rifles of this captured party, but he failed to return.

At last the cold spell broke — this cold stretch was stated at the time to be the longest spell of severe weather experienced in France for 30 years — and rain set in, making conditions very muddy and miserable. Breastworks began to crumble, thus adding to the already heavy work necessary to keep the trenches habitable, and the shell holes at the bottom were solid blocks of ice with water on top, so that if one stepped into a shell hole the consequent slide resulted in a watery seat and a good ducking. Detachments of regiments of the 66th Division from Lancashire, which had just come out from England, were posted to us for instructional purposes, and at the same time various members of the Portuguese expeditionary force were seen in the vicinity. The Lancashire boys seemed very keen and anxious to learn, and although they appeared very ignorant of the ways of warfare, it made us realize what greenhorns we ourselves must have appeared at Carnoy. We were very busy wiring and putting the trenches in order, ready for handing over. We had completely repaired the wire and added more, and during our rests at Gorre and in support, the whole battalion had been engaged in making concertinas of barbed wire to be taken up the line and put into position. In fact, the whole of our stay in this sector had appeared to be one long fatigue in straightening up the line. At the end of February, we side-stepped to the left and had two headquarters in the O.B.L. This meant extra work in reconstruction of defence systems and wiring for signals. About this time a new signal instrument appeared known as the Fullerphone, which was introduced to prevent tapping of signals on the wires, and no ordinary telephone, even if attached to the wires, could intercept any messages sent through. The battalion only had one more tour of the front line, and during this period one company of the Lancashire battalions was sent up to us each day for instruction in trench work. On 15th March, the battalion was relieved by the 3rd-5th Lancashire Fusiliers, and this commenced the relief of the 5th Division by the 66th. Some officers and N.C.O.'s were left behind for a few days to help the newcomers, and they came back with some odd stories. The line consisted only of breastworks with elephant type shelters built in and covered with a layer of sandbags. A captain of the new division, fearing his men might be cold, began to move sandbags from the parapet to put on top of the shelters and, if left to his devices, he would have made the parapet about 5 feet high with rows of shelters showing up like towers. This alteration in the appearance of the line would have had the effect of drawing enemy shell fire.

We marched out to Beuvry, the first stage for the rest area, where strenuous and intense training would prepare us for more active warfare. Our stay in the Bethune area had been on the whole very quiet. Coming straight from the Somme, as we had done, the peace of the first few weeks was very restful, but later on matters livened up considerably, and patrols and raids interspersed with heavy artillery bombardments were frequent. Gorre provided very comfortable rest billets, and the proximity of Bethune permitted frequent excursions by way of the canal to this busy town, which appeared to us then the height of civilization. So civilized was it indeed that just prior to the divisional relief, two members of the water squad — the water squad, be it noted — lost their way in the town one night and did not reach the transport lines until 7 a.m. next morning. Unfortunately the transport officer had required their services during their absence, and they were put under open arrest, and later expiated their offence by sweeping roads in Marles-les-Mines. The canal was a very prominent geographical feature of this sector. It was very wide and deep

Bethune and Festubert

as is usual with French canals, and the brickstacks sector on our right suffered from floods. Two powerful pumps on barges were established in the canal between Cuinchy and Gorre and succeeded in lowering the level of the water two feet or so, but in spite of continued efforts, the nuisance did not abate, and it was discovered that the pumped water was running back into the canal nearer the line.

VIMY FRONT

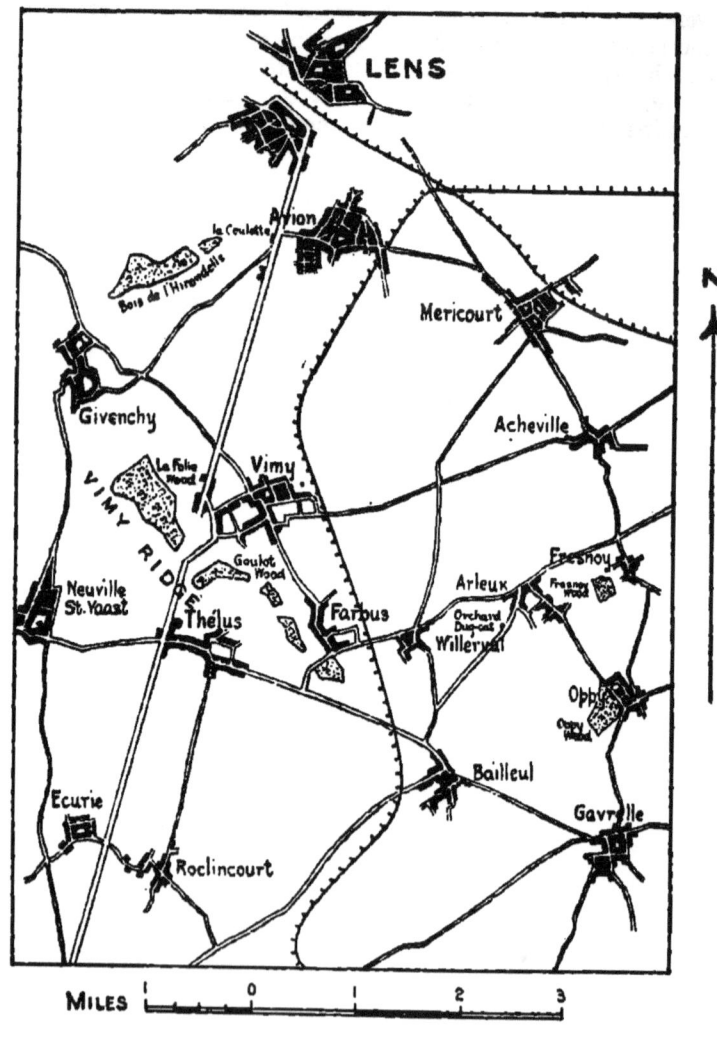

Chapter VIII.

VIMY RIDGE AND ARRAS.

After a night's rest at Beuvry, the battalion marched back nine miles through Bethune to Marles-les-Mines, a busy mining town, where very comfortable billets were found. Immediately upon arrival, we began training in a new organization for attack, and, despite wretched sleety weather, whole days were spent out on the training area and in route marching. It was the first real opportunity the battalion had had since leaving the Somme of training and reorganizing, and although few of the 1st Birmingham Battalion men remained, the recruits who had come along with the drafts were a very fine type of soldier. We were able to go to the pit head at Auchel, near by, and enjoyed excellent shower baths. That this should be worthy of note may seem remarkable in days of peace, but the fact remains that these baths did leave a lasting impression. In winter a visit to the baths meant undressing in a cold room, followed by a visit to another room, either to stand under a small trickle of lukewarm water, or to squat in small tubs of water none too clean or warm. In the case of the former, when the body had been soaped after much effort, the trickle of water would generally cease and leave one to find other methods of cleansing before one could return to dry oneself in the cold and draughty outer room. But here at the pithead baths provided for the miners, there were plenty of cubicles with an unlimited supply of hot and cold water. They were certainly the best baths we encountered in France. Our curiosity was aroused by a squadron of the R.N.A.S., who were equipped with triplanes, the first aircraft of this variety we had seen.

After an enjoyable rest, with strenuous periods of training, the battalion left Marles-les-Mines and marched via Bruay and Houdain to the area of the Canadian Corps and went under canvas in the Bois d'Ohlain. Directly after our arrival, heavy falls of snow made conditions uncomfortable, and the subsequent thaw made things worse. The roads were crowded with traffic, which churned up the mud and added to the general discomfort. The time here was spent in practising over a taped-out course for the attack on Vimy Ridge, and from the training ground a fine view eastward was obtained of the country stretching from La Bassée southward to the northern edge of the Vimy Ridge, where so many French attacks had been launched in 1915, and ground had been gained with terrible losses.

The operation in which we were to take part had for its objective the capture of Vimy Ridge. The success which attended this venture was both immediate and lasting. The spectacular capture of this renowned stronghold had a sound moral effect, and Vimy Ridge remained in our hands all through the war, and was a very tower of strength in the dark days of 1918. It formed a hinge on which all our operations turned in those days when the fate of the Empire hung in the balance. Running south easterly from Givenchy-en-Gohelle, the ridge gradually falls away, losing itself in the country north of Arras. The western slope, except in front of Souchez, is fairly gradual, but over the summit the ground falls abruptly to the east, and from the top of the ridge an expansive panorama of the plain stretches away as far as the eye can see.

The 13th Brigade and the 5th Division artillery, with all its guns assembled in the village of Neuville St. Vaast, were attached for the attack to the 2nd Canadian Division. The remainder of the 5th Division remained in reserve, ready to move forward if wanted. In the capture of Vimy Ridge, there was only one British Brigade concerned — the 13th — and thus two Birmingham Battalions helped to maintain the prestige of the Motherland in that historic attack. Many conjectures had been made as to why a brigade of the Imperial troops (as our Colonial Friends termed us), should have been asked to help the Canadian Corps, but it is probable that the assistance given by the 13th Brigade to the Canadians, during the gas attack at St. Julien in 1915, may have had something to do with this. There was a great concentration of artillery of all calibres. Our own divisional

Vimy Ridge and Arras

batteries did not open fire until the second objective had been taken, and it was at this time that the 13th Brigade went through and carried on the advance to the final objective.

On the morning of 8th April, the battalion left the bivouacs and marched to the Bois des Alleux between Villers-au-Bois and Mont St. Eloi. The day was very sunny and warm, and at the Bois des Alleux final preparations were made before the night march to assembly trenches just north of Neuville St. Vaast. A very cold night followed the warm sunny day, and as overcoats had been dumped, the low temperature was a very severe trial for troops lying out in the open. Just as dawn broke at 5.30 a.m. on Easter Monday, 9th April, the bombardment, which had hitherto been steady, swelled out into a tremendous crescendo, and the attack on Vimy Ridge commenced. The whole line from the south of Arras to Lens was lit up by bursting shells and S.O.S. enemy rockets, but except on the left where the 4th Canadian Division was held up at the Pimple, the attack went forward like clockwork. The Canadian infantry took the Red line exactly on scheduled time, meeting with little opposition, and at this point the 13th Brigade and the 5th Divisional Artillery came into action. The K.O.S.B. and the Royal West Kents were in the front line, the 15th Royal Warwicks in support, and the 14th Royal Warwicks, for the first time in an attack, were in brigade reserve to provide carrying parties. "A" and "B" Companies provided these, while "C" and "D" Companies made two strong posts on the Arras-Lens road. The brigade advanced through Thelus and Goulot Woods, and when the final objective had been taken, the reserve battalions took over the line. From the top of the ridge many good targets were picked up, and the artillery and machine guns were kept busy and seemed to be having the time of their lives. Captured machine guns, and enemy artillery with stacks of ammunition, were used to good effect by our men. The Germans were completely demoralized and fled in confusion from guns and trenches. The whole of the day the weather was vile, with snowstorms and blizzards, creating wretched conditions, and the whole area was soon in an appalling state with churned-up mud. Great difficulty was experienced in getting up guns and transport, and it can be stated confidently that but for the vile conditions prevailing, the advance would have penetrated much farther into enemy territory. The German resistance was feeble; his artillery was conspicuous by its absence, consequently the casualties of the battalion were very light. The Battle of Arras had opened very successfully and the first day's work was one of the best in any attack during the war. Everything had gone as planned on the time table, but the weather interfered with the fullest exploitation of the initial successes. The battalion had carried out its duties successfully and when relieved on the 10th, marched back to Villers-au-Bois and spent the night in tents. Next day a move back to Gouy Servins was undertaken in a heavy snowstorm, and here the battalion remained in close billets for three days.

At the end of this period we marched out to an open space on high ground in front of the Bois de Berthonval and between Carency and the Arras-Bethune road. It was a case of making one's own shelter, and very soon pieces of old corrugated iron and empty ammunition boxes appeared from nowhere, and section bivouacs were quickly erected. In view of the inclement weather, it was essential that they should be more or less weatherproof, and some very creditable edifices were built. From our position we could see through the gap between Vimy Ridge and the spur of Notre Dame de Lorette, a vast expanse of the mining country near Loos. A cluster of red-roofed houses was pointed out as Lievin, a suburb of Lens. Away on our right, a village was blazing like a beacon on a distant hill top. This proved to be Monchy-le-Preux around which much fighting was then in progress. During our stay in the bivouacs we were in reserve to the 95th Brigade, who, with the 15th Brigade had relieved the 4th Canadian Division during the advance and had pushed forward until held up by a very strongly entrenched position in front of Avion. The battalion provided large parties for road making near

Vimy Ridge and Arras

Souchez, of which village very little remained above ground. The bad weather made this an arduous job but a change of locality took us into close support trenches, in front of Angres, to allow the brigades in the line a rest before their attack on 23rd April.

The position was a very difficult one, for opposite us the strong line consisted of a steep circular railway embankment, and an electric power station had been strongly fortified. The railway embankment carried a branch line from the main line at Lens to the mine at Angres in our rear, and after curving to the left, it ran straight through our position. To our right rear lay the Bois d'Hirondelle, which was heavily shelled, as also were the mine and the village of Angres. This mining country north of Vimy Ridge, with its compact villages and mine shafts, reminded us of our own Black Country, near to the battalion's birthplace. If one looks north from Dudley into Staffordshire, a very fair idea can be obtained of the type of country in which we found ourselves and the difficulty of the position will be readily realized. The enemy artillery had recovered, and shelling was heavy and accurate. The writer well remembers looking back one afternoon and seeing the road at Angres, along which the battalion would have to pass that night when relieved, being pounded with heavy shells. Fortunately, anticipation was not realized, and we had a peaceful march back to the Quarries at Souchez. Here we rested for the night in the wonderful tunnels which had been hewn out right under the ridge and which led up to the old front line — marvels of engineering skill, cut out in the chalk and equipped with maps giving directions to the many passages which were named after the London tube railways. To-day, many of these have been reopened and can be inspected from the park on Vimy Ridge, which has been given by the French Government as a memorial to the Canadians.

On the 23rd, the battalion returned to the front line trenches, just north of Avion, to relieve the 1st D.C.L.I., who had suffered heavy casualties in the attack earlier in the day. The battalion was very much worried by shells,

The First Birmingham Battalion in the Great War

snipers, and rifle grenades, and when we were relieved by the 50th Canadian Battalion in the evening of the 24th, the casualties had amounted to 2 officers wounded, 3 other ranks killed, and 26 other ranks wounded. In view of the strenuous day, we were fortunate in having so few casualties. A company had reported seeing the enemy leaving their trenches in preparation for an attack. The S.O.S. was sent through and in $2\frac{1}{2}$ minutes an excellent barrage was put down, and this was continued for half an hour until everything was reported correct. Colonel Murray received a letter from Brigadier-General Lord Esme Gordon-Lennox, commanding the 95th Brigade, expressing his thanks and gratitude to the Colonel and the battalion for the assistance given to the 95th Brigade during two anxious days. When the battalion was relieved, the code phrase signifying that the relief was complete was " spades are trumps " : very appropriate words in those surroundings and under those conditions.

The division handed back the line to the 4th Canadian Division, and went into reserve, the battalion going back to Guoy Servins, where we were favoured with good weather. The cricket season started with some good games, while general training formed the serious part of the day's work. A concert was given to the battalion by the party of the Princess Patricia's Canadian Light Infantry, and on another occasion the band of the Royal Canadian Rifles entertained us. Throughout our stay with the Canadian Corps, we were treated with the warm hospitality for which this Dominion is famous, and the Imperial troops were the honoured guests of the Canadians. Whilst out on our training schemes, we noticed that the French civilians had followed up closely behind the advance, and were tilling land behind Vimy Ridge that had been the scene of fierce encounters in several battles of 1915. Albain St. Nazaire, Carency, and Souchez had appeared frequently in French communiques, and here peasants were hard at work on the ground in an effort to obtain a harvest in the autumn.

On 2nd May, our rest came to end and we moved away southwards. The 13th Corps, under Lieut.-General Sir W.

Vimy Ridge and Arras

Congreve, V.C., had been formed of the 2nd, 5th, 31st, and 63rd (Naval) Divisions and was in position in front of Arleux and Oppy. This, then was our destination, and after a tiring march in very hot weather over field tracks, we reached Roclincourt, where the remainder of the day was spent. Camps, water-tanks, dumps, and the various auxiliary services were scattered over ground where it had been impossible in 1916 to show one's head. The Germans were now far over the ridge out of sight and, although the village had altered little since our stay there in the previous year, it seemed strange to be able to move about freely above ground.

The weather was perfect and the battalion remained resting all day until the evening, when we moved up to a position on the ridge near Thelus, in support to the 2nd Division who were attacking next day. The following night the battalion moved up to relieve the 2nd Division as front line battalion of the brigade, with the 31st Division on our right. Trenches were practically non-existent: the front line consisting of posts 30 yards apart connected by shallow trenches, and the communication trenches and ground near were full of the dead of the composite battalion of the 2nd Division. The enemy systematically shelled our front line, and especially the portion held by " D " Company, who came in for very heavy artillery fire. At first only one battalion of the brigade was in the front line, but on the 7th, the K.O.S.B. came into the front line on our left, while we side-stepped to the right and took over a portion of the line from the 31st Division. Very heavy and continuous shelling continued all through the day and, with the wet weather conditions, made things none too pleasant. Next morning, at 3.15 a.m., a very heavy enemy bombardment opened out. Signal wires were broken and at 3.50 a.m. S.O.S. signals were sent up from Fresnoy on our left. A strong enemy counter-attack developed in front of the 95th Brigade, but owing to the heavy ground mist prevailing, the S.O.S. signals were not seen by our artillery and despite a very gallant defence Fresnoy was lost. The 95th Brigade had to fall back and the K.O.S.B. had to retire to conform

The First Birmingham Battalion in the Great War

with the line north of them : the 14th Royal Warwicks were able to remain in their position but experienced heavy shelling, which continued all day. At 7 p.m., an increased and heavy bombardment heralded a further attack, but in reply to the S.O.S. signal, the artillery got quickly on to the mark, caught the enemy in mass, and frustrated the attack which was easily repulsed. This was the climax to a very anxious day, for the position had been very uncertain, and for the last attack, battalion headquarters turned out to man trenches under the willow trees on the bank as a last line of defence, so desperate did the position seem. We were relieved by the Royal West Kents at night, and moved back to a reserve position in front of the Lens-Arras railway, which ran just under the ridge. In the sunken road near by, large dug-outs had been built in the banks : here the accommodation was good and the relief from the strain of the last few days was very welcome. The continual bombardments had been very heavy and nerve-racking, and it is safe to say that the first tour of the Oppy sector was one of the sharpest experiences of the battalion. The cost of merely holding the line had been very heavy ; the casualties totalling 115 — made up of officers killed 5, wounded 1 ; other ranks killed 32, died of wounds 1, wounded 76.

During our stay in reserve, working parties had to be provided for digging new trenches, and on the 16th we returned to the front line to relieve the K.O.S.B. The situation continued to need very careful watching. Both sides were very jumpy, as was shown by the frequent S.O.S. signals which produced barrages and heavy bombardments. There was much aerial activity, and the German red scouts were unusually aggressive. Our own airmen did excellent work by using the lie of the land to swoop up suddenly and surprise enemy observation balloons.

Our second tour in the sector proved much quieter so far as the front line was concerned, but the back areas and the artillery on the railway embankment suffered considerably from shell fire. Battalion headquarters in Orchard Dump dug-out came in for some very heavy bombardments,

Vimy Ridge and Arras

as the Germans knew its exact position, and battalion runners coming back from the front line would sit at a safe distance under the willow trees and watch the shells bursting on top of the dug-out. Fortunately the dug-out was cut deep into the side of the sunken road running from Bailleul to Arleux and, although the earth on top became perilously thin, no great damage was done. We were unable to bring the cookers up to the line and there were no facilities for making positions for fires, so that all rations were sent up to the trenches after being cooked at the transport lines.

The weather was now very gracious to us. Spring was coming on apace, and although the fighting was fierce and the shelling heavy, the landscape was not the abomination of desolation usual in a battle area. This hillside and valley had, until a few weeks previously, been well behind the German lines, and in spite of smashed buildings and shell-marked roads, the utter ruin and ancient wreckage of a long established sector were absent. The trees were bursting into leaf ; the fields and orchards were showing the fresh greens of early spring ; and the extensive panorama of the plain of Douai, as seen from the ridge top, gave a sense of freedom and activity which was always lacking in the long-established sectors which we had previously held.

It was about this time that we lost Regimental Sergeant-Major G. F. Downes, who had been with the battalion from our very earliest days at Sutton. In those early days, because we were new to army discipline, he had appeared very strict and a veritable martinet, and we certainly did not then appreciate that what he did was for our good : but " Dicky," as he was affectionately spoken of among the rank and file, loved the battalion, and in France he always proved our very great friend. He worked very hard to make the battalion efficient, and " On Parade " was always " On Parade " with him, but off parade no one was more ready to give a helping hand or friendly word of advice. No one was more grieved than he, when he knew that the battalion which he had cared for so assiduously had been cut to pieces by machine gun fire at High Wood. For behind that seemingly fierce manner of his was a

The First Birmingham Battalion in the Great War

generous and affectionate nature, and those of us who remained with the battalion till he left, witnessed his departure with many regrets and much misgiving, knowing that we were losing a real friend whose place would never be filled adequately. He was leaving us to take up a commission, and some unit gained by our loss. The Distinguished Conduct Medal awarded to him in June, 1917, was a well-deserved recognition of devotion to duty and of work done faithfully and well.

After a period in reserve trenches on the ridge near Farbus Wood, the 2nd Division relieved the 5th. A short rest in bivouacs near Roclincourt followed, and then the battalion was transported in omnibuses to the pretty little village of Camblain Chatelain which lay in a little valley with wooded slopes, then in full leaf, and with a pretty stream running through it. After the mud of Guoy Servins, the eternal snow blizzards of Vimy and the intense bombardments of Oppy, it appeared the most beautiful place in the world, and the rest and change in this delightful spot combined with the glorious weather, made life well worth living. The brook provided some excellent bathing pools, and here our natatory efforts received encouragement from the inhabitants of the village. Cricket matches were played, and a battalion sports meeting, at which the band of the 5th Dragoon Guards provided music, proved very successful, " A " Company finishing second to H.Q. Company on points. The C.O. gave a dinner at battalion headquarters and invited the commander and the two senior subalterns of each company. Not to be outdone, one junior subaltern of " C " Company issued invitations to the two junior subalterns of each company to dinner at his company mess — we are sure that both occasions were equally enjoyable. Another successful function was the dinner given by the C.O. to the battle section of headquarters company, followed by a smoking concert and very felicitous speeches. Colonel Murray was in great form and sang for us " Lucky Jim," which was enthusiastically received. Much unsuspected talent came to light at this function. One H.Q. officer sang " Old King Cole," and one of the runners

Vimy Ridge and Arras

brought down the house by a serious attempt to sing a comic song about Wellington and Waterloo, while one of the signallers retired into a corner of the room and proceeded to "Ha! Ha!" and "Ho! Ho!" in a dramatic fashion, while he rubbed his hands together in a weird manner and gibbered about "Mr. Copperfield." This, he asserted, was an imitation of "Uriah Heap," much to the enlightenment of the assembly and the astonishment of the café patrone who witnessed this amazing exhibition from the doorway. They were spacious days!

All too soon our rest came to an end, and the same 'buses took us back to Roclincourt, where we took over from the 12th Gloucesters in Leeds Camp at the side of Wednesday Avenue, the old communication trench to Roclincourt in 1916. It was here that all trousers were cut down to shorts, providing greater comfort and freedom in the warm June weather. During our stay in Leeds Camp, we had to provide large night working parties for the corps, and heavy marches, sometimes as long as 12 miles, were necessary in addition to the various fatigues. In the daytime we played cricket matches and, with a hard chalky subsoil, the pitch proved very fast, and one is reminded that in the course of a certain game a quarter-master, one Jack Denham, when playing a good innings, was astonished to receive delivery of a Mills bomb.

Arras was very close, but visits revealed a different town from the Arras of 1916. Then the town had seemed almost deserted, but now one found streets thronged with troops, civilians had returned, and many more shops were open. A gloomy romance had hung around Arras in 1916: it was then a deserted city with only sufficient life to indicate what it had been, but now that the Germans had gone back, Arras became more lively, and shops were doing a good trade. It was interesting to revisit the old spots, both in Arras and Roclincourt; but during the hot weather, the most popular excursion was to the open-air baths of the Ecole de Natation National on the banks of the Scarpe, where excellent bathing could be enjoyed.

The Division took over the front line on 13th June,

The First Birmingham Battalion in the Great War

with the battalion in reserve on the ridge. On taking over the front line before Oppy Wood, a special raiding party of volunteers from each company under Lieut. H. D. Rees, attempted a raid on the German lines. The party was divided into two detachments, one under 2nd Lieut. J. P. Turner, and the other under 2nd Lieut. J. P. Ivens. This latter party succeeded in reaching the German lines but found the enemy so well prepared that they were forced to retire, while Turner's party had to return without reaching their objective. Unfortunately, Ivens did not get back and was reported missing, but we heard later that he was safe and a prisoner of war. Two days after, on 28th June, the 15th Brigade attacked Oppy Wood in conjunction with the attack of the 31st Division on trenches south of the wood. All objectives were gained and numerous prisoners taken, the 15th Brigade's share being 200. While this attack took place, the battalion was at Springvale Camp, in front of Ecurie, and a rifle range was constructed in one of the mine craters in the old front line, the remains of which can be seen to this day. During this spell, games of cricket were played just behind the old front line, and fielding in a shell hole or on the edge of one proved very exciting work. On 5th July, the battalion again took over the front line of Arleux, which village was explored by the supporting companies who found, in addition to countless signs of Boche occupation, red currant trees in full bearing. A Quarter-Master was posted to the battalion about this period, for we had been without one for 15 months, during which time Q.M.S. A. Tomey had carried on very successfully. Major Charles Playfair left us early in July on being appointed to command the 7th Battalion Royal Fusiliers, and this was the second of our few surviving original officers to leave the battalion within a short space of time. Major Playfair was the original second in command, and in the course of his duties he had always looked after the creature comforts of the battalion in a very efficient manner. His pride in the 1st Birmingham Battalion was manifest, and from the very early days his help was appreciated by all ranks.

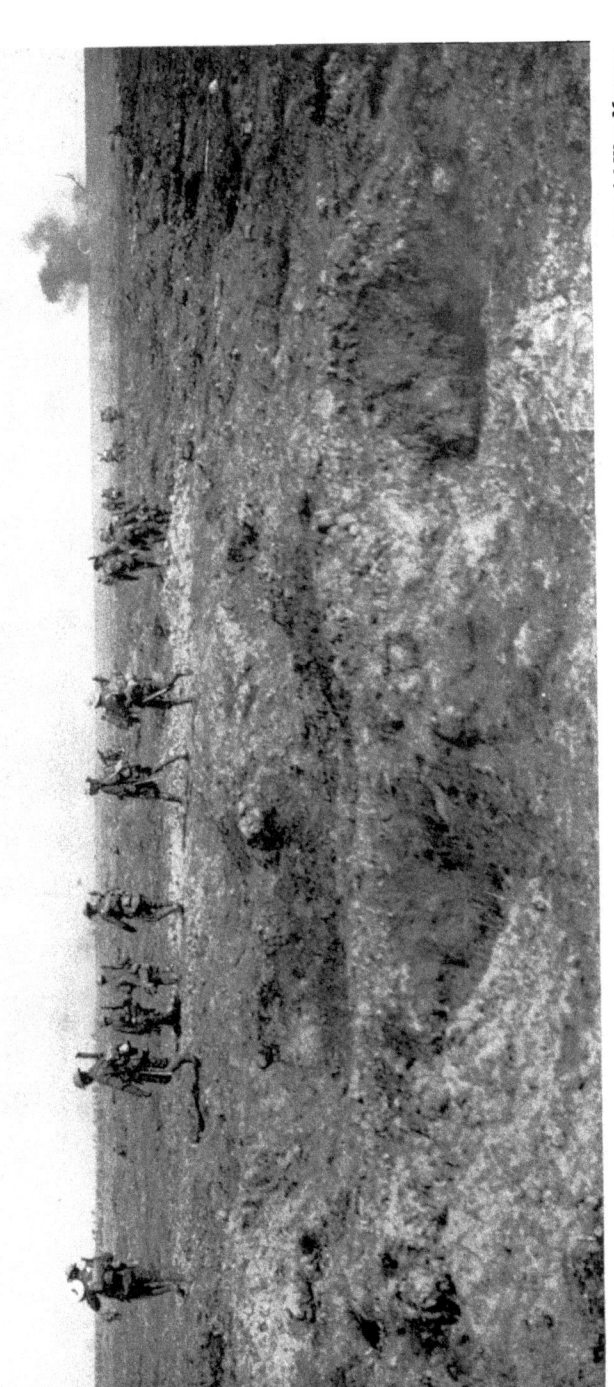

MORVAL. 25TH SEPTEMBER, 1916. THE BATTALION ADVANCING.

Imperial War Museum.

Vimy Ridge and Arras

Colonel Murray started building one of his famous overland tracks, whereby mules could take up rations to the front line, thus doing away with the ration fatigues. It speaks well for his judgment that in this work we never had a man or animal hit. On 11th July, His Majesty King George V, accompanied by Sir Douglas Haig, came to Ecurie to inspect the troops, and it is rather significant that two days later, when the battalion was in Cavalry Camp, the railhead at Ecurie, about 500 yards away, was pounded by 5.9's for a considerable period. As the shells were going directly over the camp, any sign of the range being shortened produced a very uneasy feeling. It was about this time that the authorities thought that the enemy was going to retire to the Drocourt-Queant line and, in preparation for this contingency, we indulged in a delightful game termed " bounding." The idea underlying this particular form of military sport was that one line of attack should advance, then stand firm while a succeeding line should go through the first line and carry the advance a stage further and hold their ground until the first line could again go through: this process would be repeated *ad infinitum*: a delightfully easy game, but as the enemy did not oblige us, we were unable to put the plan into action.

The scheme of holding the line was reorganized: only one battalion of the brigade held the front line, with another battalion in support in front of the ridge, one in reserve on the ridge itself, while the fourth battalion was at rest near Ecurie. The battalions in support and reserve provided working parties for the line, and from the battalion in reserve one company went down each day to Roclincourt for baths and rest. As each tour was for six days, we were consequently in the front line once in 24 days: but there was much work to be done on the front line and many fatigues to fill in time. The support position was just in front of the railway line which now carries the Dunkirk-Paris trains, and we had Willerval to our left rear. Long communication trenches starting behind the ridge and known as " Tired Alley " and " Tommy Alley " went

The First Birmingham Battalion in the Great War

right up to the front line, permitting day reliefs, while the trenches in the reserve position on the ridge bore such familiar names as " Hagley Road " and " Summer Lane," with the shelters in them named after well-known Birmingham establishments. From this reserve position, perched high on the forward slope of the Ridge, one had an excellent view of the enemy country. The prospect stretched from Mont Kemmel in the north to Douai away to the south-east. Villages, fields, woods, and roads, all lay open to view, and on this sector at least we were in the unusual position of being able to observe all enemy movement. Railways, mines, and factories could be seen at work ; all movements of troops could be observed ; and for once we enjoyed the superiority afforded by observation which the enemy had commanded when he held the Ridge and which he still had in such sectors as the Ypres Salient. Through those long summer days we were able to check our watches by the clock tower of Douai Cathedral, which brooded over the plain, ten miles behind the German lines. Telescopes and field glasses were much in demand.

July and August were very hot months and the walk along the interminable communication trenches was an exhausting affair. The vegetation in this sector was luxuriant and masses of poppies, daisies, and cornflowers waved in the breeze ; while in August, blackberries were picked in Farbus Wood on the left of the reserve position. In No Man's Land the grass had grown so long that parties had to be sent out at night to cut it down, thus depriving enemy patrols of cover.

The authorities had developed a mania for salvaging material of every description, from bits of leather or webbing equipment to 18 pounders, and the battalion entered into this worthy pastime with great spirit. The value of the salvaged material was published in routine orders and the battalion usually headed the list. Catchwords were framed and all ranks were urged on by such phrases as, "What did you salvage in the Great War ? " One day we had a great find and salvaged a large quantity of 18 pounder shells, which were sent back and put to our

Vimy Ridge and Arras

credit. By a strange coincidence, a certain battery reported next day that its forward dump had disappeared and could not be found anywhere.

In the early morning of 5th August, the enemy attempted a raid on No. 1 post of "A" Company, and I am indebted to Major R. H. Baily, who was commanding "A" Company, for the following description :—

"In the early morning of 5th August, we had quite an exciting little adventure. The wiring party had been gone out about an hour, Holley was out with a patrol near the Boche wire, north of Fresnoy Road, and Tommy (2nd Lieut. Thompson) was out with a grass-cutting party between Nos. 1 and 2 posts. Meredith (my servant) and I were strolling along the top, as was our wont, and had just reached the Fresnoy Road on our way to No. 1 post when I heard someone excitedly calling to me to get inside the trench as there was a large party of Boche in the wire outside No. 1 post. 'Hallo! some excitement' thought I: so I speedily made my way into the trench and went back to warn No. 2 post. Verey lights were being sent up from No. 1 post and there was a burst of Lewis gun fire and a few isolated shots. On the way a bomb fell on the parapet just above my head, so I drew my revolver and doubled back to the sunken road which I knew to be unguarded. We crawled out to the wire to see what we could, and when things had quietened down, I went along to No. 1 post to see the damage, and found none. Tommy was there as cool as ever, and Lance-Corporal Palmer was trying to get the gun in working order again, as it had jammed. The Boche had evidently withdrawn, so Tommy, House (his servant), and I crawled out through the wire to investigate. We found no bodies and no wounded as we had hoped to do, but discovered some empty cartridge and pistol cases, and a couple of stick-bombs. There were also three tracks as if helpless men had been dragged through the long grass, and I also found a bomb near the tree on the roadside. The sketch overleaf will indicate roughly what happened. The first to spot the Boche coming was House, who was out on the grass-cutting party. The

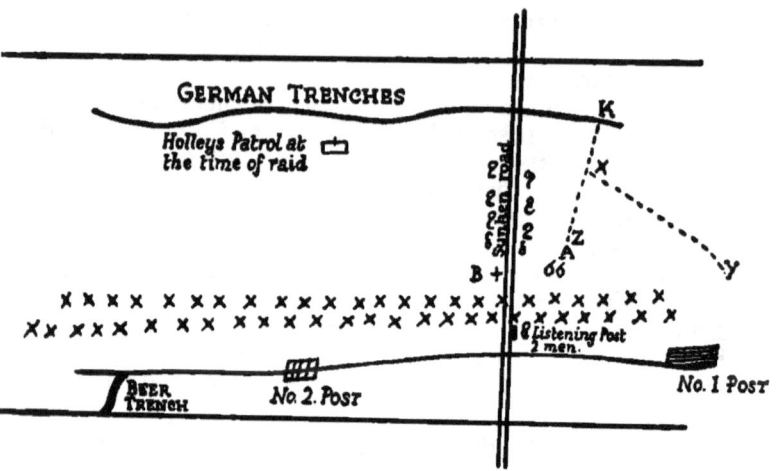

Distance between trenches along the road 500 yards.
No. 1 Post—100 yards from road (*approx.*).
No. 2 Post—70 yards from road (*approx.*).

A—Tommy & Co. grass cutting.
B—German bombs and cartridges found here.
KXY-KXZ—Tracks of enemy party during their advance.

leading Boche was crawling through the wire opposite No. 1 post before the grass-cutting party withdrew, and the enemy's action was evidently as follows. A party of approximately 40 left the enemy trenches in the neighbourhood of 'K' and halfway across No-Man's Land the party divided into two, the southern party, 'A,' being the stronger. The intention was for 'A' to enter the trench south of No. 1 post and cut in behind it, while 'B' prevented communication between Nos. 1 and 2 posts. Lance-Corporal Palmer withheld his fire until the enemy were actually crawling through the wire. The Germans were evidently surprised and fully thought that they were crawling through at the appointed place where there was no post. Meanwhile, party 'B' were carrying out their part of the programme, but were surprised by the outburst of fire from No. 1 post,

Vimy Ridge and Arras

which was promptly followed by similar fire from No. 2. A somewhat hasty retrograde movement of their comrades in the bright moonlight decided the enemy party to beat it. Holley's patrol saw them returning and confirmed the numbers; our men had wondered what all the pother was about. Lance-Corporal Palmer was made full corporal for his steady action, and Private Smith, a stretcher-bearer, did stout work by running between the two posts with messages although he was carrying no arms."

All this was condensed in the official British communique to " the enemy attempted to raid one of our posts north of Arleux-en-Gohelle, but was repulsed."

Very early the next morning, the enemy heavily bombarded our front line with 5.9's and gas shells, and heavy machine gun and rifle fire opened out. It is quite possible that, but for very prompt artillery retaliation, we should have received another visit.

In our reserve and support periods, we were still hard at work on the front line, and I am again indebted to Major Baily for this description of a night's activity on this work :—

"We were continually employed on working parties in the front line, which was still far from complete. I used to take the company up overland to the dump, and then straight up the main street of what used to be the picturesque village of Arleux. Now it was a sad scene of desolation, the street which was pavée is now a mass of shell holes and overgrown with grass; bricks and timber are strewn across the road, and not a house remains intact. A shell screams overhead and falls with a crash amongst the ruins, scattering a shower of brick and fragments. A few machine gun bullets crack past my ears and patter with a hollow noise against the shell of some house. The flickering of Verey lights and flashes of guns cast fantastic shadows amid the gloom. The front line is reached and we start to deepen Beer Alley. Work is difficult as the ground is still sodden with the recent rains. Meredith and I stroll on the top, as it is so much easier than floundering in the trench. At about 1.30 a.m., we return to our dug-outs by the same route and get in just as the first streaks of dawn are

The First Birmingham Battalion in the Great War

reddening the eastern sky and the first flight of aeroplanes is droning overhead."

On 13th August, we received news that Sergeant E. W. Williams, who was killed in action on 22nd July, 1916, had been awarded the Military Medal.

Our stay in the Arleux sector was coming to an end and, on 24th August, the battalion went into this front line for the last time. This tour provided an occasion for a very successful gas projection by a special company of the Royal Engineers. Livens projectors were used in Devon trench, and the objective was Fresnoy Park. This was the latest British invention in chemical warfare, and for the purpose of the bombardment a line of small mortars was placed in position in a trench behind the front line. The mortars were loaded with gas shells and the whole battery was fired simultaneously by electricity. There was no retaliation whatever although it was evident that considerable damage had been caused. After relief and a few days in Wellington Camp at Roclincourt, the 5th Division said farewell to Arras, and moved back for hard training in preparation for its share in the Third Battle of Ypres, which had been in progress since the beginning of the month.

Our second stay in the Arras district had started under very unfavourable conditions, with vile weather and very heavy shelling, but the latter two months had been much pleasanter. A warm summer had followed with congenial atmosphere, and except for a few lively periods, we had experienced peaceful trench warfare. Much of our time had been occupied in fatigue work to put the trench system into a good defensive state and this involved many heavy fatigues and working parties.

Since we had left Camblain Chatelain in the early spring, all our time had been spent in an uninhabited countryside — Roclincourt being our farthest point back from the line — and except for very occasional visits to Arras, we had been completely out of touch with French civilian life. However, the divisional baths and canteen had been established at Ecurie, and the " Whizz-Bangs," in their own concert hall, gave performances which were thoroughly appreciated. As

Vimy Ridge and Arras

the fine weather and the amenities of the sector made our stay in the district less irksome than usual, it is doubtful whether there was any special desire to get back to a French village, as excursions to Arras were very few both as to occasions and numbers — although when it was actually known that we were going back, we did appreciate the prospect of seeing French civilians again. So that our move provided not only a change of scenery, but a change of outlook in meeting the people in their own villages. For three-and-a-half years the only human beings we met who were not wearing khaki, were the French peasants. They were our one link with civilization.

Our first halt after a march overland was Frevin Cappelle, where we renewed our acquaintance with close billets and estaminets. Next day we moved on to Magnicourt, whence the battalion had made a forced march to the Somme in July, 1916. Much of import had happened since then: very few men remained who had been with the battalion in those seemingly far-off days, and the return brought poignant memories of that happy band of warriors who had left Magnicourt with such high hearts. Those who came the second time to Magnicourt were but a small part of the First Birminghams. The battalion had given of its best on the uplands of the Somme and in the meadow lands around historic Arras.

Amid the delightful surroundings hard training commenced, relieved by six-a-side football matches and rugger trial matches to select a team for the divisional league. After a few days, we moved to Le Souich, a village nearer Doullens, where better manœuvre facilities could be obtained, and here we shared billets with the 15th Battalion. Musketry and field practices were carried out during morning parades, which lasted from 7.15 a.m. to 1 p.m.; and the afternoons were devoted to football and sports. Several interesting matches in both codes were played, and at soccer we beat our old rivals the K.O.S.B. who came to meet us with a great record of achievements. Under the handling code, we scored victories at the expense of the 6th Argyll and Sutherland Highlanders and of the brigade

The First Birmingham Battalion in the Great War

headquarters; a composite team of brigade machine gunners, 15th Royal Warwicks and headquarter staff. Our first match against the Argylls created a sensation in the division as our opponents were reported to have a very strong team with a sprinkling of internationals, and they were backed heavily by the rest of the division to win easily. Rumour has it that our very genial and robust Roman Catholic padre, one " Jim " Evans, refused to be bluffed and put his shirt on the 14th. Suffice it to say that after a fast and strenuous game, the battalion emerged victorious by 1 goal and 5 tries (20 points) to 1 try (3 points). It is interesting to record that with two exceptions the battalion team was composed of Old Edwardians of the various schools of the Foundation, and many were seen out, after the war, playing for different Birmingham clubs. The match against the brigade was a very much closer affair and the battalion only emerged victorious after a gruelling contest. A successful sports meeting was held and our very pleasant rest in ideal weather ended on 25th September, when orders were received to entrain at Petit Houvin for active service in the Ypres area. " A " Company were left behind at Le Souich to clear up and joined the battalion next day at Wizernes, near St. Omer, just in time to move up with it to support positions at Vlamertinghe on the famous Poperinghe-Ypres road.

Chapter IX.

YPRES.

Much controversial matter has been written about the Third Battle of Ypres, but this history is not concerned with the rights and wrongs of that great conflict. The Salient had always been a lively part of the line and even when offensives further south were in full swing, Ypres still maintained its reputation of being a "warm spot." Now a full offensive was being staged here. The Vimy and Messines ridges had been captured earlier in the year and the present objective for the British Army was the Passchendaele Ridge and the country between it and the newly won Messines Ridge, whilst in the background of the scheme was the dim hope of pushing through to the German submarine bases.

Since the beginning of the offensive in August, the weather had been vile, turning the flat land into a veritable sea of mud. The postponement of the original date for the opening of the offensive, owing to French unpreparedness, had robbed us of several days fine weather, and when the offensive did start on the altered day it heralded in also the wettest autumn that had been known in Flanders for nearly forty years. Constant shelling had broken down the barriers which held the water courses in position with the consequence that the ground became flooded and shell holes formed series of small lakes. Incessant rains converted the already waterlogged ground into a quagmire so that duckboard tracks were the only means of moving about in the forward areas. Any straying from these marked paths meant serious trouble and for the heavily-laden infantry, journeys up to the front line were grim adventures, but even these were not to be compared with the return journeys when the men were soaked with mud and exhausted by attacks and front line work. These duckboard tracks were well marked and proved excellent targets for enemy artillery. Many wounded never reached the casualty

YPRES

Ypres

clearing stations but perished in the mud, some after many hours of agony, gradually sinking lower and lower until they were finally completely immersed. However, the mud sometimes proved to be a blessing in disguise, for shells would often embed themselves so deeply in the mud before exploding that one would receive only a plastering of mud: uncomfortable, but distinctly better than flying steel.

Continuous trenches in the forward areas were impossible, either to dig or maintain: companies would take over lines of shell holes and then would hang on in these with no shelter of any description, at the mercy of the continual rain and ceaseless shelling. In fact these lines of water-logged shell holes were at once a danger and a defence. They were the only possible method of holding the ground, but were dangerous to their occupants inasmuch as they often contained sufficient water to drown a man.

It is impossible to convey an adequate impression of the physical conditions prevailing in the Ypres salient in the memorable autumn and winter of 1917. To move at all demanded the greatest physical pluck and endurance, but when the extra handicaps of darkness and incessant heavy shelling were added to the appalling state of the ground, then the achievements of the regiments who carried through the operations in that stricken area assume the proportions of an epic struggle, and stand out as heroic achievements, even in those days of great events.

Advances were made under these conditions, but the objectives were necessarily very limited. The Germans did not rely on the generally accepted form of trench system for defence, owing to the nature of the ground and the heavy casualties they had suffered. They had decided on defence in depth, and constructed lines of small concrete forts known as " Pill-boxes." These had walls and roofs about 3 feet thick and were proof against direct hits from the smaller-sized shells, although some of the larger ones survived direct hits from 8 inch howitzers. These " pill-boxes " were manned by machine gunners who fired through narrow loopholes: thus they were themselves practically immune from rifle and machine gun fire which

The First Birmingham Battalion in the Great War

did not penetrate these slits. These miniature forts needed very special attention, and in consequence, our training at Le Souich had been directed specially with a view to the reduction of these strong points.

Such then were the conditions of the Salient when the 5th Division arrived — and we were destined to experience to the full the horrors of the climatic conditions and the heavy shelling. At Wizernes, we received orders to entrain next day for Vlamertinghe as the 13th Brigade was to support an attack by the 59th Division east of St. Julien. Bombs and ammunition were issued and all preliminaries gone through ready for an immediate journey up to the front line to take part in an attack. At Vlamertinghe we remained in tents on the side of the famous road from Poperinghe to Ypres. On our first night we experienced our first taste of the enemy air bombing, which we soon found out was to be a regular nightly routine during the whole of our stay in the Ypres area. There was no peace for us at any time, even when out at rest ; for however far back we went enemy airmen seemed to penetrate and make our nights in the back areas more unpleasant than the days. The drone of the aeroplane engines would be heard, searchlights would search the sky for the invaders, and an appalling din would break out, made up of machine gun fire, bomb explosions, and the rapid firing of countless anti-aircraft guns. In addition to the danger from bombs, there was also the likelihood of spent shrapnel finding a mark. Transport lines suffered very heavily from these visitations and, to minimize casualties in such vicinities as Ridge Wood, low sandbag parapets were built round tents and horse lines to stop flying splinters from the bombs. Our own airmen were not inactive and at night these could be distinguished by the small lamps they carried on the tips of their wings, which they extinguished when crossing the line.

The attack of the 59th Division was quite successful and, as our services were not required, we moved back on 28th September through Poperinghe to rejoin the 5th Division near Eecke. Next day we marched over the Mont

Ypres

des Cats, with its monastery dominating the landscape, and famous for a cavalry encounter in 1914, involving the death of a German prince, but now quiet and undisturbed. At Berthen we went under canvas for a few day's training. Here we received a draft of 196 men, transferred from the cavalry, who were all of fine physique and very anxious to learn all they could of infantry drill. The rumble and roar of the guns in the Salient seemed very loud and clear, and we wondered what it would be like when we were in the midst of things, if the artillery sounded like this from 15 miles or so away.

On the morning of 2nd October, the 5th Division moved up to take over the line to the left of Gheluvelt and the Menin Road, and the battalion embussed at Berthen for Ridge Wood. At first, the roads were fairly good, and clear of traffic, but as we progressed they became worse and more crowded until the last mile was just a crawl through a sea of mud. After a hurried dinner at Ridge Wood, the battalion moved off at mid-day to take over the support line, preparatory to an attack by the 95th and 13th Brigades. The objective for the 13th Brigade was the ridge between Gheluvelt on the south and Polderhoek Château on the north.

In the peaceful days before the war, Polderhoek Château was a residence of some importance, situated in large grounds and just north of the Menin Road. A photograph of the château before the war, issued just prior to the attack, showed a charming house and a picturesque garden with a large lawn bordered with tall trees and shrubs, with here and there ornamental flower beds. But when we arrived all these had disappeared; in their place was found a ruined shell of a building reinforced with concrete and converted into a strong fortress, standing up conspicuously as an island, surrounded by swampy ground pitted with countless shell holes full of water. So that in the succeeding pages, when mention is made of the château grounds and the château itself, the reader must put aside all thoughts of a charming house with pleasant surroundings, and substitute instead a waterlogged dreary waste and a grim

The First Birmingham Battalion in the Great War

low ruin strongly fortified to resist attacks. To-day the château is represented by the remains of a pillbox, and the name Polderhoek Château conveys little or no meaning to the residents on the Menin Road, less than half a mile away.

The Royal West Kents were on the right with the K.O.S.B. on the left, and the 14th Royal Warwicks in close support. The weather was bad and as we moved forward we made the acquaintance of the terrible conditions of the thick, seemingly bottomless, muddy morass that constituted the Ypres Salient of 1917. Enemy aeroplanes were flying low, bombing and machine gunning, and combined with the muddy surroundings and shelling, conditions were very far from comfortable. It was while passing through Dickebusch that we renewed acquaintance with the triplanes we had seen first at Marles-les-Mines. They were very fast and could rise quickly and climb to an altitude faster than the biplanes, although offering a bigger target for enemy fire.

Just after we topped the ridge near Zillebeke, S.O.S. signals were sent up from the front line, and we soon found ourselves in the middle of a good artillery strafe, but fortunately our casualties were light, mainly owing to the swampy nature of the ground. One of the first casualties was our popular R.C. padre, who was wounded in the stomach. From hospital he wrote to say "The shell is still buried some three inches in the adipose tissue of my stomach, but to me three inches is nothing." We were sorry to lose our padre; he had been with the battalion in the days of the Somme, always up at the dressing station, and his cheery and unofficial outlook on life made him beloved by officers and men alike. Battalion headquarters was situated in the tunnels at Tor Top, from which point one could obtain a comprehensive view of the Salient from St. Julien in the north to Hill 60 in the south, with Passchendaele away to the east and the ruined city of Ypres to the west. The tunnels were a masterpiece of military engineering, covering a large area, with accommodation for a brigade.

Ypres

There were several entrances cunningly concealed in shell holes.

The roar of gunfire was incessant, and at night the eastern horizon was lit up with the flashes of guns and the Verey lights. By moonlight the Salient appeared very startling, with tree trunks, stranded tanks, and every yard of ground just shell holes half-full of stagnant water, the result of heavy shelling. " C " Company went up to the line in charge of their sergeant-major, " Brummie " Heath and Sergeant Davenport. The latter had been up to the line previously to survey the route, and gave his sergeant-major the direction for one half of the company while he took up the other half. When Davenport had got his men in position, he went along to the left to see how the other party had fared. On making enquiries as to the whereabouts of Heath he was told, " Oh ! we've buried him." Further enquiry elicited the facts that there were no signs of wounds or blood but that the buried man's helmet showed a big dent from a piece of shell. Davenport surmised that Heath was only suffering from concussion and ordered the men to disinter the body. The surmise proved correct, and the sergeant-major was found to be still alive, though suffering from concussion.

At 5.30 a.m., on 4th October, the 5th Division, with the 21st Division on the left and the 37th Division on the right, moved forward for the attack. The already continuous gunfire developed immediately a thousandfold, and hell itself seemed to be let loose. The attack started well and by 7 a.m. our troops reported the capture of the first objective with many prisoners. The attack on Gheluvelt had failed on our right, and the right-hand battalion of the 13th Brigade suffered severely from flanking fire. The attack did not succeed in reaching all of the objectives and the line of the brigade finally ran along the western edge of Polderhoek Château. "A" and " C " Companies, under command of Captain R. H. Baily, were moved up in close support to the attacking battalions and in reinforcing these they did valuable work. The enemy counter-attacked insistently in mass formation, but our accurate artillery barrage caused him heavy losses. Although all objectives were not gained, the attack had been a success as a considerable advance had been made, many prisoners had been taken, and severe losses had been inflicted on the Germans.

It was learned later from prisoners that the Germans had planned a big attack to take place almost at the same time that our advance commenced. One of the German prisoners remarked that we English did not know what an artillery bombardment was like as we had not experienced one of our own. An elderly unarmed German soldier was found wandering about near the support lines. After patient enquiry, it was learned that he was looking for his son who was in the same regiment and had taken part in the attack. The boy was eventually found lying wounded, and a party of German prisoners with an improvised stretcher of overcoats and German rifles without bolts, started down the line accompanied by the father. Unfortunately no further news was received of them, but one would like to have known that they reached safety.

For gallant conduct during the attack the following decorations were awarded to members of the battalion :— Military Cross — 2nd Lieut. C. H. Platt, 2nd Lieut. R. G. Warren. Military Medal (Bar) — Corporal W. E. Tongue. Military Medal — Sergeants J. H. Davenport, S. Burke ; Lance-Sergeants J. Howe, W. Robertson ; Privates W. Lunn, F. T. Shirley, A. Smith, F. E. Ralphs, W. Webb, R. H. Holloway, T. Williams, A. A. Cooper. The casualties were : officers, killed 1, wounded 5 ; other ranks, killed 24, wounded 96, missing 3, total 129.

The battalion was relieved on the night of 5th-6th October and withdrew to huts and tents in Ridge Wood, with a further loss of 9 men wounded. The accommodation in Ridge Wood was poor and very crowded and continual rain each day added to the already foul conditions A certain section of battalion headquarters, in an endeavour to improve matters, decided to dig in on a high piece of ground outside the wood and thus be safer from shell fire, bombs, and the general wet conditions. They settled themselves comfortably for the night, but on waking in the morning

GORRE CHATEAU, 1930.

Ypres

they were disagreeably surprised to find they were lying in six inches of water, which had percolated through the earth. So that, even on comparatively high ground, one was never free from the eternal water and mud. Further misfortune was in store for them, for on the same morning, when the junior member of the section was bringing back the porridge which formed part of the day's breakfast, he found difficulty in gaining access to the dug-out, and the contents of two plates found a resting place in the boots of the corporal of the section, much to this worthy's disapproval, expressed very forcibly.

Our rest was only of very short duration for, on 8th October, the battalion returned to the front line to take part in a further attempt to capture Polderhoek Château in co-operation with the Anzac Corps. After a very rainy night, the attack was made early in the morning. The château grounds were entered, but here very heavy machine gun fire was encountered and the attack was held up. Despite desperate efforts to go forward, the appalling muddy conditions made further advance impossible, and the attacking troops were forced back to their original positions. The battalion was relieved on the 10th, withdrawing to Ridge Wood, having lost Captain Clements and 2 other ranks killed, and 9 other ranks wounded.

Next day we moved out from Ridge Wood and marched via Kemmel to huts at Chippewa Camp near La Clytte for a very happy few days welcome respite. Although we were still troubled with air visitations by day and night, we were glad to be out of the mud and away from the shell fire. We received a strong draft here, including more cavalry men. Major Parry left us on appointment as instructor to the Corps Infantry School, and Captain R. H. Baily became the acting second-in-command of the battalion.

Training was carried out for our next attack over a taped out course with coloured flags. One day, when out practising, a German 'plane came over us flying very low. At the time, the battalion was scattered over a wide area waiting for the signal to go forward to attack the taped out objective, and as the 'plane came overhead, the battalion let drive with rifles and machine guns from all angles. The 'plane came down beyond a neighbouring windmill and the pilot, who had been wounded, was taken prisoner.

We were destined for more heavy work in the front of Ypres. Polderhoek Château still remained in the enemy's hands and we were about to make another attempt to capture it. We left the huts at La Clytte on 22nd October and marched to Bedford House. Bedford House must be remembered by many units which fought in the Ypres Salient. Originally it had been a château of considerable proportions, but at one time and another it had been gradually demolished by shell fire. However, there were many shacks and shelters in the ruins, and situated as it was out of enemy view and some two miles behind the front line, it formed an excellent halting place for troops passing up and down to or from the front line. It lay on the Lille Road, just to the south of the Menin Road and close to Shrapnel Corner, and the ruins of Ypres and the old Lille Gate could be plainly seen from the grounds. On the 24th, the 9th K.R.R. were relieved in the line; Colonel Murray had been slightly wounded in the leg by shrapnel at Bedford House, but he went up to the line with the battalion. Since our last tour there had been no improvement in the general conditions; it had rained incessantly for the whole of October and the ground steadily got worse. The route to the trenches was extremely bad and caused much fatigue, mud in places being over the knee. All around were visible signs of heavy losses of mules and horses, and the duckboard tracks were receiving constant attention from enemy artillery. On one occasion a shell was seen to drop on the track in front of a horse and limber. The horse was wounded and plunged off the track with the consequence that horse, limber, and driver were quickly swallowed up in the mud and lost. Enemy aeroplanes, flying low, were very active and they frequently opened fire on single men or small parties. It was a ghastly experience being chased in this manner down the Menin Road with no prospect of shelter, for shell holes would afford little or no protection from machine gun bullets fired from the air.

Ypres

At 5.20 a.m., on 26th October, the battalion, as part of the 13th Brigade, advanced against Polderhoek Château. Three battalions were in the front line, the Royal West Kents on the right, the 14th Royal Warwicks in the centre, and the 15th Royal Warwicks on the left. At the same time the 7th Division, on the immediate right of the Royal West Kents, was attacking Gheluvelt. In addition to the usual artillery barrage, the machine gun barrage had been thickened to one gun for every ten yards of front. The 14th Royal Warwicks had for their immediate objective the capture of the château and the ground to the south and east of it. " D " Company were to capture the château buildings while " B " Company were to make good the ground to the left. "A" Company were to pass through " D " Company and capture the outbuildings to the east of the château with " C " Company in reserve and under the direct orders of Colonel Murray. The battalion assembled in perfect order but before dawn the weather broke and heavy rain began to fall.

" D," "A," and " B " Companies advanced through the heavy mud with " C " Company following up closely in support. At 6.22 a.m. a report was received that platoons were on to and past the château although machine gun fire from the right flank was very severe. " B " Company sustained very heavy casualties and the advance of the Royal West Kents was retarded as the 7th Division had not succeeded in capturing Gheluvelt. This allowed the enemy to concentrate on the advance of the 13th Brigade and, as soon as the Germans learned of the capture of the château, a very heavy, well-directed fire was put down on this spot. " B " Company took their first " pill-box," but could advance no farther against a stubborn resistance, and " C " Company was sent up to reinforce. At 7.15 a.m., prisoners reported that the château was surrounded by our troops and that the Germans had suffered heavy casualties. A request was received for more rifles and Lewis guns, as those in the front line were useless on account of the mud. It was impossible to get further supplies of these and the only weapon left was the Mills bomb, which was used to good effect. Unfortunately, the château had acted as a sort of magnet to the attacking troops and instead of one company taking it, elements of five companies were drawn towards it. " C " Company was absorbed into the line and a platoon set out to attack a " pill-box " about 200 yards south of the main building. The whole of "A" Company, who soon lost all their officers, was drawn into the attack and eventually struggled forward to their final objective with one sergeant and twenty men. One company of the 15th Royal Warwicks was attracted by the château and left a gap in the line between this point and their own battalion on the left.

Reinforcements were asked for from the supporting battalion to form a defensive flank on the battalion left as there was a considerable gap in the line at this point. At 11 a.m. news was received at battalion headquarters that our troops were withdrawing from the captured positions. Captain Watts was sent up to reorganize the front line and Colonel Murray followed with the two companies of the support battalion. Unfortunately, this was too late for the enemy had reoccupied the château, and it was impossible to move the troops forward again. The line had, therefore, to be consolidated on our original position and this was successfully done. It transpired that the officer in command of the attack of the battalion on our left had gone down severely wounded. The junior officer left in charge had talked over the situation and he decided that in view of the conditions prevailing (the gap on his right flank, the useless conditions of the rifles and machine guns, and the threatening attitude of the enemy, who were forming up in front), the only thing to do was to retire. Without consulting his own battalion headquarters, he carried out this withdrawal, and the 14th Royal Warwicks had to retire afterwards to conform with the new line. It was a very unfortunate decision, as Colonel Murray had made all arrangements to form a defensive flank to protect the left battalion and had reinforcements arrived in time, this would have been done before their withdrawal. If a reference had been made to his own battalion headquarters, which was shared with the

Ypres

14th Royal Warwicks, this officer would have been told of this reinforcing move, and the loss of the château would most probably have been prevented. As it was, the good results of an excellent attack were swallowed up by the unfortunate circumstances of the subsequent withdrawal.

With the recapture of the château, the Germans swept the ground to the west with machine gun fire and counter attacked with such effect that by nightfall our troops had been pushed back to their original line. The battalion had experienced heavy casualties with a very big percentage of missing, owing, no doubt, to the treacherous state of the ground. The numbers were: officers — killed 4, wounded 4, missing 2; other ranks — killed 30, wounded 100, missing 106, making a total of 246.

The 1st Bedfords relieved us on 27th October, and we began our weary journey back to Ridge Wood. Exhausted men, struggling down from the line, tired out, with scarcely enough energy to drag one foot after another out of the clinging mud, were met by transport personnel and conducted to the field kitchens for rum and tea. When parties of a dozen were made up, they were taken to the huts and lay there, just as they were, to sleep off their exhaustion.

On the 28th, the battalion marched to rest billets at Wood Camp, near La Clytte. Only tents were available here, and on account of the exceptionally cold weather and the dampness of the surroundings, the battalion had to move on 1st November to MicMac Camp, near St. Hubertshoek. Here a very welcome rest was enjoyed after our recent strenuous experience. Major Waterworth joined as second in command. For gallant conduct, on 26th October, Private F. Shirley received a bar to his Military Medal, and Military Medals were awarded Privates H. Coles and J. W. Haynes.

In the cold and wet weather which persisted, braziers and fuel were scarce, and in consequence very valuable assets to those fortunate enough to possess them. One section possessed a brazier and fuel which had been acquired after careful " scrounging." In addition, some bacon had been " won " from the company cooks while they had been listening to stories of front line conditions related to them by a member of the section. Two new officer reinforcements, spotting the glow of the brazier, decided to make investigations, and stayed to partake of the good things provided, as they had no fire in their own tent. The section stayed up till the early hours of the morning and then turned in with a request to the officers to be careful of the very valuable fuel. However, on awakening in the morning, the section were astonished to find that not only had the officers disappeared, but the brazier and fuel had gone as well. After half-an-hour's search, one of the section located the officers' tent and found the brazier and fuel inside. It was then only a few seconds' work to retrieve the valuable articles, which were taken back to the section with much joy. Unconstitutional behaviour perhaps, but neither party could say anything, and needs must when the devil drives.

The short rest came to an end on 5th November when the battalion moved up to the line in preparation for a further attack on Polderhoek Château. The main attack was to be by the Canadian Corps some miles further north against Passchendaele, but it had been decided to make one more bid to capture the château, and the 95th Infantry Brigade were deputed to carry out the attack. On the 6th, the battalion moved to Bedford House, and next day the 95th Brigade was relieved by the 13th Brigade. Two companies of the 14th Royal Warwicks took over the left subsector north of the Reutelbeek from the 12th Gloucesters, and two companies remained near Northampton Farm in support. Passchendaele Ridge was captured by the Canadians, but no further progress was made at Polderhoek. The capture of this position would have given us wonderful command of the country, and in consequence the Germans spared no efforts to retain this point.

Five days were spent in the line, and the tour was far from comfortable. No proper trenches existed and the only shelter obtainable was under a ground sheet, stretched over a shell hole or in deserted and battered " pill-boxes." These latter certainly had drawbacks, for their scanty cover always attracted people towards them, and those who

Ypres

could not find accommodation inside would crouch near the doors or on the side furthest away from the enemy. Inside the "pill-boxes," which were usually small, accommodation for a company headquarters was very limited. So crowded did it seem that one could neither lie nor sit up straight. With the exceptionally wet weather, the bottom became covered with a pool of water, necessitating continual baling out. As these miniature forts had been captured from the Germans, the doorway faced towards the wrong way and enemy snipers were continually on the alert to pick off men who tried to enter or leave. Round the door of each "pill-box" a sad sight met the eye. A dozen or so men of various regiments would be stretched out on the ground, their sightless eyes turned towards the door through which they would have reached safety, and their still hands stretched out as though to warn others to avoid the journey. One of the saddest sights in the great British cemetery at Tyne Cot on Passchendaele Ridge is near the "pill-box" over which the Cross of Sacrifice is built. Near the point where the door was situated one comes across graves of men buried where they were found, only a few yards from the shelter of the "pill-box."

On 11th November the 5th Division was relieved by the 39th and the 21st Divisions. The two front line companies were relieved by the 16th Royal Warwicks of the 15th Brigade and the two companies in support by the 1st Cambridgeshires. The relief was carried out without casualties, but during our tour we lost the following officers and men: officers — wounded 3; other ranks — killed 8, wounded 18.

This was our last appearance in the line at Ypres, and it is interesting to record that the battalion were the only troops to capture the château, for from 28th October this stronghold resisted all subsequent attempts, and it remained in enemy hands until August, 1918, when it was finally captured in the German retreat from Belgium.

The conditions for the advancing infantry during the period at Ypres were too bad almost to be imagined, but tribute must be paid to the work of the stretcher-bearers who carried out their work in a very gallant manner, overcoming seemingly unsurmountable difficulties in carrying wounded men down the line. Nor can we forget the heroic work of the gunners who carried on without shelter, with their guns sunk so low in the mud that when relief was carried out guns had to be left in position and handed over to the incoming unit, and subjected to continual heavy counter-battery bombardment. Despite these hardships, barrages were never allowed to be interfered with and adequate artillery support was always forthcoming when called for.

The battalion withdrew to Scottish Wood, but Scottish Wilderness would have been a better name, for not a blade of grass was to be seen, nor could a stick or any object likely to be of use for making a fire be found anywhere. The battalion base details, who had been stationed at Ridge Wood during the attack, moved to Scottish Wood to rejoin the battalion and hereby hangs another tale of a brazier. Wonderfully useful things were braziers in those days, and almost worth their weight in gold. A corporal of the dumped personnel, knowing the bleakness of Scottish Wood and the shortness of braziers, decided to take his own with the necessary fuel. The move took place at night and, as the weather was very wet and cold, the fire was still burning when it was time to move. The help of a comrade was enlisted, and with a stout stick thrust through the handle of the brazier, the fire was taken, still burning. The route to Scottish Wood lay through one of the largest ammunition dumps in the district, with large notices displaying cautions — "No Smoking," "Danger," "No Lights." Unmindful of these, our worthy firebearers hastened through this area with sparks flying in all directions. Pandemonium was let loose; sentries, sergeant-majors, and the whole world seemed to be yelling, "Put that light out," but the brazier escaped their clutches and reached Scottish Wood safely, where it was the only fire in the camp. For hours after, the tent was full of various people trying to get warm, so that the corporal saw very little of his fire until the fuel had been practically exhausted.

Ypres

After two days' rest, a move was made to tents at a camp near Westoutre. This was another bleak spot, but on the 15th, the battalion entrained at Ouderdom for Nielles les Blequin. This mode of transport was a decided improvement, for marches in the Salient were definitely uncomfortable. Heavy traffic impeded movement and churned up roads, making very heavy work for the heavily-laden infantry in the soft muddy surface of the rough country roads. Our transport was often bogged in the morasses encountered, and this involved hard labour in extricating their vehicles.

During the rail journey in the usual 40 hommes cattle trucks, the train was bombed by aeroplanes whilst in St. Omer Station, but fortunately no damage was done. From Nielles the battalion marched to billets in the villages of Bollescamp, Harletts, and Fromental, situated on the main St. Omer-Boulogne road.

The villages were situated in very charming country, hilly and well-wooded, and the rest in billets in these peaceful surroundings was very welcome and beneficial. To be in comfortable billets with straw to sleep on seemed luxury after the cold huts and tents on muddy ground. Visits were made to Desvres, a small country town close at hand and also to St. Omer, a fine town with good buildings, shops, and a charming cathedral. A rugger match was played between the officers and sergeants and the rest of the battalion — the first game to be played since leaving Le Souich in September. The Rest won an exciting game by 1 try to nil, much to the great satisfaction of the other ranks.

Only one thing tended to mar the very pleasant rest. At the back of everyone's mind was the thought that away to the east was the Ypres Salient, and that a return there was not improbable. However, this was not to be, for the word "ITALY" seemed to take a prominent part in cook-house rumours.

It was reported unofficially that the 5th Division had been selected to form part of the British Army which was being sent to reinforce the Italian front. So that when orders were received to move to St. Pol we felt almost certain that we were going to leave France. This march through quiet villages and charming scenery was very pleasant and much appreciated.

We hoped, and future events justified our hopes, that we were definitely leaving the Ypres sector behind us. If any name is indelibly inscribed on the records of British soldiery, it is Ypres. No place on any of the war fronts holds such memories for most British infantry units, and the 14th Royal Warwicks among them. Mud and misery to an extent undreamed of, were the main features of all the winters in the Salient, and especially of the winter of 1917. Incessant shelling, and intense aerial bombing were the added horrors of 1917. Sanctuary Wood, Inverness Copse, Polderhoek Château; what names to conjure up a nightmare! Was there ever a road in the world like the Menin Road? Of the thousands who tramped east along that way of desolation, how few returned. The waterlogged wilderness that was the Ypres Salient exacted from the British Army hundreds of lives for every yard of muddy desolation which was wrested from the Germans. And, behind it all, the gaunt ruins of the ancient Flemish city lay open to the sky, and the splintered ruin of the Cloth Hall Tower pointed skyward through all the weary months during which the British Army guarded those ruins and kept them inviolate from the invader. The motto of the French before Verdun was that of the British before Ypres — " They shall not pass ! "

CHAPTER X.

ITALY.

It was now definitely confirmed that the Division was under orders for Italy. Warm clothing was issued, and officers and men were being recalled from courses and leave — in the latter case some were returned before they had left France on their way home. At first we were assured that this was a normal procedure, but eventually the truth came out that Italy was to be our destination. Everyone was delighted at the prospect of the change.

The Italian Army, whose morale had been weakened and undermined by insidious propaganda, had been pushed back from the Isonzo front to the Piave River, which enters the Adriatic Sea just north of Venice. In the mountains about Asiago and Mont Grappa, they were standing firmer, but were still being hard pressed. It was decided therefore, that twelve divisions (five British and seven French) should be dispatched at once from the Western Front to the aid of the Italian Army.

The Fifth was one of the British divisions chosen, and together with the 48th (South Midland) Division, which included four battalions of Royal Warwicks, formed the 11th Corps. As the 7th Division with the 2nd Royal Warwicks was in the other Corps, there were thus eight battalions of the Royal Warwickshire Regiment sent to Italy, and six of these were originally composed of Birmingham men.

On 29th November, the battalion left St. Pol in two trains, made up of the usual cattle trucks (40 hommes and 8 chevaux). Each man had two blankets for the journey and accommodation was less cramped than usual; thus conditions generally were not uncomfortable. In view of the long journey in front of us, visits had been paid to the canteen to buy extra rations to supplement the army supplies. The journey occupied six days, and to men whose outlook had so recently been confined to the Ypres Salient,

The First Birmingham Battalion in the Great War

a journey through the heart of France came as a visit to another world. Although the trains crawled along, with no heed to scheduled stops, the leisurely pace suited our mood. There were numerous unauthorized halts, and the troops took advantage of these to get hot water from the engine driver to make tea; or to obtain food from the natives; or to roam about the permanent way in the casual fashion peculiar to the British Tommy. Some of these halts were of several hours' duration, but invariably the engine driver started off again without giving any warning. Even then, for the most part, one could catch up the train, so leisurely was our progress. If tea was being made, one had time to gather up the utensils, sprint along and board the train before it had gathered speed.

In the evening of the first day we skirted Paris and could see the lights of the great city. On leaving the capital behind, the train displayed an unusual outburst of energy, and we were soon heading south for Dijon and Lyons. Down the valley of the Rhone we rolled, and on to Tarascon: here we entered the charming countryside of Provence, with its sunny southern atmosphere and beautiful autumn tints, which still defied the grip of winter. Arles was passed, and Marseilles was reached just as night was falling. It was feared that the beauties of the Riviera would be passed during the night, but on awakening next morning the train was found to be still in the vicinity of the seaport city. Then followed a wonderful run along the Riviera coast, in perfect sunny weather with cloudless blue skies. Through Toulon, Nice, and Cannes we progressed, and as one man put it, "It seemed like Heaven after the horrors of Hell." Everywhere we were cheered on our way by the inhabitants of the towns. English people met us on the stations with tea and cigarettes; and at Nice we were welcomed by the wife of the Town Major of Bethune. When we crossed the border and ran along the Italian Riviera, the same enthusiasm was displayed. Our first stop of importance in Italy was Turin, where we enjoyed a long halt. And so the journey continued eastward across Italy to Est and Montagna, at which places the two halves of the battalion

Italy

detrained on 5th December. We found ourselves in the northern extreme of the wide plain which stretches up from the River Po to the foothills of the Alps, and in the clear air the beautiful snow-capped mountains seemed very close, although actually they were thirty miles or more away. The air seemed very much colder here. During the day, the sun shone in a blue sky, and the atmosphere was warm, but at night we experienced frosts and bitter cold.

On the 6th, the battalion was re-united in Noventa Vicentina where we found the village placarded with posters in Italian and English, " England for Ever," and eulogising the altruistic intentions of England in showing she was fighting, not for mere mercenary gain, but for the rights of the smaller nations by sending some of her best troops to Italy's aid. The corps was not yet functioning, and the battalions were thrown more or less upon their own resources. No English rations, except bully and biscuits were obtainable, and we were without cigarettes and bread for three weeks. While we had been moving, the Battle of Cambrai had been launched, and railway material which would otherwise have been sent to Italy, had been used on the Cambrai front for reinforcements of men and supplies of ammunition. The day after we left St. Pol, all movement to Italy was temporarily suspended. In fact, Colonel Murray's train, with brigade headquarters, was the last to run. The remaining units of the Division were formed into an emergency brigade, and held in readiness to move at 6 hours' notice. Had it not been for the fact that our artillery had already left for Italy, we should probably have been thrown into the furnace round Bourlon Wood, and have never seen the olive groves of Italy at all.

We had a new language difficulty to combat, but with the usual resource of the British Army, this was soon overcome. It was not long before we acquired a smattering of the language, and by pantomime and a few phrases from " Italian in a Month," we were able to make ourselves understood. In the early days, Q.M.S. Denham of " D " Company, went on a shopping expedition, accompanied by one of the cooks, to purchase some pork. Neither of them understood a word of the language, but Denham pointed to the joints hanging in the shop, and the cook proceeded to cut up what was required, while the shopkeeper looked on. Denham wrapped up the meat, and then by signs asked how much there was to pay. More signs indicated the amount required and when this was paid up, the shopkeeper smiled and our men departed, with everyone satisfied. Surely, true economy of words!

New foods and drinks were tried. We made an early acquaintance with Polenta. This was the staple article of diet among the majority of Italians. It resembled stiff batter pudding, being made from Indian maize flour. It found favour with the omnivorous British soldiery, although it was regarded in some quarters as a barbarous survival of the Middle Ages. One old lady informed us that polenta had been popular in the time of the Medicis. During one of the then common poisoning epidemics which added interest to life in Renaissance Italy, the peasant folk, for safety's sake, began to make their own bread immediately before it was consumed. Thus only could they be sure of what they were eating, and the quickly made polenta became a national dish. We could not vouch for the accuracy of the old lady's story, but it certainly deserved to be true. Wines, of which the Vino Nero appeared to be the most popular, were very cheap, the equivalent of eightpence being charged for a quart, while for the modest sum of half-a-crown a four-course meal with wine and coffee could be procured.

The plain stretched uninterruptedly to the north and north-east, but as we marched nearer to the line, we approached the snow-capped mountains north of the Piave River. The weather continued biting cold but dry, and the sharp air which came straight from the mountains was very invigorating.

On 7th December, the battalion marched to Italian hutments at Mossano, at the foot of the mountains. The scenery was truly magnificent, for around us was the plain, dotted with picturesque old-world Italian villages and vineyards, rising in the north and west to the snow-capped peaks.

Italy

It was at Mossano that a new way of overcoming the language difficulty was discovered. Two of the signallers found themselves one evening in a large inn on the hillside. The place was crowded with Italian troops, and our two worthies had difficulty in attracting the notice of the landlord. At last, he deigned to spare them a moment and by pantomime and broken Italian they tried to order a meal. The landlord, either very dense or slow, was unable to make anything of the weird noises and weirder actions and called a group of Italian soldiers to his aid, but with little success. The Italians knew no English, our signallers knew no Italian; the signallers had some French, but no one else had. It looked hopeless for our signallers' dinner until one of the Italian soldiers happened to remove his cap, thereby disclosing what looked like a tonsure. " By Jove," said signaller No. 1, " a priest, for a quid ! What about Latin ? " And then began the most unusual process of an Englishman trying to order a dinner in Latin. " Shades of King Edward's, and jolly old B—— taking the classical sixth ! " The Italian troops turned out to be some sort of theological students, who were serving with the Red Cross, and were quite at home in speaking Latin. Our signallers obtained their dinner and spent a convivial evening with the Italians into the bargain.

General training was carried out, and on the 10th the battalion played a rugger match at Nanto against the 13th Brigade H.Q. Group. Our previous victories at Le Souich and our rugger reputation had induced our opponents to whip up a strong team to stop our run of victories at any cost. This they were successful in doing, for after a game which early on developed into a maul, the battalion was defeated by 15 points to nil. This was one of the very few defeats sustained by the battalion rugger team.

On the 17th, we continued our move forward along frost-bound roads to St. Giorgio di Brenta, which was reached on the 19th. Our progress through the hamlets and towns was indeed interesting. Romantic names appeared on the signposts — Padua, Piazzola, Barbarano, Verona. The never-ending vineyards, and the great grey

The First Birmingham Battalion in the Great War

oxen slowly drawing the cumbersome farm carts, the dark-skinned, cheerful " bambini," and the quaint arcaded streets, all helped to smother recollections of the Salient. Polderhoek seemed far away ; we were in a romantic country, the land of the Caesars. Halts were made at Pojana for the night of the 17th, and at St. Giorgio di Bosco on the 18th. A long stay was enjoyed at St. Giorgio di Brenta, and it can safely be said that this period was one of the most pleasant periods spent by the battalion on active service. Everyone was comfortably housed in billets, although the village being straggling, these were somewhat scattered. Houses were possessed of only a single fireplace each, a huge affair in the kitchen, and wood was the only fuel obtainable. The only method of heating the rooms appeared to be by means of iron grids filled with embers from the kitchen fire, carried from room to room, so that it proved a really trying business to get a good fire.

The Italian troops in the vicinity appeared to be very dissatisfied with their lot, after they had watched the issue of food to our own men. Our issues of bacon and beef were so much superior to the horseflesh — which was all they had in the meat line. Civilians, too, regarded our commissariat as bountiful, and in this connection the following incident may be of interest. Horseflesh was scarce, and consequently desirable. One of our transport horses sickened and died late one wintry afternoon. Owing to the approaching dark, the task of burial was postponed until the following morning. The news evidently quickly spread amongst the villagers, for next morning we were surprised to find only the skeleton of a horse — the meat had been cut off by the inhabitants. This meant less work for the burying party, and the Italians had extra meat.

The roads were very narrow, and our motor transport, in contrast to the Italian short base Fiat lorries, had great difficulty in negotiating the sharp corners and steep hills. The Italians were certainly adept drivers. They took the narrow mountain roads at top speed, ignoring the sheer drop of hundreds of feet which loomed below. No fatalities

Italy

occurred, however, but motoring in the Alps was certainly not good for the nerves.

The battalion was now engaged on general training, and particular attention was given to musketry. During this period, Colonel Murray rejoined the battalion from his temporary command of the 13th Brigade, in the absence of Brigadier-General L. O. W. Jones. Colonel Murray had been in command of the brigade during the move to Italy, and Major R. H. Baily had commanded the battalion, and became second-in-command on the C.O.'s return. There were no afternoon parades, but everyone was expected to support the many rugger and soccer matches which were arranged, and which provided much enjoyment.

On 24th December, the first issue of the *Warwick News* appeared as a Christmas number. This paper was edited by Lance-Corporal Harper, of canteen fame, and was issued practically daily, the printing being undertaken by the Orderly Room staff on their duplicator. Unfortunately, we are unable to reproduce a copy of the paper, which contained all the sport news, daily events, and matters of interest to the battalion. The *Warwick News* had a short but vivid career, and was appreciated by all ranks. The last issue was on 21st January, 1918, the day before our move from St. Giorgio. In the columns one reads the results of platoon six-a-side soccer matches, and of a competition to spot the winners of the final tie in these games. In the last issue we learn that No. 1 platoon won the final game, but the name of the winner of the prize is not handed down to posterity. In this issue there is also an account of a soccer match between the 14th Regg. Fanteria DIMARCIA and " C " Company of the 14th Royal Warwicks, which was won by " C " Company after an excellent game. A rugger match between H.Q. Company and the Rest is reported to have been won by the H.Q. Company by 8 points to 3 points; and, as a final social gossip item, one was asked, " who was the officer who, after being inoculated, stayed in bed with watch in hand waiting for his 48 hours off duty to expire ? " Does anyone remember ?

The First Birmingham Battalion in the Great War

We were subjected to bombardment from enemy aeroplanes, which made Padua (British Army headquarters) their special target, and this place was bombed almost every night. Bombing was very common in Italy, and trenches, back areas, and villages were bombed indiscriminately and continuously, Treviso and Castel Franco being favourite targets. On this account we found later that Treviso was very sparsely inhabited.

Citadella was very near, and to this old-world town, surrounded by ancient walls with towers practically intact, visits were paid for excellent meals in the cafés there. The main streets were wide, with arcades running along each side.

Christmas arrived, and everyone had a thoroughly enjoyable time. Each company had its own special Christmas dinner, consisting of roast beef or pork, cabbage, Christmas pudding, fruits, and wines. Oh! shades of Blighty! all thoughts of war were abolished for the day. Boxing Day was also a general holiday, and without doubt this Christmas time was by far the best the battalion spent overseas. Not content with the splendid fare provided for Christmas, many gatherings took place at private houses and cafés, where chickens and other succulent fare were put on the table, and the evenings usually finished up with impromptu concerts.

The battalion took part in a divisional scheme on 27th December, and were inspected by General Sir H. Plumer, who was in command of the British forces in Italy. Next day the battalion attended a ceremonial parade at which medal ribbons were presented.

On New Year's Eve, the headquarters company had a supper and smoking concert, at which Colonel Murray and other company officers were present. Headquarters company partook of this dinner in the dining-hall of the old château, which served as battalion headquarters. This was a fine old room, panelled in dark oak, and the old timbers, which shone in the candlelight, were reminiscent of the bygone days of the Borgias, and had probably seen many a noble feast and gay company. Certainly it had

Italy

never seen a more cheerful or convivial crowd than the khaki-clad Midland men who feasted there the last day of that eventful year — 1917. The commanding officer made a speech, and gave us a real breezy and amusing quarter of an hour. Afterwards, he insisted on all officers present making a speech. At midnight, Colonel Murray mounted the table and led the singing of "Auld Lang Syne." The concert finished with the C.O. being carried shoulder high to his mess, not a very regimental procedure, perhaps, but a very popular one. The weather was intensely cold at this period, and on New Year's Day a heavy fall of snow occurred. Although soccer matches could be played, the hard, frosty ground prevented many rugger games.

The New Year Honours contained the following awards for the battalion :—

M.C. — Captain R. C. Watts.

D.C.M. — Com.-Serg.-Major C. B. Plenderleith, Corporal A. G. Smith, Private A. H. Hudson.

Mentioned in Dispatches — Sergeants C. J. Brown, B. V. Davies, D. W. Tuffley.

A further distinction applicable to the whole British Army in Italy was also received at this time. An official memorandum was received stating that Italy had been much impressed by the excellent discipline of the British troops, their delicacy of feeling when dealing with the inhabitants, and with the cleanliness of the billets and the general appearance of the men.

Peace and quiet continued to prevail, and general training was carried out. In fact, life was reminiscent of training days in England. Reconnaissance parties were sent up to the front line on Mount Grappa to survey the ground and general conditions, in case we should have to take over any sector. The parties found that the front line life was very tranquil, with little shelling. The lines were far apart and wonder was expressed that such positions on the heights could ever be captured. The journeys up and down the mountains, climbing on mule tracks, were very arduous and thirsty work, and the wine shops, which were to be found at intervals, were decidedly popular. There was a very grave danger from colic if lumps of snow were picked up and used as thirst quenchers, and precautions were taken to stop this practice.

On 22nd January, much to everyone's regret, orders were received to leave the village as the 5th Division was moving up to the forward area. On the first day, we marched 24 kilometres to Resana, the next day another 30 kilometres to Pederno, finishing up on the third day with a 6 kilometre march to Povegliano. The roads were bad, the surface had been affected by the thaw, and the heavy traffic had not improved matters. Povegliano was a village quite deserted but barely touched by the war, although several buildings had horrible gaping openings caused through bombs and shells.

The 5th Division relieved the 58th and 48th Italian Divisions on 25th January, in the Piacenza Tevere sector, with the 13th Brigade on the left and the 95th Brigade on the right. The British artillery took over the Italian positions gradually, the artillery relief not being completed until the 30th. The 13th Brigade relieved the 58th Italian Division, with the 14th and 15th Royal Warwicks in the front line, the K.O.S.B. in support, and the Royal West Kents in brigade reserve. It will thus be seen that one British brigade was taking over a sector previously held by an Italian division, and in many cases three or four of our men were taking over posts which had previously been held by eighteen or twenty Italians. This caused the Italians considerable alarm, and in many cases difficulty was experienced in persuading the Italians to leave, as the idea of leaving a post usually manned by twenty Italians in charge of three or four Englishmen appeared too ridiculous to be permitted. However, the relief was eventually carried out, although a great deal of congestion took place. Italian helmets were worn by the British sentries for the first few weeks, and captured Austrians expressed great astonishment to find that the British troops were in the line.

The position taken up by the battalion was on the south bank of the Piave, with the Austrians on the other bank. The river, which at this point constituted No-Man's Land,

Italy

was about ¾ mile to a mile wide, and on either side of the river the banks, with steep sides facing the water, had been built up as high as 40 or 50 feet in some places to protect the country from flooding. This was a very necessary precaution, as the melting of snow in the mountains caused a rapid rise in the river. Stone stairways led from the tops of the banks down to the river and these were used by patrols to reach the river bed. Behind us the level plain stretched right back to Venice, but in front the prospect was entirely different. Behind the Austrian lines the country rose up to the snow-capped mountains. The clear sunlight with the intensely blue skies and the vivid colourings of the mountains made a gorgeous picture. From the foothills of these mountains the Austrians dominated our back areas and the good visibility helped their observation, so that all roads behind our lines had to be camouflaged with netting and sacking.

We found the trenches in good condition. The sentry posts themselves were built on the top of the river bank, but the small garrison manning the post was accommodated in trenches below and behind them. On our side, the Piave consisted of a series of rivulets winding among stretches of shingle. Plank bridges, built just under the water, were provided for patrols to cross these streams, and near the Austrian bank there were proper bridges where the water was deeper and ran swiftly. The noise of the running water deadened the crunch of the feet of patrols on the shingle. Life in the front line was quite comfortable and very little like the Western Front. When we first took over the line, the Austrians were seen parading on the opposite side of the river, and apparently very little activity had taken place recently. However, the enemy were not long left in peace, for matters soon livened up, and the Austrians found it unsafe to show themselves.

At night, four-hour patrols in the river bed were undertaken; the chief danger experienced by these patrols was the risk of a slip off the small bridges. But, as the antidote to likely chills consisted of doses of rum, immersions were not unpopular. During the daytime, targets were hung out

The First Birmingham Battalion in the Great War

on the barbed wire in the river bed, and rifle practice indulged in, the spent bullets going over to the Austrian lines. This practice ultimately proved of great value, for the proficiency in quick firing gained on the Piave was of immense value in April, 1918, at the Fôret de Nieppe, when the battalion was called on to repel many heavy German attacks with little or no artillery support. So quiet were the conditions that one company headquarters occupied an untouched house 100 yards behind the front line and used the upstairs rooms, while the transport brought rations up to a point 300 yards from the river. Water for drinking and washing was obtained in buckets from No-Man's Land.

After four days, the battalion was relieved by the K.O.S.B., and on 2nd February the 1st Bedfords relieved us in the support position, from which point we moved back to Visnadella. The weather was ideal and several enjoyable days were spent, football matches being the main item on the programme. The soccer team played the 2nd K.O.S.B. under the eyes of the Austrian observation balloons on the 5th, and on the following day the rugger team beat the 13th Field Ambulance. During the progress of the match against the K.O.S.B., the enemy had dropped shells near the playing field, so that in the notice relating to the rugger match the following paragraph appeared: " It is requested that spectators either lie or sit down in order to minimize enemy observation." The story went that at a nearby playing field trenches had been dug around the pitch so that the spectators could stand in them to watch the game. The rugger team continued its victorious career by defeating the 1st East Surreys on the 8th by 20 points to 8 points, but on the 9th defeat was suffered at the hands of the King Edward's Horse by 17 points to 3 points. This team contained some of the members of the famous Springbok team which visited England just prior to the war. However, on the same day, the soccer team upheld the battalion tradition by winning the Brigade league final.

These pleasant times came to an end on the 10th, when the 13th Brigade relieved the 95th Brigade in the right

Italy

subsector, the 14th and 15th Royal Warwicks taking over the front line. A few casualties were sustained during this tour, but all these were caused through Italian bombs left in the trenches. Regular trench tours now took place: reliefs in and out of the line being carried out at definite periods in conjunction with the Royal West Kents. Reserve billets were at Visnadella, where we were troubled by shelling and continual night bombing. This village was on the main road to Venice, and the enemy planes followed this route on their nightly visits. Rarely did a night pass without visits from the enemy airmen. The effect of the bombing was cumulative and nerve-racking, and an illustration of this is provided by the following incident. Early on arrival in Italy, a sergeant was sitting in the room of a house in Visnadella when an enemy 8.9 shell dropped near, killing and wounding several men in the room behind him, but, imperturbably, he carried on with his work. Later on however, in March, after continual experience of the bombing and shelling, the sound of bombs dropping anywhere in the neighbourhood caused an undignified and hurried retreat out into the open fields. Few things are more terrifying than aerial bombing, for one cannot calculate where a bomb will fall, whereas an old soldier generally has a very good idea where a shell will land.

As leave to England was very scarce, special leave was granted to Rome, Nice, and other large towns, but all those wishing to avail themselves of this opportunity of seeing the country had first to submit to vaccination. Several men spent their leave in Rome, where they had a very pleasant time, and were well received. The Riviera also was visited and one company-sergeant-major went with his quartermaster-sergeant to Nice and Monte Carlo to sample the delights there. Unfortunately, Monte Carlo was visited first and the temptations of the casino proved too much for the sergeant-major. The remainder of the holiday was spent quietly in Nice, where he had to rely on his companion to pay all expenses.

By this time we were pretty well settled down and found life on the Italian front far from unpleasant. The wines of the country were cheap and good, and we were well treated by the natives, who were not averse from selling wines and food to the well-paid " Ingleesi." Indeed, they were so eager to oblige us that on one occasion a party in a restaurant were served with a dish of meat, the bones in which aroused some suspicion. Sergeant Moretti, who was of the party, made enquiries and informed the diners, after they had dined, that a portion of dog had been served. Sergeant Moretti, who will be remembered as the Battalion Sergeant Tailor, was back in his native Italy; and very useful he was in acting as interpreter on billeting parties. British troops were always welcome in the farmhouses, where wine was invariably taken in the stable as being the warmest place. The large, grey oxen kept the stable at a pretty high temperature, and here the family would congregate in winter, and over the flagons of Vino Nero would discuss the European situation with any Tommies who called: and callers were frequent. Occasionally, the presence of Italian troops, together with the family, the oxen, and the wine would warm things up to a considerable extent, and there are one or two stories of lamps kicked over and "rough-houses" in the dark. However, although the 1st Birminghams were a peaceful crowd on the whole, they were well able to take care of themselves.

At the end of February, preparations were commenced for an operation to be carried out early in March in order to help the Third Italian Army to recover lost ground between the old and new Piave Rivers, near Venice. With a view to drawing off the enemy's attention from that place and pinning his reserves down, the 5th Division were to send a brigade across the Piave on the day of the Italian attack, establish a bridge head and hold the ground for forty-eight hours. This was to be carried out by the 15th Brigade, while the 14th Royal Warwicks made a demonstration. Our men were practised in aquatics and other necessary training, and patrols were constantly out reconnoitring the ground. Extra bridges were built just under the water level, and everyone was looking forward to an interesting operation, on mobile lines. By March 1st,

Italy

all was ready, but unexpectedly heavy rains came on and the mountain streams which fed the Piave became roaring torrents: the Piave itself rose rapidly, and became a really formidable obstacle; the temporary bridges were washed away and the operation had to be abandoned.

Our stay in the Visnadella district came to an end on 16th March, when the 5th Division was relieved by the 48th Italian Division; the 13th Brigade being relieved by the Aquila Brigade. The battalion handed over Visnadella to the K.O.S.B. and withdrew to Ponzana, five miles away. Next day we marched ten miles to Castagnola and moved on again the following day to Le Pittoche, a further twelve miles march. Here we stayed until the 23rd March, spending the time in training, and bathing in the numerous streams in the vicinity. The weather was rapidly becoming warmer and bathing was very popular. This in March! The Italian climate was certainly not half-hearted. At Christmas it had been almost Arctic, but in March we were bathing and sitting out in the open as if it were midsummer. On the 23rd, we moved back to Castagnara for training in mountain warfare, and to obtain the necessary extra equipment. It was understood that we should take over positions in the lower Alps north of Vicenza, and the prospect of spending the spring in these delightful surroundings was pleasant in anticipation.

On the 26th we marched 11 miles to Veggiano, and while in this village the Divisional Show was held. The battalion transport took second prize, and " A " Company represented the battalion in the marching contest, taking third place in the division. This test consisted of an eight-mile march in full pack, with inspections of kit at various points.

Rumours were reaching us of the German offensive on the Western Front, with the captures of ground and prisoners. We heard that the Germans were shelling Paris. This we refused to believe; even our susceptibility to rumour would not accept this; but it proved all too true, and we began to anticipate a return to France, hoping against experience that the 5th Division would not be required. Our worst fears were realized, however, and on

The First Birmingham Battalion in the Great War

1st April — an auspicious day — the 5th Division commenced entraining for France. The 13th Infantry Brigade left from Pojana, the first half of the battalion starting at 3 a.m. and the second half following five hours later. The weather, as if in sympathy with the general mood, broke up, and marked our exit from the Italian front. This had been the most pleasant part of the battalion's activities overseas. In clean country, under sunny skies, we had enjoyed ourselves to the full. The war had been a "good war," and our four months' absence from the Western Front had done much to remove the war weariness, which was beginning to show itself after two-and-a-half years' of active service. So we entrained for France in good form and fettle, but at the same time we realized that things were far from quiet on the Western Front, whither we were bound.

Chapter XI.

NIEPPE.

NEEDLESS to say, we did not find the return journey so exhilarating as the outward journey. We were by now sufficiently experienced campaigners to understand the full significance of the official reports, and, reading between the lines, we realized that things were serious. The Italians viewed our departure with considerable misgiving; they seemed to think that we were leaving them " in the lurch." Just at this time, however, news began to come through of the large American forces that were on their way to Europe, and the prospect of aid from the " Americani " did something to compensate the Italians for the loss of the " Ingleesi."

The train journey followed the same route that we had come by. When we crossed the frontier into France, our reception was distinctly friendly. Everything seemed the same as when we passed through in the previous December, but it seemed strange to see life pursuing its normal course, while further north momentous events were taking place, and division after division was being shattered in attempts to hold up the great German advances on the Somme and at Vimy.

On 6th April, we reached Amiens to find that the Germans were within 10 miles of the town. Shrapnel bursts were observed just over the eastern suburbs, while, from what we could see, the town was deserted. Continuing our journey, we passed on through Doullens, and one-half of the battalion detrained at Petit Houvain, and the other half at Frevent;. re-uniting at Bonnieres, a village about six miles east of Le Souich, which had been our rest billets before going up to Ypres in the previous September.

The weather was dull and cold and in marked contrast to the warm sunshine of Italy. We realized only too well that we were back on the Western Front, for the situation

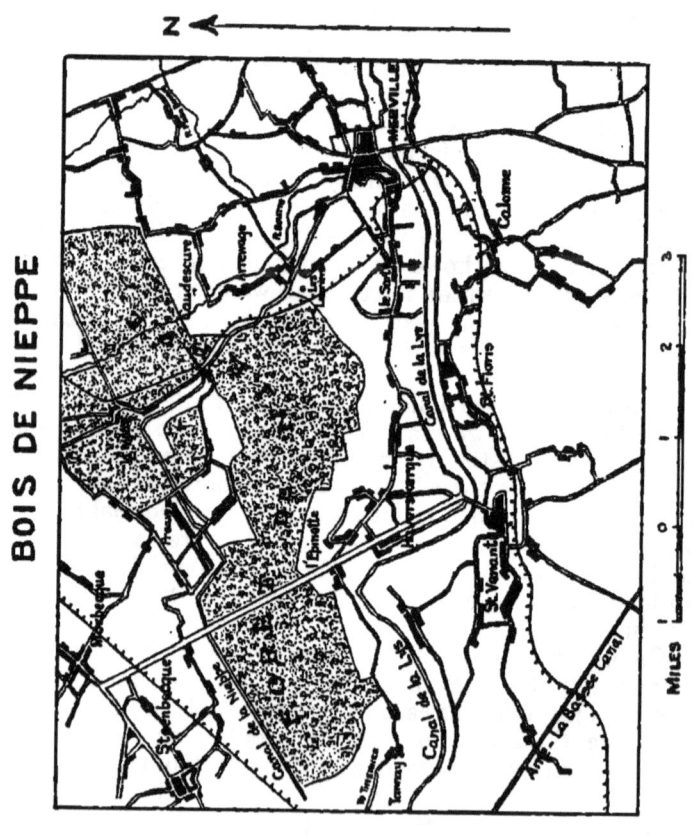

Nieppe

was in keeping with the gloomy weather. We were still very much in the dark as to the tactical situation, but the Colonel gave us a talk on the recent operations and the importance of musketry, after which we did realize more fully what was before us.

On the 10th, orders were received to relieve the Canadians south-west of Arras, and the battalion marched away from Bonnieres en route for Mondicourt, preparatory to taking over the line near Wailly. When we had nearly reached our destination, dispatch riders arrived with orders to cancel the relief and return to billets to be ready to move at once as the Division was wanted for more urgent work further north. So for the second time in the battalion's history, a Wailly stunt was cancelled for more urgent matters. After an hour's rest, during which dinner was served, the battalion turned back and marched to Humberscourt, but as no billets were available here, the march was continued to Beaudricourt, where excellent billets were found. Altogether, twenty-four miles had been covered in the day, but the battalion had marched in good style, and retired for rest, tired-out but full of excitement, and not displeased at the prospect of mobile operations.

News was received that a heavy German attack had been launched against the First Army between the La Bassée Canal and Armentières. The Portuguese had been driven in near Neuve Chappelle, and the Forêt de Nieppe and Hazebrouck were being threatened. In connection with this, it is interesting to note that had the Germans delayed their attack by one day, the Portuguese would have been out of the line, as it had been arranged that British troops should take over the Portuguese sector.

At 11 a.m., on 11th April, the battalion again set out for Mondicourt, and there entrained at 6 p.m. for the Aire area. Thiennes was reached about 2.30 a.m. next morning. Portions of the line on the way up showed signs of war, for in one place a train had been cut in two by a shell and Chocques station was badly knocked about. The battalion detrained in pitch darkness, and went into bivouacs in a field close to the station. No one seemed to know anything, and the situation was very obscure. There were no signs of warfare, artillery fire was conspicuous by its absence, and over all pervaded an ominous silence as though the world itself was waiting with ears strained for the first note which would herald stirring events. The intention was for the battalion to bivouac in the wood all day, and to return to billets at Thiennes at night. So we marched into the wood, posted sentries, settled ourselves down for a rest, taking off boots and puttees, and made ourselves thoroughly at home, with visions of manœuvres in Upper and Lower Nuthurst in the good old Sutton days. But these fancies were soon scattered, for patrols reported that German outposts were moving near the eastern outskirts of the forest. Up till then we had been under the impression that the Portuguese were between us and the Germans, but our patrols found no one, and information was received that the Portuguese had absolutely given way, while enemy patrols were moving freely over a wide range. The exact position of the main body of the Germans had not been located, but we realized later that when we detrained there had been nothing between us and the enemy troops, who were busy ransacking the wine cellars of Merville, which had been captured on the 11th. If the Germans had but realized the situation, our plight would indeed have been a desperate one.

One patrol returned to battalion headquarters with this information, and found there the Commander-in-Chief, who himself received the report. We had a chance here of noticing (and it was confirmed by others who had had an opportunity of observing it before), that Sir Douglas Haig always carefully returned a salute, no matter what one's rank might be. It was always a full salute in the proper style, an index to the character of the great soldier he was.

The information received from the patrols caused great excitement and hustle, for orders were received to move forward at once. Packs and extra equipment were dumped and the battalion prepared for action. The 5th Division had received orders from Corps to re-capture Merville, and with this task in front of them, the 13th Brigade moved south of the forest via Tannay. Attempts were made to

Nieppe

obtain artillery support, as our own divisional artillery was still on the march; but at La Motte Château everything was in chaos, and we had to carry on without any guns. Two hours later, the attack on Merville was cancelled, but the 13th Brigade, with the 14th and 15th Royal Warwicks in the front line, had already begun to move through the forest in open order. The weather was fine now, and as we crashed through the undergrowth, we contrasted the bustle and movement with the stagnation which had prevailed on the Piave. Occasionally, through a clearing, we would catch a glimpse of the open country away to the east and, although it was impossible to see any great distance, yet the ominous black columns of smoke which rose up from behind the trees, told a tale of burning villages and dumps. There was no sound of firing. Wherever the German infantry might be, their artillery was certainly far behind them. The only gun to be heard was a solitary howitzer which was firing from a mile or two to the south of the forest; beyond this there may not have been a gun within a hundred miles. A few stragglers of other divisions were met, and pathetic sights were witnessed when streams of refugees, taking with them what household goods they had managed to gather, passed through the battalion lines. This was the first time that most of us had seen a civil population fleeing before an oncoming enemy. Women, children, and a few old men plodded by, pushing their possessions in carts and trucks. Fear, desperation, and courage alternately showed in these usually stolid faces. The sight of the familiar khaki seemed to hearten them a little, and here and there some brave soul found it in his heart to wish us " Bon chance! " Progress through the forest was difficult, low branches stung the face, and very few escaped without bruises or scratches. Pheasants and deer in plenty were disturbed but there were no signs as yet of the enemy troops.

Orders were received to take up a line from Robecq in the south, through the forest north to La Motte Château, but by this time the front line battalions had advanced through the forest and established themselves 100 to 200 yards outside. General Stephens then urged the advantage that the line at present held would have over a line through the forest, and obtained the sanction of the Corps Commander to consolidate the position in the open. The wisdom of this course was amply demonstrated in the days that followed.

Consolidation of the line on the eastern edge of the forest was commenced, and by the evening our line was firmly established facing Merville, with the 61st Division on our right and the Guards Division on our left. We had to dig in with entrenching tools, and the line consisted merely of a number of holes hurriedly dug out; there were, of course, no established support positions. Behind the division there were as yet no reserves and, as our artillery had not yet come up into position, we had no guns to rely on for support. During the advance, Lieut.-Col. L. Murray, D.S.O., was wounded by shrapnel and had to go down the line: Captain R. C. Watts, M.C., taking over command of the battalion.

The morning of the 13th found the battalion posted and ready for any emergency. Two hours after dawn a supposed patrol of men, wearing field grey, was seen on our left. The patrol was fired on, but they proved to be a collection of Portuguese stragglers. Later on a patrol of German cyclists was seen approaching and they were followed by German infantry, who extended into open order when fired on. At 11 a.m. the enemy delivered a determined attack on the battalion front at Les Lauriers, but this was repulsed everywhere except at Le Vertbois Farm, into which the enemy penetrated and from which we were forced to withdraw. More attacks followed, but the enemy could gain no further advantage. The gap in the line had been filled in and attack after attack was repulsed during the day, merely by rifle and machine gun fire. The Guards Division on our left were attacked very heavily, but the battalion was able to render very useful help by firing half-left and enfilading the attacking enemy lines.

The supply of ammunition often proved a source of great anxiety, for at times the front line was reduced to five rounds per man; all spare ammunition was kept for the

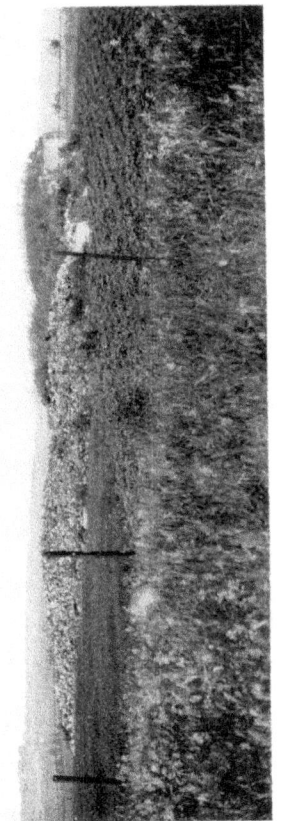

Polderhoek Chateau, 1930.

Nieppe

Lewis and machine guns. Officers' servants, grooms, and all extra men were used to carry up ammunition, which was dropped at the edge of the wood and from there it was fetched by the front line companies. Urgent demands were also being sent back for tools and barbed wire. The divisional transport, carrying the divisional supply of tools was still on the march, but a big dump was found at Aire and eventually tools from here were sent up. Here, also, was found a large dump of ammunition, and on this day no less than $2\frac{1}{4}$ million rounds were sent up to replace expenditure in the front line.

We were fighting in a country hitherto unscarred by war, and we found a cow and fowls cheerfully carrying on in No-Man's Land. The cow remained there, quietly grazing and seemingly unconcerned for two or three days before it was killed. A patrol was sent out to reconnoitre a farm in front of the battalion — a château-like building, which appeared to be untouched. Pigs and fowls were found roaming about the farmyard, and entrance was made into the farmhouse. Here a normal farm interior was found, just as the inhabitants had left it, with dinner laid on the table ; and an open piano proved irresistible to the musician of the party. Before the patrol returned, a fowl was killed and taken back to the front line, together with bottles of wine.

In the evening of the 13th, Major St. J. S. Quarry arrived to take over command of the battalion, and orders were received for " B " Company to attack Le Vertbois Farm that night. The farm was successfully re-captured, but in the attack we lost our new C.O., who was killed whilst gallantly leading his men. Unfortunately the farm had to be evacuated later as it formed a too exposed salient in the line. Captain R. C. Watts again assumed command of the battalion.

Determined attacks were resumed against us on the 14th, and one attack caused a slight withdrawal on part of the battalion front, but a support company of the Devons immediately counter-attacked and promptly restored the situation. Very heavy attacks were delivered on the left, and several times during the day concentrations of infantry and mounted detachments were seen. Our artillery, with plenty of ammunition, had now come up into position, and put down some accurate and devastating barrages, thereby smashing up several attacks.

* "All the attacks were preceded by bombardments, and it was extremely difficult to move up any reinforcements through the belt of fire. The task of breaking up attacks devolved upon the infantry and machine guns in the front line, who had been there from the beginning and who stolidly stood their ground with the utmost gallantry and coolness."

The practices in musketry indulged in on the Piave front had yielded excellent results and the tradition of the British army for rifle-shooting was well maintained.

The artillery, too, deserved praise for they had carried out a rapid march and on arrival quickly got into action. We felt much happier in having their support, for when they did start, they did excellent work and proved of the greatest assistance in repelling the heavy attacks. The front line battalions were relieved on the night of the 14th-15th, the 14th Royal Warwicks being relieved by the Royal West Kents, and the battalion moved back into the wood, as reserve. It had been a very trying time for all ranks; seven attacks had been beaten off in forty-eight hours and the casualties had been very heavy. Our losses were: officers — killed 2, wounded 4; other ranks — killed 25, wounded 109, missing 29.

Again, on the 15th, the Germans were several times seen massing for attack, but in every case they were dispersed, and, on the 16th, it was apparent that the force of the enemy thrust was dying down, for they were engaged in digging and wiring their front. The dead lay thick in the fields in front and stretcher bearers were continually at work. The battalion had played its part in assisting the 5th Division to hold up the German advance, and in the history of the Fifth Division one reads: "In these three days the 5th

---

* "*The Fifth Division in the Great War,*" by Brig.-Gen. Hussey and Major Inman.

Nieppe

Division had saved the situation on this part of the Western Front, and had stopped the German thrust on Hazebrouck. The infantry, fresh from their four months in Italy, had gone into the attack with a marvellous dash and spirit, and their steadfastness in withstanding the furious and continuous onslaughts of the enemy was magnificent."

A message was received from Lieut.-General Sir R. B. Haking (commanding the XI Corps): " Well done, 5th Division ! The Corps Commander congratulates all ranks on their steadiness and gallantry." The Army Commander sent congratulations in which he expressed his appreciation of the great bravery and endurance with which all ranks had fought, and held out during the past five days against overwhelming numbers."

In *Sir Douglas Haig's Command*, by C. A. B. Dewar and Lieut.-Col. Boraston, the authors refer to the position at Merville as follows :—

" That evening (April 12th), the 5th Division, fresh from Italy, arrived and took over that portion of our front. Thereafter, all the enemy's efforts to make further progress in this sector were in vain."

In a footnote, the authors add :—

" The arrival of the 5th Division afforded another example of the immediate effect produced by the intervention of fresh British troops in the later stages of a German attack.... The 5th had very heavy fighting on the 13th in particular, but never looked like giving ground. At the time they did not get their fair share of credit with the public; because, being but lately arrived from Italy, it was not desired to advertise their presence. It is probably for the same reason that the division is not named in the text of the dispatch which, it must be remembered, was written and sent home some months before it was published in the *Gazette*."

For the next few days matters were very quiet and we returned to the line on the 18th to relieve the Royal West Kents in our original sector. One company of the West Kents remained as reserve company to the battalion on account of our numerical weakness. Little movement was possible by day, as we had no continuous front line, and communication trenches were conspicuous by their absence. One is pleased to note that the morale of the men was excellent and our early experience at Nieppe had kept our tails well up. After three days, the Brigade was relieved, the 12th Gloucesters took over our position, and the battalion moved back to bivouacs in the wood for rest. During the relief, the enemy sent over a quantity of gas shells, causing about 20 casualties.

We now had time to carry on with the full consolidation of our position, and to realize something of our surroundings. The forest extended behind the front line for about five miles to our rear. Most of the trees were low oaks and hornbeams, and in places the undergrowth was so thick as to be impassable. It had the advantage of concealing movement and artillery positions, but communication with the rear was very difficult, as only established paths and a Decauville railway, laid by the 7th Canadian Railway troops, could be used. Later on, radiating branches of the railway were built by our own divisional engineers, and these were of immense value in bringing up supplies. In front of the wood, the flat Flanders plain stretched out to our old front line, and neither we nor the Germans had any superiority of observation. Most of our time at Nieppe was spent in and about the wood, and camps began to spring up in support and reserve positions. Deer-stalking was indulged in, but the danger of bullets hitting unwary troops stopped this pastime. However, the numerous livestock running loose provided excellent extra rations, and meals were extraordinarily good. Orlando and his merry men in the Forest of Arden could not have fared better. Rations were taken up to the front line on mules, and one enterprising Q.M.S. made use of a local farmer's gig to take up his company rations. It was probably this gig which gave rise to a story related in Major C. A. Bill's history of the 15th Royal Warwicks, which runs as follows :—

" No 16 platoon (15th Royal Warwicks) formed the left flank of the battalion and rested on the main Merville road.

Nieppe

On the other side of the road lay the right flank of the next battalion, which was in echelon about 200 yards nearer the enemy. The gap was covered by a Lewis gun, mounted on the left flank post. On taking over from the West Kents, Corporal Harriot, in charge of this Lewis gun section asked, as was usual, whether the outgoing N.C.O. had any information to impart. In very disgusted and hoarse Cockney tones came the reply, ' Yus, I 'ave ! Every night abaht 2 o'clock in the mornin', a bloke comes down this 'ere road wiv a 'andsome cab wiv rubber wheels. And when yer says, ' Alt ! 'oo are yer ? ' 'e just says ' Aerbut ' and 'ops on dahn the —— road. If 'e comes that gime on yew, Corpy, yew just turn the ol' Dicky Dunn on 'im, the cheeky monkey." The apparent phenomenon was easily explained. It appeared that when the houses on the edge of the forest were evacuated, there was left behind, *inter alia*, a large yellow-wheeled rubber-tyred gig. An enterprising C.Q.M.S. of the 14th Warwicks conceived the idea of bringing his ration party to just within the edge of the wood, loading up his rations on the gig, and sending it along the road by means of only two men, one to pull and one to push." Major Bill goes on to explain that the reply " Aerbut " was given because at one time the City Battalions were known as " Aerbuts," after the famous " Brum " character created by Graham Squiers and exploited so successfully by Will Kings. In the early days, when the line was newly formed and positions difficult to locate in the darkness, one quartermaster-sergeant, on his usual trip up the line, felt that he had travelled a long way without reaching his company. In front of him he saw a collection of houses which should not have been there, and voices in a strange tongue broke on his ear. Thereon he beat a hurried retreat back to our lines, and discovered later that he had been very close to Merville, well inside the German lines.

Our greatest enemy in the forest was gas. The Germans drenched the front part of the forest with mustard gas shells, causing many casualties and often temporary blindness. The R.A.M.C. did excellent work providing gas patrols to locate gas shell-holes, which, when found, they sprinkled

The First Birmingham Battalion in the Great War

with chloride of lime and filled in. It was now as much as any time during our stay, that we realized and were thankful for the foresight of General Stephens in having the line located outside the wood. A front line in the wood, with gas so prevalent, would have been an awful experience. A string of gas-blinded men being led to the dressing station by a wounded man, was not an unusual spectacle in Nieppe Forest.

During our period in rest, we provided parties to work on the support line, and on the 27th April we moved back into the front line to relieve the 16th Royal Warwicks in our original sector. Matters had quietened down somewhat, but the enemy artillery continued to be very active. Brevet Lieut.-Col. R. H. C. Nunn, D.S.O., assumed command of the battalion on the 29th, but his tenure of command was very short-lived, for, on 4th May, he went down to hospital badly gassed. Much work was done on the trenches and wire entanglements, but no movement was yet possible by day as the front line was not continuous, and the enemy was very close. Two raiding parties from the battalion were sent out on 2nd May; one party brought back useful information, but the other was heavily fired on and was unable to penetrate the enemy wire.

On 3rd May, the 15th Royal Warwicks relieved the battalion, and we withdrew a few hundred yards inside the wood in reserve, where we stayed until the brigade was relieved by the 95th Brigade. We then went back into bivouacs for rest and once again during the relief we were shelled with gas, sustaining further casualties. Regimental Sergeant-Major Taylor, who had been with the battalion since Oppy, was wounded and died a few days later.

A Brigade Church Parade was attended by the battalion on 12th May, and after the service the Corps Commander, Lieut.-General Sir R. C. B. Haking, K.C.B., K.C.M.G., presented company banners to all the battalions. The next few days were spent in erecting huts at Spresiano Camp and in general training and cleaning up. Captain R. C. Watts, M.C., had again taken over command of the battalion, but on the 13th May, Major W. Wilberforce, M.C.,

Nieppe

of the Royal West Kents, was posted to the battalion to command, and Captain Watts became second-in-command. During the period at Nieppe, Captain Watts had been called on to command the battalion on three occasions, and he showed marked ability and courage in this position.

The weather was gloriously fine and bathing in the Lys canal was enjoyed. Life in the sylvan glades of Nieppe was quite pleasant in spite of the constant considerable shelling. The "Whizz-Bangs" came along to cheer up the troops by giving open-air concerts under the trees.

On 16th May, we returned to the line, relieving the 1st Bedfords of the 15th Brigade. The Germans still had a large reserve of 29 Divisions against us, and it was not known at what spot they would attack next. Heavy assaults had been delivered near Ypres, and about this period it seemed quite likely that a further blow would be aimed at Hazebrouck, the most important point on our lines of communication.

Preparations were being made for any eventuality, and in this relief the battalion took over the front line in fighting order, packs and overcoats being left behind. A neat little raid was planned out by "A" Company on the night of the 22nd-23rd to ascertain the enemy position. At 11.50 p.m., Corporal Lawton worked forward to the first objective, a house in front of our line. On reaching the house, one of our bombers flung a Mills bomb through the window aperture, and at the same moment a carefully-aligned Lewis gun barrage opened up, accompanied by slow artillery fire. At zero hour, which was midnight, the whole party went forward, flung more bombs into the house, and finally rushed the house. On investigation, it was found that the house was deserted, so the whole party moved forward to a hedge, and reconnoitred the surrounding ground, but finding no trace of the Germans, they returned to our lines. The enemy did not retaliate.

And so things continued; patrol work in No-Man's Land and beyond was not hazardous; prisoners were easily picked up, and it was gradually becoming apparent that the morale of the Germans was deteriorating; although their artillery harassed us very considerably, and the battalion was badly exposed to gas shelling; "D" Company especially suffered heavily. In the vicinity of the front line there were many thatched farm houses, and the Germans used incendiary shells, which set the roofs on fire. As they usually chose night-time for this practice, the burning buildings lit up the countryside, to the discomfort of working parties and patrols. On the 29th, the East Surreys relieved the battalion, and we marched back to billets at Steenbecque. Next night the town was bombed by enemy aircraft, and a heavy bomb fell on one of "C" Company's billets, killing four men and wounding six: the barn was completely destroyed.

The weather continued fine, and our rest at Steenbecque was thoroughly enjoyed. News was received that the Corps Commander had made the following awards for gallantry and devotion to duty: D.C.M. — Sergeant D. W. Tuffley; M.M. — Corporal N. Mooney, Privates W. S. Sharman, G. J. Smith, and G. O. Smith.

Whilst we were at Steenbecque, detachments of Portuguese stragglers arrived daily, escorted by our troops. Parties of Portuguese had been found roaming all over the country and were brought back to Steenbecque for concentration. Very much to our disgust, we were informed by the inhabitants that these excellent troops had been telling them that they had been brought back to prevent the British troops from running away. This proved too much for us after our heavy fighting in making up the Portuguese deficiency, and an exciting night followed, with the result that the "Pork and Beans" were interned in a large field, where, unfortunately, they were bombed by enemy aircraft.

On 4th June, we returned to the reserve position in Spresiano Camp, and on 9th June moved forward into the forest. Then commenced a very trying time for the battalion. An epidemic of a form of trench fever, called P.U.O., broke out, and casualties from this cause became very heavy. The fever took the form of influenza, causing complete impotence and utter uselessness. Every day batches of forty or fifty men were sent down the line, and so serious

Nieppe

did matters become that the battalion was sent back to Thiennes for disinfection and bathing. The epidemic did not die down until 20th June, and by that time 15 officers and 340 other ranks had been admitted to hospital. It was learnt afterwards that 'the enemy had suffered from the same cause, and called it Merville fever.

In the meantime, the battalion, seriously depleted, relieved the K.O.S.B. in the front line on 11th June, and as the total strength of the battalion was only 280, the battalion was organized in three weak companies, " C " and " B " Companies forming one company under the command of Captain D. Neal. On 12th June, further casualties went down with the fever, so that " D " Company had to take over more of the front line and "A" Company, of the K.O.S.B., took over the line vacated by " D " Company. Fortunately the situation was quiet, but the shortness in numbers meant heavy work for all concerned. Going up for the relief, the battalion suffered a heavy loss. The route into the line for some distance followed the canal bank. A shell dropped very close to one of our limbers while on this part of the journey : the horses took fright and overturned the limber. Most of the contents were tipped into the canal and these included valuable stores in the form of two jars of rum. Great heroism was displayed in endeavours to recover the rum, but as the bed of the canal was littered with barbed wire, all efforts proved fruitless, much to the consternation of all ranks. This melancholy incident proved a topic of conversation for some considerable time.

After six days in the front line, the battalion moved back to bivouacs at Tannay, and two days later withdrew to La Lacque Camp for rest. Football matches were arranged here, and general training was carried out. Birthday honours were published on 16th June, and the following awards were made to members of the battalion :—

M.C. — Captain H. D. Rees. D.C.M. — Regimental Sergeant-Major F. W. Hayes. M.S.M. — C.Q.M.S. A. C. Denham, Sergeant H. Lee. Mentioned in Dispatches — Major R. H. Baily, C.S.M. A. Lucas, C.S.M. W. J. Blower,

The First Birmingham Battalion in the Great War

C.Q.M.S. F. P. Cornforth, S. J. Neighbour, Sergeant F. J. Patrick, Corporal H. H. Lyons.

Urgent orders were received on 25th June for the battalion to move up to the support positions of the 95th Brigade, and the journey was made by the Decauville Railway. The position of the division since April had not been too comfortable. The edge of the forest was very close to the front line, leaving very little room for manœuvre, so it was decided to carry out an attack to improve the situation and enable an outpost line and main line of resistance to be formed well clear of the forest. The attack took place on the morning of 28th June, on a front of three miles to the depth of one mile, and was carried out by the 5th and 31st Divisions — the same two divisions who made the successful attack on Oppy on the same date twelve months before. The 13th and 95th Brigades with two platoons of the Cheshire Regiment formed the 5th Division front line, and the 31st Division attacked on the left. In the 13th Brigade, the K.O.S.B., the Royal West Kents, and the 15th Royal Warwicks from left to right, in the order named, formed the front line, with the 14th Royal Warwicks, still very weak in numbers, in support. "B" Company, of the 14th, went over in the attack, with the K.O.S.B. and the remaining three companies supported the attacking battalions, moving forward as the attack progressed. The operation was completely successful, and all objectives were gained on time. At first there was some opposition from machine guns, but this was soon overcome. Heavy casualties were inflicted on the enemy, and many prisoners and much material were captured. "B" Company played its full part in the attack and captured a machine gun, and its share of prisoners. At night, parties from "A" and "D" Companies began to wire the new front line, and the 29th was occupied by the battalion in consolidating the captured position.

* "The Division was greatly elated by this victory, which was the first successful operation of any size under-

* *"Fifth Division in the Great War,"* by Brig.-Gen. Hussey and Major Inman.

Nieppe

taken by the British since the Retreat, and congratulations poured in. Almost immediately after this, General Stephens left the division on promotion to the command of the 10th Corps — it was an appropriate send-off to the beloved commander, who had led them to so many triumphs on previous occasions. He was succeeded by Major-General J. Ponsonby of the Coldstream Guards."

After this attack, the situation on our front remained quiet : the enemy made no attempt to recapture the lost ground, and life followed the ordinary trench routine. The weather was very hot, and in the surrounding fields crops were ripening. Efforts were made to garner some of these, and special officers were appointed to supervise this work. Patrol work was carried out continually in order to capture prisoners for identification purposes and, as mentioned previously, this proved a simple matter. Large drafts were arriving to make the battalion up to strength. Many of the men arriving were only eighteen or nineteen years old, but they were very keen and made good soldiers.

Major R. H. Baily rejoined the battalion on 5th July, after a course in England, and on 14th July he took over temporary command of the 1st Cheshires. On the 5th we relieved the 1st Bedfords in the front line. The transport had very bad luck on the 8th July, for an aerial bomb dropped in the transport lines, killing 14 men and wounding 16. A move back to rest at Arcadia Camp was made on 11th July, but the huts were found to be leaking very badly, and the battalion was employed for several days in making them rainproof.

Little more remains to be said of our stay in the Nieppe area, for on 1st August, the battalion went back to Steenbecque, where it was inspected by the new divisional commander, and on 6th August, the 61st Division took over the front from the 5th Division, who were destined to move further back for a divisional rest. With this relief ended our Nieppe experiences, which had opened full of excitement, and ended after a burst of activity, in peaceful trench life conditions.

Chapter XII.

THE FINAL ADVANCE.

WHEN we said "good-bye" to Nieppe, very few of the battalion had any inkling of the tremendous events in which the battalion would take part in the next three months. There seemed to be no end to the war, and even with the large drafts of American troops coming over weekly, it did not appear that there could be any termination of hostilities before the autumn of 1919. But the future had many surprises in store, and the month of August, 1918, was to show a definite turn in the fortunes of the war. As far as the battalion was concerned, the early part of the month provided a series of hurried moves culminating in a return to the line in the third week of the month. On 4th August, orders were received for a quick move and the battalion marched to Wittes and Cohem. The billets there were scattered and far from comfortable. Two days later a further move was made to better billets at Campagne, near St. Omer, where the battalion stayed for a week, carrying out general training. During this period passes were granted to St. Omer, and every advantage was taken of this privilege. Big drafts had been joining the battalion, and with 37 officers and 875 other ranks, it was stronger than it had been since the days of the Somme in 1916. During the intervening period, we had never received large drafts, so that the battalion was always under strength, a situation that compared unfavourably with the regular battalions of the brigade. The rest at Campagne was very welcome; it was quite refreshing to get away from the precincts of the Forêt de Nieppe, with its gas, mosquitoes, and fever.

We were not left idle for long, for further south, on 8th August, a magnificent victory had been gained near Amiens, and our immediate job was to take part in exploiting

The Final Advance

this success. In the days following the big advance, Sir Douglas Haig decided to extend the attack northwards, where, by striking in a south-easterly direction between Albert and Arras, it would be possible to turn the line of the Somme. This attack was to be made by the Third Army under Sir Julian Byng, and the 4th Corps under Lieut.-Gen. Sir G. Harper, containing the 5th, 37th, 63rd (Naval) — replaced later by the 42nd Division — and the New Zealand Division was to take part.

On 13th August, the battalion entrained at Wizernes for Doullens, which was reached early next morning. A march to Vacquerie-sur-Canche followed, and here the Royal Air Force rendered substantial assistance in providing tents for our accommodation. Great secrecy was being observed as to the immediate arrangements. Movement was permitted only during the hours of darkness, but all ranks knew that a big attack was impending. News of the break through further south had been received and the battalion felt that stirring times were coming. To know that the British Army was to advance in mass over ground already several times strenuously contested, keyed everyone up to concert pitch, and after months of comparative inaction, interspersed with heavy defensive work, the prospect of a move forward was comparatively pleasing. It was at this point that we were informed that the Third Army was to take part in the attack on Bapaume, and in this attack the 5th Division was to play its part.

To preserve a correct sequence of the events during the next four months, it is necessary to devote a fair amount of space to the doings of the larger units. Operations were on such a large scale that the battalion's part can be assessed only by considering it in relation to the whole.

Orders were received at 8 p.m., on the 18th, to leave Vacquerie at 9.30 p.m. and move to Remaisnil by a night march. As with all the previous orders, this entailed a hurried move, and on arrival at our destination at midnight, the battalion was put under one hour's notice for a further move. However, we had breathing space until 3 p.m. next day, when orders came to move to Couin, another stage nearer the front line. The dumped personnel of the battalion marched back to Doullens, where they were billeted in the Citadel, while the rest of the battalion marched to Bouquemaison, from whence they were conveyed in 'buses to Sarton. From this place, a further march was made to Couin, which was reached at 3 a.m. on the 20th. Orders were received that the battalion was to take part in the attack on the 21st.

The plan of attack was for the 5th Division to pass through the right brigade of the 37th Division after this division had captured the high ground east of Bucquoy, and then to continue the advance. The 63rd Division was to pass through the left brigade of the 37th Division, and on the right of the 5th Division the New Zealand Division was to carry the attack right through. The 95th and 15th Brigades were to form the divisional front line with the 13th Brigade in support.

On the night of the 20th, the brigade moved to its assembly position, the order of battle being the 14th Royal Warwicks, 15th Royal Warwicks, the 1st Royal West Kents, and the 2nd K.O.S.B. During the night the mist thickened, and by zero, at 4.55 a.m., a dense fog covered the ground, making the advance of the infantry very difficult. Ninety minutes after zero, the 95th and 15th Brigades passed through the 37th Division, and by 7.40 a.m., a line west of Achiet-le-Petit, representing an advance of two thousand yards, had been made good. The attack was supported by twelve Mark IV Tanks. The fog became thicker than ever, and in the second advance, which was supported by Mark IV and Whippet Tanks, it was almost impossible to keep direction; units became intermingled and it was difficult for the infantry to keep close to the tanks. At the end of the day, however, the division had advanced over two miles, capturing many prisoners and much material. The night and the day following were spent in consolidating the positions gained.

During these two days the 13th Brigade remained in the support positions as the G.O.C. had decided not to use the

The Final Advance

brigade until the 23rd, on which day the other two brigades were ordered to continue the advance. The position to be attacked was one of great strength, and defended by a large number of machine guns. After heavy fighting, the 15th Brigade made good their objectives and during the advance two tanks rendered valuable help, while the 16th Royal Warwicks advanced without a halt to their final objective. On the extreme right of the attack, the East Surreys gained their objective but the 12th Gloucesters were held up in front of Irles. The strength of this position may be judged from the fact that at one point 23 machine guns were captured on a front of fifty yards, each with a great heap of empty cartridge cases by its side.

Despite repeated attacks, Irles remained in the German hands, and it was decided to move up the 13th Brigade to complete its capture and exploit the success of the morning's attack as far as Loupart Wood. During the day the battalion had moved up nearer the front line, occupying positions in the valley south of Bucquoy, and in the evening orders were received for the attack. The 14th Royal Warwicks were in the centre of the brigade front line with the Royal West Kents on the right and the 15th Royal Warwicks on the left, the K.O.S.B. being in support. The attack was completely successful; the Gloucesters, determined to carry out their part in the day's work, joined in the attack, and had the satisfaction of going right through Irles and gaining the objective of their original attack. Later in the day, " B " and " D " Companies, at only ten minutes' notice, continued the attack and passed through the first objective: the intention was for these two companies to capture Loupart Wood in conjunction with an advance by the 15th Royal Warwicks on Grevillers, but by the time " C " Company arrived at the support position, it was too dark and further advance was held up. Thus the line had been advanced past Irles and up to Loupart Wood, and had not darkness stopped the advance, the brigade would have pushed right through Loupart Wood, which was cleared next day by the K.O.S.B. The three days' fighting had been crowned with success, and the captures of the 5th Division included nearly 3,000 prisoners, 25 guns, over 350 machine guns, and 37 trench mortars, besides anti-tank guns and much material.

The positions captured were held on the 24th, and next day the New Zealand Division passed through the front line, capturing Grevillers, and carrying the advance forward. Later in the day, orders were received to move up and relieve the 111th Brigade at Favreuil. The orders for relief were received very late on the night of the 25th-26th and the suddenness of the orders and the dark night made the relief very difficult, but the battalion moved off just in time to avoid some heavy shelling. At noon on the 26th orders were received for the battalion to support the attack of the K.O.S.B. on Beugnatre by protecting their left flank and keeping in touch with the division on the left. The K.O.S.B. advanced under a creeping barrage and, after some resistance, obtained their objective by capturing Beugnatre. " C " Company of the 14th Royal Warwicks took over a portion of the front line and later in the day " D " Company was sent up east of Beugnatre to fill in a gap between " C " Company and the K.O.S.B. The enemy counter-attacked several times, but were repulsed, and on the 27th the front line held by the battalion was reorganized. At night, the Royal West Kents took over the front line, and half the battalion marched back to reserve positions, leaving " B " and " D " Companies in the line to hold strong points.

On 29th August, in conjunction with an attack on the right by the New Zealand Division, the 15th Royal Warwicks and the Royal West Kents continued the advance, the role of the battalion being to keep in touch with the latter unit. Apparently this attack was not successful, for at about 8 p.m. the battalion was ordered to reoccupy the old positions. Three hours later the battalion was relieved by the East Surreys, but no sooner was the relief completed than verbal instructions were received cancelling the relief, and the battalion returned to the front line, remaining there until they moved back into support on 31st August.

In the meantime, the New Zealanders on our right had

TRENCHES ON VIMY RIDGE TO-DAY.

The Final Advance

pushed patrols through Bapaume on the 29th, while in the ten days of the battle the Germans had been driven from one side of the old Somme battlefield to the other; Bapaume and Peronne had been captured and the line of the Somme turned. The battalion had taken its full share in this advance, suffering heavy casualties amounting to 20 officers and 280 other ranks, but during the advance captures had included 4 officers and 273 other ranks prisoners, together with nine heavy machine guns, twenty-three light machine guns and one trench mortar.

The attack was continued on the 30th by the 95th Brigade, and this was followed up by an attack by the 15th Brigade on 1st September. The results of these two attacks were exploited on 2nd September, when it was found that the Germans had made a hasty retreat. As a result, at the end of the day, the total advance by these brigades was seven miles. On the 2nd, the battalion followed up the advance to a position east of Beugnatre, but two days later the division came out of the line for rest. The battalion was relieved by the 4th Middlesex and moved back to bivouacs on the main Arras-Bapaume road south of Sapignies. Accommodation was provided in old trenches which were none too comfortable, but the rest was thoroughly enjoyed, and the battalion felt particularly gratified that, after heavy fighting, they had succeeded in penetrating so far into the enemy occupied territory. It was realized that there were still many prepared positions to be taken before we could reach open country. Cambrai was still in enemy possession, and he was still hoping to hold us up by his great bulwark, the Hindenburg line.

The supply of water was a pressing and difficult problem. During the advance, the weather was intensely hot; such wells as the enemy had not destroyed in the tiny villages were totally inadequate to meet our needs. The divisional engineers had followed up the advance closely to reopen water supplies and bore new wells, and in addition, tank lorries were used to bring up water. The supply of ammunition was another vital matter for the advancing infantry. Two schemes were very successfully evolved to meet this emergency. The 59th squadron of the Royal Air Force dropped boxes of ammunition by parachutes at points where they were required, and this worked so satisfactorily that ammunition was supplied in nearly all cases within half an hour from the time of demand. Tanks were also of the greatest assistance. During the advance in the battle of Bapaume three gun-carrying tanks were allotted to the division to carry forward stores. They followed up close on the heels of the infantry and were of great service in keeping up supplies.

The tanks were extensively used for all sorts of jobs during 1918, and for the following account of their activities, I am indebted to Captain V. G. Sanders of the Royal Tank Corps, who was a member of the battalion till 1916.

"Towards the end of 1917, the Tank Corps had grown from four companies and forty-nine tanks in July, 1916, to five brigades, thirteen battalions, and with a total of 320 heavy and 50 light tanks fit for action, concentrated at Bray-sur-Somme.

"In January, 1918, all the battalions from Roisel to Bethune, moved up behind the front line, a frontage of about 60 miles. They were to act as reserves and were to be used to counter-attack against tactical points.

"When the German advance started in March, the battalions in the Bethune district were not called upon, but on the 5th Army front, on the right of the line, the battalions did excellent work in delaying the advance by making repeated counter-attacks, and suffered very severely both in tanks and personnel. So much so, that several battalions were re-formed as Lewis gun detachments and joined up with the infantry.

"Near the Arras-Bapaume road in front of Boisleux, the infantry had retired too far south, leaving a gap in the line, which was held only by a company of tanks (sixteen), a battery of 8 inch howitzers, and a second company of tanks; there was also a battery of anti-aircraft guns. For some reason unknown, the advance was not continued, and the gap was closed during the night.

"On 24th April, the Germans attacked again along the

The Final Advance

line south of the Somme, and for the first time used their own tanks. One which had advanced on Cachy came up against two British female tanks, which were armed only with machine guns, and put them out of action, but it was itself put out of action by the first male tank that appeared on the scene.

" The corps was withdrawn from the line in May, to take over new tanks which were arriving from England, to re-equip and be ready for action by the end of July. One brigade was actually in action on 1st July with the Australians at Hamel, where 1,500 prisoners were taken as against the Australian losses of 672 officers and men. Another battalion operated with the French in a successful advance. Both these attacks were made in order to get a suitable jumping-off line for the big advance in August.

" This advance started on 8th August, when 415 tanks advanced from Amiens. The surprise effect was complete; the enemy line was penetrated to a depth of over seven miles and 200 guns and 16,000 prisoners were taken. The cavalry, light tanks, and armoured cars continued the advance, and by 10th August, the old trench system of 1916 was reached. This eventually stopped any further advance. This old trench system was the cause of over sixty tanks getting knocked out by direct hits, and out of a total of 688 tanks used since the 8th, 480 were handed to Salvage.

" The attack then moved north, and on 21st August all available tanks attacked between Beaucourt-sur-Ancre and Moyeuneville. They took 2,000 prisoners. Unfortunately the ground mist lifted as the tanks were crossing the railway in front of the guns, and 37 out of 190 received direct hits.

" On 22nd August, an attack was made along the Bray-Albert road, as well as on a 30-mile front from Lihous to Mercatel. These minor attacks were made daily from 22nd August to 4th September. Gomiecourt was captured by moonlight; Hamlincourt, Sapignes, Behagnies, Mory, Ervillers, and numerous other villages were taken.

" After a temporary withdrawal for refitting, two tank brigades joined the 3rd and 4th Armies in an attack on a

The First Birmingham Battalion in the Great War

17-mile front in which Epehy was taken. The Hindenburg line was attacked on 27th September, 53 tanks were used successfully against Gouzeaucourt, Flesquiers, Graincourt, and Bourlon Wood. Sixteen tanks managed to cross the Canal du Nord at Moeuvres and attacked Bourlon village and hill. On the 29th, the St. Quentin Canal was crossed by the Midland Territorial Brigade, and the 175 tanks used included the 301st American Tank Battalion. The Americans were unfortunate, their tanks ran into an old minefield at Guillemont Farm, and ten machines were blown up, while their infantry were not successful. Further south the attack succeeded, Lauroy and Bellecourt were taken, as were Magny and Etricourt. Further successful attacks were made later with the tanks against Joncourt, Montrehain and Magnies-la-Targette.

"At Awoingt, the Germans counter-attacked with captured British tanks. A piquant situation arose when a captured British tank was knocked out by a shell fired from a captured German field gun. Another was knocked out by a British tank, and the remaining two got away in the mist.

"Owing to these continuous attacks by the corps, the number of fighting tanks was rapidly diminishing and, on 12th October, five tank battalions had to be withdrawn from the line: they handed over what tanks they had to the battalions who were to remain in the line.

"On the 20th of October, 48 tanks attacked between Le Cateau and the Scheldt Canal, and on 4th November, 37, the remains of four battalions attacked at Mormal Forest. On 6th November the remains of the light tanks, eight in number, attacked with the Guards Brigade, this being the last tank action of the war.

"Since 8th August, the Tank Corps had been in almost continuous fighting, 2,000 tanks and armoured cars were used and, in these ninety-six days, the losses amounted to 598 officers and 2,826 other ranks."

To return to the doings of the battalion, we find that they remained in the trench line bivouacs, carrying out general training, but there was much sickness, which was

The Final Advance

attributed to poor accommodation and inclement weather. During this period, the 37th Division had carried on the advance to beyond Havrincourt Wood and orders were received on 13th September to take over positions from the New Zealand Division in front of Gouzeaucourt. Before we returned to the line we had suffered the loss of our brigade commander, Brigadier-General L. O. W. Jones, who died of pneumonia. He had commanded the brigade since September, 1915, and his loss was felt by all ranks. Brigadier-General A. T. Beckwith succeeded him in command.

The following awards were made by the Corps Commander for gallantry during the operations August 23rd-31st :—
Bar to Military Medal — Lance-Corporal T. Williams, M.M. Military Medals — Sergeants J. Leach, H. R. Martin ; Corporals C. E. Rudge, J. W. Bubb ; Lance-Corporals H. Morris, H. Williams, W. Shepherd, C. Sparkes ; Privates W. Hocking, A. C. Pilgrim, T. H. Vernon, G. Nicholls, J. Woolsey, T. Powell.

The 13th Brigade moved up on the 13th to take over the front line running from east of Gouzeaucourt Wood to south-west of Trescault Spur. On our march up to the forward positions, we passed through Bapaume, which had been completely demolished. The roads through were all clear, but on either side of them were huge piles of bricks and debris from the smashed buildings. The Germans had been very thorough in their destruction, and left behind numerous devices for causing more damage. In one of the cellars at Bapaume was found a piano. This proved irresistible to an officer of the battalion, but as soon as he touched the keys there was a tremendous explosion and officer and piano completely disappeared. A bomb had been concealed inside the instrument, and only needed the touch of a finger on the keys to set off the explosive material. Much more of this kind of devilish ingenuity was found in the later advances.

It was a great experience to march through Bapaume. The name had a strange fascination for all who had taken part in the Battle of the Somme in 1916, for in those days

The First Birmingham Battalion in the Great War

Bapaume was far behind the German lines; a name to conjure with.

The battalion arrived at Neuville, near Ytres, in the evening, where they billeted for the night, and the next day the 2nd Wellington Battalion was relieved in the left sector of the front line. The 15th Royal Warwicks were in the centre with the K.O.S.B. on their right, the Royal West Kents being in support. This position was maintained until the 18th, but considerable casualties were suffered each day. Further awards were made to the battalion, and the following received Military Medals — Sergeant B. J. Cope; Lance-Corporals B. T. Langford, F. J. Stephens, and Private G. Lawton.

On 18th September, the attack was resumed by the 13th Brigade. This was to take the form of an advance of some 400 yards to form a defensive flank for the larger operations by the Corps and Army to the right. The K.O.S.B. carried out the attack and started out in pouring rain at 5.20 a.m. on a two-company front. Their immediate objective was African Trench, a very strongly fortified position. Despite desperate efforts, the attack failed and the K.O.S.B. had to retire to their original position. However, the attack on the right had been completely successful, and it was very probable that the K.O.S.B. attack had been of assistance to them.

On the same day, Major R. H. Baily left the battalion to take over command of the 1st Royal Warwicks. It was a decided loss to the battalion, for since December, 1916, when he joined us at Festubert, he had made himself indispensable in all the battalion activities, and he had a great affection for the old 14th. We were pleased to know that he had been given command of his old battalion, but we feel safe in saying that he regretted his departure, as much as did the rank and file.

After the failure of the attack on the 18th, the position remained quiet and uneventful, and on the 20th the battalion was relieved by the D.C.L.I. and marched back to billets at Haplincourt, where cleaning up and general training were carried out. During our rest period two

The Final Advance

soccer matches were played against the Royal West Kents and the 63rd (Naval) Division artillery; both matches were won by the battalion. It may seem incongruous that football should be played in the middle of a big advance, but wherever the battalion went, every opportunity was taken to play matches in either code. It was a great change from the more serious matters in front of us and afforded considerable relief to both players and spectators.

While we were at rest, the consolidation of positions recently won had been taking place, and on 25th September, in preparation for further offensive action, the 13th Brigade moved up to relieve the 95th Brigade in the right sector of the divisional front. After a march from Haplincourt and tea at Ytres, the 12th Gloucesters were relieved in the support position and, on the night of the 26th, the battalion moved up into assembly positions for the attack next day.

A determined effort was to be made to advance past African Trench and, in addition, the Division with the 15th Brigade on the left and the 13th Brigade on the right, formed the pivot for an attack by the Corps and Army on the left. In the front line of the 13th brigade the order of battle from right to left was Royal West Kents, 15th Royal Warwicks, 14th Royal Warwicks. African Trench, which had defied us in spite of many attacks, was the immediate objective of the Royal West Kents, and this position proved a stumbling block in the day's operations. After the Germans withdrew from African Trench, we had a chance of looking at it from both points of view. It was sited as perfectly as a trench could be sited, and must have been the work of an expert.

The attack opened at 7.52 a.m. on the 27th, when the battalion started well, and after some opposition made good their objectives on the centre and left, but they were presently bombed out of the greater part of it, owing to the battalion on the right being held up. The advance had been difficult, since it had to be made diagonally across three parallel lines of trenches, and at the ultimate position it became necessary to form a defensive flank to the right. In the advance Captain C. W. Hughes, commanding "A"

Company, was sniped whilst making sure of his direction. The enemy barrage came down fairly quickly, but the battalion got east of it in time and few casualties occurred until they came under view of the Smut trench system on the right flank, which was still manned by enemy machine guns, one or two at least being pushed well forward out of our creeping barrage. Some expert enemy snipers were also posted in this part of the trench system. The battalion on the right failed to clear this trench and the right platoon of "C" Company, marching on tapes, could not reach their objective, having lost three-quarters of their number. Meanwhile "A" Company on the left went on and reached their objective, but suffered heavily during their advance from machine gunfire. "D" Company advanced through "A" Company, their right platoon losing heavily as they followed that part of "C" Company's line of advance which had come under fire from Smut trench. "D" Company reached Dunraven trench and many prisoners, estimated at 130 at least, were sent back. Within thirty minutes of zero the battalion held Dunraven trench, but were out of touch with the brigade on the left. At this time, Captain Izon went along to get in touch with "C" Company or the battalion on the right. The enemy were still holding this part and Captain Izon was hit by a stick bomb and killed.

At 9.30 a.m. the enemy commenced to bomb out our men from Dunraven trench, but were unsuccessful. An hour later, a determined hostile attack was made with picked bombers and riflemen on this point, and this was successful, causing "D" Company to retire. The enemy had apparently worked his way round Soot Trench, and the troops on the left were withdrawing. Our men were in a trench not stocked with German bombs and had used all their own and also many of the enemy stick grenades at Dunraven Post. Moreover, this was a case where it was impossible for our men to get out of the trench and deal with this bombing attack in the usual manner, owing to the severe and accurate sniping and machine gun fire coming from Smut Trench and other trenches occupied by the enemy commanding a fine field of fire.

The Final Advance

The situation seemed very obscure, and it appeared that the companies were very mixed up, and even the officers on the spot were somewhat in the dark owing to the extreme difficulty of reconnoitring in view of the well-chosen sniping posts which the enemy held. " B " Company was ordered to counter-attack with two platoons; this relieved the situation, causing a slight withdrawal on the part of the enemy. The enemy machine gun fire was still very accurate and heavy, and as we could not have advanced during the day without further losses, which had already been very heavy, the commanding officer decided to hold his position and reorganize. By midnight reports were received that this had been done; posts were out and stops in the trenches had been completed whilst the enemy was quiet.

Heavy artillery fire broke out on the brigade front early next morning, and at 5 a.m. orders were sent out to watch the enemy closely. At 8.30 a.m. news was received that the companies were advancing without opposition, and by 11 a.m. all the objectives of the previous day had been re-occupied. On the right, the Royal West Kents had captured African Trench, and during the morning, as the enemy had finally withdrawn, the 95th and 15th Infantry Brigades passed through in pursuit while the battalion was left in position as part of the reserve brigade. During the morning of the 28th, the entire headquarter staff of the 15th Royal Warwicks were seen walking slowly to the rear with their eyes closed and evidently in a sad plight. They had all been gassed, including the H.Q. cooks. The 14th Royal Warwicks, who occupied the next dug-out, were entirely untouched.

The day of the 29th passed uneventfully and on the 30th the brigade was relieved by the 37th Division and moved back to rest billets at Ytres. The division had advanced on the 28th to a line along the Gouzeaucourt-Villers Plouich railway. In view of the weakening of the enemy resistance, the advance was continued further next day and, before the division was relieved by the 37th Division, the front line and support trenches of the famous Hindenburg line had been captured, together with high ground overlooking the canal.

The First Birmingham Battalion in the Great War

Thus ended the second phase of fighting. The enemy, though being steadily driven back, had put up a very strong resistance, as exemplified in the defence of African Trench. The enemy machine gunners had taken very heavy toll and their defence was of a very stubborn character. Very brave men were the enemy machine gunners; they held their posts till the last, inflicting the maximum of casualties, and one was compelled to pay tribute to their courage. The division had a full chance of getting rest, and the time was spent in cleaning up and general training. Awards to members of the battalion were notified as follows:—Military Cross — Second-Lieutenants H. H. Kaye, M.M., H. Ford; D.C.M. — Acting-Sergeant H. Newey, Lance-Corporal R. Wright, Private B. Harman. Captain C. W. Hughes, one of the original members of the battalion, died from his wounds received on 27th September.

This was the last offensive action in the war in which the battalion took part as a fighting unit, and it is pleasing to know that, after heavy fighting, the battalion's efforts were successful. For his successful handling of a difficult situation, the commanding officer, Lieut.-Colonel W. Wilberforce, M.C., deservedly received the D.S.O.

In February, 1918, owing to the lack of adequate reinforcements from England, the divisions of the British Expeditionary Force had been reduced from a 12 infantry battalion establishment to one of 9 battalions. For over seven months the 5th Division had evaded this change, but eventually peremptory orders were received that this change must take place at once. In consequence, on 5th October, the 15th Royal Warwicks and the 12th Gloucesters were disbanded, and the 1/6th Argyll and Sutherland Highlanders, the divisional pioneers, returned to their old division, the 51st. The 14th Royal Warwicks took their place as pioneers to the division and the 16th Royal Warwicks became the third battalion in the 13th Brigade. The personnel of the disbanded battalions was split up amongst the remaining battalions and seven officers and 200 men of the 15th Royal Warwicks joined the battalion.

The Final Advance

* "Although, with the exception of the Argylls, practically all the personnel of the disbanded units remained with the division, it was a sad parting, and it is a lasting regret that they could not have kept their identity, and that the 5th Division could not have completed the remaining six weeks of the war with the twelve battalions of which it had been so long composed."

Henceforth the battalion carried on work as pioneers for the division, and was organized in three companies, " D " Company being disbanded and its personnel distributed between the three remaining companies. Events were moving rapidly in other theatres of war — in Palestine, General Allenby had carried out a huge drive towards Aleppo, causing Turkey to sign an armistice, and on 30th September, Bulgaria signed an unconditional surrender. All along the Western Front the Allies were driving back the Germans, and the end seemed to be drawing near at last.

Until 9th October, the battalion remained in Corps reserve and during this period Cambrai was captured and the advance was being carried on in open country. All the villages were inhabited and the problem was how our artillery should deal with them and inflict the minimum amount of damage. To avoid civilian casualties, shelling was confined to the outskirts of towns and villages, where, as a rule, German machine guns were posted, and the inhabited area was covered with a light shrapnel barrage. The inhabitants were safe from this in their cellars and they were so overwhelmed with joy at their deliverance that a few broken windows were neither here nor there.

The division moved forward on 9th October to take part in the further advance, and the battalion marched to a position east of Bantouzelle, across the Escaut River, where accommodation was found in the support system of the Hindenburg line. Opportunity was taken of inspecting this stronghold, which was a masterpiece of military

---

* " *The Fifth Division in the Great War,*" by Brig.-Gen. Hussey and Major Inman.

engineering. The trenches were wide with deep, comfortable and roomy dug-outs, which were all boarded with the thick planks common to all German dug-outs. Telephones were installed in each dug-out, which was furnished with bunks for sleeping, while the rats could be heard running about in the cavities between the boards and the outside earth, not inside the dug-out, as had been our usual experience. At night, away to the north, Cambrai could be seen on fire, and further away the glow from fires in Douai was observed.

The following day the march was continued to the Haucourt-Esnes area, the battalion being accommodated in a sunken road just west of Lesdain. On 11th October we continued the march to the Caudry area, preparatory to the division taking over the line from the 37th Division. The battalion was very comfortably billeted in Caudry, and marched in during the afternoon as the Germans had evacuated the town during the morning. The inhabitants were delighted with our arrival, signifying their release from captivity by unfurling Tricolors and singing the Marseillaise, as our troops marched in.

Caudry was the first inhabited town of any size on the divisional front to fall into our hands. It was a strange experience both for us and the civilians. We had crossed the old wilderness of the Somme. Mile after mile of that tragic desolate area that had been swept by the ebb and flow of war for four years. And now the enemy was in retreat and the civilians saw again friendly faces and heard cheery greetings after four years of isolation and misery. One old French veteran, a survivor of the war of 1870, told us how he had never given in during the whole four years. With tears streaming down her cheeks, his old wife poured out a pitiful yet heroic tale to any of us who could understand French. " Yes, M'sieur, we have been French. Mon mari, here, would never salute them. We walked proudly in the streets. They have struck him, M'sieur, but he has replied, ' Vive La France ! ' Ah M'sieur, we have suffered." And so the tale went on, told between tears and laughter. It was a great day for them, and we ourselves felt that it was worth while.

The Final Advance

One man, so overcome with joy, was seen running about the streets with a hatchet, shouting with glee and smashing with his axe all the German notice boards. Immediately, on entering Caudry, a huge crater was found in the middle of the road, evidently a nice little trap laid by the Germans, which fortunately exploded before our arrival. Several days later, however, a delayed mine exploded under the railway bridge; it brought down the bridge and caused a few casualties, but did not seriously hold up the advance.

The 5th Division, with headquarters at Caudry, relieved the 37th Division on the 12th and the battalion remained at Caudry to supply working parties for road repairs, filling in craters and doing general pioneer work in the advanced areas. We were notified that awards had been made as follows:—Private W. G. Sharp received the French Croix de Guerre and Lance-Corporal F. J. Stephens a bar to his Military Medal. Military Medals were awarded to Sergeants R. French, F. C. Usher, H. Dance, P. Bristowe, Lance-Corporals S. Manning, L. Nicholson, Privates J. H. Anderson, G. Fiefield, A. S. Brown, W. G. Beere, W. G. Sharp.

For some time we had been singularly free from enemy gunfire or aircraft for which, of course, everyone was duly thankful. On 18th October, a soccer match was arranged with another battalion in the district, but when the match had only just commenced an enemy shell, the first for days, dropped right on the football pitch, wounding two of the players and bursting the ball. Whereon, because there was nothing to kick, the game had to be abandoned.

Another big attack was launched on the 20th by the Third Army, and in three days the IV Corps advanced ten miles in pouring rain. The battalion followed up the advance, moving up to very good billets at Bethencourt. Although not in the actual fighting, the battalion was constantly in the forward areas working on roads and tracks, and in this work suffered casualties. The division was relieved on the 23rd and moved back to Caudry, but the battalion remained at Bethencourt, doing pioneer work. The advance had been carried out by the 37th

Division, and the battalion moved forward to Viesly to work on roads near Briastre.

Many stories were afloat of cunningly set booby-traps being found in all sorts of places. Delayed fuses were usually resorted to by the Germans, and everyone became extraordinarily cautious. At one billet a sergeant was found prodding a bed with a long stick from the next room, as bombs had been known to be found in beds. In another case, a section of men were filled with consternation when, after retiring for the night, they could distinctly hear a ticking in the chimney, which had been blocked up. With the usual nonchalant spirit, which always prevailed, and thinking that "if it blows up, well, we shall be asleep, and know nothing about it," no notice was taken and by the morning the ticking had ceased.

Several pioneer N.C.O.'s joined the battalion for duty and lectures were given to the companies on pioneer work by an R.E. officer. Only two companies were engaged each day on roads and tracks, while the remaining company carried out general training. Military Crosses were awarded to Captain W. E. Richardson, Second-Lieutenants N. Rolles, G. E. Phillpot, C. V. F. Manning, and Parchment Certificates were awarded by the G.O.C. for gallant work performed by the following on the dates stated against their respective names :—Sergeant A. L. Haddon (26-8-18), Lance-Corporal P. Mellidge (23-8-18), Private G. Jukes (27-9-18), Sergeant McHale (23-8-18), Private J. Williams (23-8-18).

The battalion moved forward on 3rd November to Neuville, marching on next day to Ghissignies. On this day the last decisive battle of the war commenced. The morning of 4th November started in glorious weather, but later in the day rain fell in torrents and the roads were soon in a shocking state. To add to the difficulties, huge mine craters had been blown in the roads, and this entailed much work for the pioneers and engineers. The advance continued through the Forêt de Mormal. This was a very extensive area of thickly grown timber, and it had been anticipated that here the enemy would put up a strong resistance. However, little resistance was met with in the forest itself, and it was

The Final Advance

now obvious that the enemy was retiring rapidly, and orders were received on 9th November that the advance was to be pressed forward closely.

In the meantime, the battalion had moved forward on 5th November to Le Rond Quesne, and two days later marched through the Forêt de Mormal to La Grande Carriere. German dead were seen on all sides of the road through the forest. The battalion was busily engaged filling in the mine craters at road junctions and making the roads fit for transport. The railway running through the forest had been mined in many places, but the engineers did such excellent work that supply trains were running through within a few hours after the advance.

The German retirement was so hasty as to be almost a rout, and it was difficult for our troops to keep in touch with them. Rations, too, were scarce and the A.S.C. had no little trouble in getting supplies up to the advanced positions. No water could be used from the wells and pumps until it had been tested, in view of the possibility of the enemy having poisoned the supplies. The ease of our advance had created difficulties, especially in the Forêt de Mormal. Cunningly concealed mines were constantly going up and the rain was incessant; these two factors added greatly to the difficulty of pushing forward supplies.

However, the end was in sight; Turkey and Bulgaria were out of the war, and on 4th November Austria signed an armistice. On the German side news came through that the country was in chaos and the Kaiser had abdicated, while Germany had appealed for an armistice and negotiations were proceeding. The battalion was stationed at Pont-sur-Sambre when news was received at 8 a.m. on 11th November that the armistice had been signed and that hostilities would cease at 11 a.m. that morning. There was perhaps a tinge of disappointment that the pursuit could not be continued, but this was of no account against the realization of the almost unbelievable — the war was over. It is difficult to describe the general impression that the news of the Armistice made upon the fighting troops. However, Mr. Rudyard Kipling in his *History of the Irish Guards* has succeeded, he says :—

" Men took the news according to their natures. Indurated pessimists, after proving that it was a lie, said it would be but an interlude. Others retired into themselves as though they had been shot, or went stiffly off about the meticulous execution of some trumpery detail of kit cleaning. Some turned round and fell asleep then and there, and a few lost all hold for a while. It was the appalling new silence of things that soothed and unsettled them in turn. They did not realize till all sounds of their trade ceased, and the stillness stung in their ears as soda-water stings on the palate, how entirely these had been part of their strained bodies and souls . . .

" Men coming up from Details Camp, across old " unwholesome " areas, heard nothing but the roar of the lorries on which they had stolen their lift, and rejoiced with a childish mixture of fear as they topped every unscreened rise that was now mere scenery such as tourists would see later. To raise the head without thought of precaution against what might be in front or on either flank, into free, still air was the first pleasure of that great release. To lie down that night in a big barn beside unscreened braziers, with one's smiling companions who talked till sleep overtook them, and, when the last happy babbler had dropped off, to hear the long forgotten sound of a horse's feet trotting evenly on a hard road under a full moon crowned all that had gone before. Each man had but one thought in those miraculous first hours :—" I — even I, myself, here — have come through the war." To scorn the shelter of sunken roads, hedges, walls, or lines of trees, and to extend in unmartial crowds across the whole width of a Pavé, were exercises in freedom that he arrived at later."

As far as the battalion was concerned, there was no excitement, just a dull numbing feeling that now, after three years overseas, we should definitely get back safely to " Blighty." We tried to celebrate the occasion and thronged into the cafés, but there was nothing to drink. Habits of caution died hard, for no one would take the risk of pulling down the blankets over the windows which were used to conceal lights, and no lights were visible in the houses for several nights.

Chapter XIII.

FINALE.

It was a strange life after the Armistice. We were still on Active Service, but now the War was over, the prominent thought in everyone's mind was as to how soon he could get home to resume civilian occupation. There still remained much to be done, for as the Germans retired back behind the Rhine, the Allied Forces advanced to take up the positions allotted under the terms of the Armistice. And above all this, we had to be prepared for any eventuality. Demobilization was in everyone's mind, but it was realized that it would, of necessity, be a long, slow process. Now that there was no very active service to be carried on the great problem was to keep the men healthy and alert, and it was at this time that sports of all kinds were encouraged throughout the whole army.

On 12th November, the division moved back west of the Forest of Mormal, and remained in this district until the middle of December, but the battalion stayed on at Pont-sur-Sambre. Little work was carried out, but every day football matches were played. Lieut.-Colonel L. Murray, D.S.O., who had been on sick leave in England, following his wound at Nieppe, rejoined the battalion on 15th November, and the battalion was pleased to see its old commanding officer once again. Colonel Murray was held in esteem by all ranks: he always showed great concern for the welfare of his men and was constantly devising schemes to mitigate the ardours of active service. He was an excellent soldier in every way. He quickly distinguished the important geographical points in a new trench system, and the essential features of a large operation. The longer we knew him, the more we liked him. He was equally efficient as battalion goalkeeper, and played a useful bat at cricket. This, combined with his efficiency as a soldier and his continual care for his battalion, entitled him to that often misapplied term, a true sportsman.

The First Birmingham Battalion in the Great War

We were glad to learn that Lieut.-Colonel W. Wilberforce, D.S.O., M.C., who had commanded the battalion since Nieppe, was to remain with us as second-in-command; and incidentally, Colonel Wilberforce proved a useful member of the battalion rugger team.

The battalion soccer team started the football season by beating the 9th North Staffords 9–0, the 5th H.T.M. 7–4, and the 42nd Brigade R.F.A. 4–2, but they lost to the 14th Northumberland Fusiliers by 3 goals to 1. The rugger team defeated the 9th North Staffords by 19 points to nil, and on a cold frosty day, after a very hard and fast game, a match against the New Zealand Tunnelling Company ended in a draw of 6 points each. The New Zealanders included some Maoris, and a noticeable feature of their game was that the full back of the New Zealanders gave a capital display, although playing in bare feet.

Our stay in Pont-sur-Sambre came to an end on 21st November, when the battalion marched back to Le Rond Quesne to join up with the 5th Division. The weather was cold and frosty, but football matches were soon resumed. Difficulty was experienced in obtaining a suitable ground, as most of the fields had been too badly shelled to be of any use. However, a suitable plot was at last found, having only some half-dozen craters, and these were quickly filled in. The slope, however, was so bad that the goal crossbar at one end was invisible from the other.

After playing two or three matches on this ground, a better one was discovered, which was quite level; but here again, a good healthy hedge across the playing area was a decided disadvantage to good football. However, this presented few difficulties to old soldiers, for in a very short time the whole of the hedge was removed, the ground was levelled, and where once the hedge had flourished now ran the centre line of the field of play. On this new ground the battalion rugger team beat the 5th Battalion M.G.C. by 9 points to 6, and the 13th Field Ambulance by 13 points to nil, and drew with the 1st Devons 3 points each. The soccer team beat the 5th M.G.C. by 4 goals to 3, and a soccer match between the officers and sergeants ended in a win for the officers by 3 goals to 1.

Finale

On 1st December, the battalion strength was 35 officers and 963 other ranks and, although full records are not obtainable, this was probably the greatest strength the battalion ever had overseas. Games still continued to be a big feature of our days, and soccer matches against the K.O.S.B. and the 13th Field Ambulance ended in wins for the battalion, while a rugger match against the K.O.S.B. ended in a draw. This last chapter in the battalion history was frequently interspersed with football matches. There was little else to do. Parades were reduced to a minimum, and football kept the men fit and cheerful. The natives did not understand the mania of "les Anglais" for "le football." They did not see much sense in filling shell-holes and removing hedges in order to chase a "ballon" to and fro on a wintry afternoon. Queer fellows, these English! During our stay, however, the inhabitants learned something of the games, for when the battalion left for home, the footballs were left with the village priest for use among his schoolboys, who had picked up quite a lot.

The division was not called on to take part in the advance into Germany to form part of the Army of Occupation, but on 8th December, preparations were made to proceed by route march to an area in Belgium near Namur. Le Rond Quesne was left on the 9th in pouring rain and on the 11th, after crossing the Belgian frontier, the battalion was billeted at Grand Reng, where the inhabitants gave us an enthusiastic reception. Continuing the march, we next reached Binche, one of the largest towns encountered for some time, and here the battalion rested for one day. The march was continued on the 13th to Courcelles, and for the fifth consecutive day it rained during the march. After three further days' marching in pouring rain, Meux, our final destination was reached on the 18th, but the billets were far from satisfactory and very scattered. There were many refugees in the village; and we found ourselves rather cramped.

On 22nd December, a party of coal miners, the first batch for demobilization, left the battalion. Christmas Day was spent very quietly, and it was not until the 27th and 28th that the various companies celebrated Christmas by holding company dinners and concerts. It was the fourth Christmas spent by the battalion overseas, and only a very small sprinkling of those who had partaken of the Christmas festivities at Froissy in 1915 were left with the battalion, and these few were mostly with H.Q. company. There was little to be had in the way of Christmas beverages. Beer and wine were practically unobtainable, but the canteen corporal managed to unearth from somewhere a supply of gin, and this had to suffice.

Demobilization was beginning to move, and from the beginning of the year men were leaving the battalion daily; while those not so fortunate proceeded to make themselves comfortable in the new quarters.

The G.O.C. 5th Division presented two cups for soccer and rugger to be played for on the knock-out system. In the first round of the soccer cup, the battalion beat the 5th Divisional Ammunition Column by 6 goals to 1.

On 3rd January, news was received that Captain A. H. Gibson and Sergeant H. F. Knight had been mentioned in dispatches. The battalion left Meux on the 4th to find better billets at Eghezee, and here we stayed until orders were received for the cadre to return to England. General training and educational classes, and of course football matches, occupied the time, and the days slipped pleasantly by.

The rugger team defeated the 1st Norfolks on 14th January by 6 points to 3. The kick-off was timed for 2.15 p.m., but it was over a quarter-of-an-hour later before this match actually began. It transpired that the team changed in a school, which also housed the sergeants' mess, and as the team was invited into the mess, great difficulty was experienced in getting the match started. Two days later the 16th Royal Warwicks were defeated by 8 points to 6. The battalion team was photographed before the match and this must have upset them, for the margin should have been larger. On the 20th, the rugger team was again successful, defeating the 1st Cheshires by 35 points to nil in the second round of the Divisional Cup.

Finale

The awards of Meritorious Service Medals to C.Q.M. Sergeants S. J. Neighbour, F. W. Dow, and Sergeant C. J. Brown were notified on the 23rd January.

In the second round of the Divisional Cup, the soccer team beat the combined Field Ambulances on the 31st by 5 goals to 0. Demobilization was steadily proceeding, and by the end of January the battalion strength had dwindled to 16 officers and 687 other ranks.

February 4th was a Red Letter Day for the battalion, for the first Colour — the King's Silk Union — was received at Leuze from the hands of the IV Corps Commander, Lieut.-General Sir G. M. Harper, K.C.B., D.S.O. The 16th Royal Warwicks also received their Colours on this occasion, which took the form of a ceremonial parade commanded by Lieut.-Colonel L. Murray, D.S.O. The day was fine but cold, with two inches of snow on the ground, and after the General Salute and a short service, the Colours were consecrated by the senior Chaplain of the 4th Army. Following this ceremony, the battalions marched past in column and close column. On the return march to billets at Eghezee, "A" Company provided the escort to the uncased Colour.

A dinner for the battalion to celebrate the presentation of the colour was held in the schools at Eghezee on 6th February, and this was a very enjoyable function.

On the 11th, the battalion played the 16th Royal Warwicks in the third round of the Divisional Soccer Cup. A heavy fall of snow had occurred, and the ground had to be cleared. The battalion entered the semi-final by a win of 6 goals to 0. Two days later, the 1st Bedfords were defeated by 10 goals to 2, and the battalion entered the final, which was played at Leuze on the 17th. The other finalists were our old friends and rivals the K.O.S.B., with whom we had fought out some strenuous games. A large number of spectators assembled to watch the match, which was won easily by the battalion by 10 goals to 1. After the game, Major-General Ponsonby, C.B., C.M.G., D.S.O., presented the cup to the battalion captain, Private B. Millard. In the progress of the competition the battalion had scored 37 goals to 4, and the names of the team, which were inscribed on the cup, were:—Lance-Corporal A. Beaver; Corporal F. Mumford, Private R. Bishop; Private F. Horton, Private B. Millard, Sergeant S. J. Smith; Lance-Corporal E. W. Bailes, Private A. E. Fletcher, Corporal C. E. Rudge, Private W. A. Jeffery, Private J. Woolsey.

The rugger team played a friendly match against the K.O.S.B. on the 19th on a soft, wet, and muddy ground and the game, which was confined to the forwards, resulted in a draw.

The battalion strength at the end of February was only 18 officers and 217 other ranks.

The final for the Divisional Rugby Cup was played at Leuze on the 3rd March, and once again the battalion's opponents were the K.O.S.B. This was the cup we had expected to win, but unfortunately, practically all the battalion team had been demobilized and only three regular members remained, so that a very weak side was put in the field. The game was played in heavy rain before a large crowd and resulted in a win for the K.O.S.B. by 9 points to 3, and so with this result honours were divided with our old friends and opponents.

On 17th March, Lieut.-General Sir R. C. B. Haking, K.C.B., and Lady Haking visited the battalion and inspected the company banners, which had been presented at Nieppe. In the middle of March, the division began to move nearer Charleroi as a preliminary move to the entrainment of battalion cadres for home. Fleurus was reached on 16th March, and while waiting for embarkation, a combined rugger team of 14th Royal Warwicks and K.O.S.B. played two matches. The first, against the remainder of the division, was won easily by 35 points to nil, but a week later, after a very hard game, Captain Gotto's 4th Army XV defeated the combined battalions by 6 points to 3.

At the end of March the battalion ration strength was 13 officers and 124 other ranks, and orders for home were received in the middle of April. The battalion cadre entrained at Charleroi for Antwerp and embarked for England on the 17th for final demobilization.

Finale

And so the 14th Battalion of the Royal Warwickshire Regiment (1st Birmingham) came home. Amid the general return of millions to civilian life, the little group of Midland men slipped quietly back to their homes. The war was over. Peace had begun; and the subsequent history of many a battalion man in these days of economic stress proves that " Peace hath her victories, no less renowned than war."

Once every year, usually in November, the survivors meet at a re-union dinner. Old memories are revived; old tales are told; old songs are sung. For a few short hours the camaraderie of the old days lives again; those old days when we swung along the high roads of France; when we wandered together among the vineyards of Italy; and when we manned the trenches at Ypres, High Wood, Arras, Festubert, and a score more places whose names are for ever written across the world's history. In all those places the 1st Birminghams remembered their city's motto, " Forward." But at these annual re-unions, a toast is drunk early in the evening: " Absent Comrades." That toast is drunk in silence. Words cannot fill the gaps in our ranks, but in silence we remember those whom we left behind in those foreign fields which are " for ever England." Several pilgrimages have been made to the battlefields and to the Gardens of Remembrance where the Birmingham men lie. They are beautiful places these gardens, and the peace that prevails is the result of the sacrifice of the men who lie there: instead of the whistling bullet, they hear the bugle blowing " Last Post " at sundown from the new Menin Gate; and instead of the crash of the barrage, they hear the peaceful evening bells from many a church tower, which they died to restore.

> " Bells of remembrance, on this summer's eve,
>   Of our relief, Peace and Goodwill ring in!
> Ring out the past, and let not hate bereave
>   Our dreaming dead of all they died to win! " *

* *John Galsworthy.*

DISTINCTIONS CONFERRED 1914-1918

Distinguished Service Order. Lieut.-Colonels L. Murray, W. Wilberforce, M.C.

Military Cross. Major R. C. Watts ; Captains H. D. Rees, W. E. Richardson ; Second-Lieutenants H. Ford, H. H. Kaye, M.M., C. H. Platt, G. E. Phillpot, C. V. F. Manning, N. Rolles, J. T. Turner, R. G. Warren.

Distinguished Conduct Medal. Regimental-Sergeant-Majors G. F. Downes, F. W. Hayes ; Company-Sergeant-Major C. B. Plenderleith ; Sergeants S. Langford, H. Newey, H. W. Perry, D. W. Tuffley ; Corporal A. G. Smith ; Lance-Corporals S. E. Hull, M.M., R. Wright ; Privates A. H. Hudson, B. Harman.

Military Medal and Bar. Corporal W. E. Tongue ; Lance-Corporals F. J. Stephens, T. Williams ; Private T. Shirley.

Military Medals. Sergeants P. Bristowe, S. Burke, B. J. Cope, H. Dance, J. H. Davenport, R. French, J. Leach, H. R. Martin, F. C. Usher, E. W. Williams ; Lance-Sergeants J. Howe, W. Robertson ; Corporals J. W. Bubb, N. Mooney, C. E. Rudge ; Lance-Corporals T. Langford, L. Manning, H. Morris, L. Nicholson, J. A. Roberts, W. Shepherd, C. Sparkes, H. Williams ; Privates J. H. Anderson, T. Bailey, W. G. Beere, A. S. Brown, H. Coles, A. A. Cooper, G. Fiefield, J. W. Haynes, W. Hocking, R. H. Holloway, G. Lawton, W. Lunn, G. Nicholl, A. C. Pilgrim, W. Poulton, T. Powell, F. E. Ralphs, W. S. Sharman, W. G. Sharp, A. Smith, G. J. Smith, G. O. Smith, R. V. Sorge, T. H. Warnon, W. Webb, J. Woolsey.

French Croix de Guerre. Private W. G. Sharp.

Distinctions

Meritorious Service Medals. Company-Quarter-Master-Sergeants A. C. Denham, F. W. Dow, S. J. Neighbour; Sergeants C. J. Brown, H. Lee.

Parchment Certificates. Sergeants A. L. Haddon, P. McHale; Lance-Corporal P. Millidge; Privates G. Jukes, J. Williams.

Mentioned in Dispatches. Majors R. H. Baily, C. Playfair, Captains A. Addenbrooke, A. H. Gibson, D. Neal, F. W. Richmond; R.S.M. G. F. Downes; C.S.M. W. J. Blower, A. Lucas; C.Q.M.S. F. P. Cornforth, S. J. Neighbour; Sergeants C. J. Brown, B. V. Davies, F. W. Dow, H. F. Knight, F. J. Patrick, D. W. Tuffley; Corporal H. H. Lyons; Private A. L. Cooke.

CASUALTIES.

	Officers.	Other Ranks.	Total.
Killed	26	328	354
Died of Wounds	7	40	47
Wounded	62	1,516	1,578
Missing	6	419	425
Died	—	2	2
Casualties not catagorized :—			
23rd-31st August, 1918	20	280	300
27th September, 1918	—	190	190
	121	2,775	2,896

ROLL OF HONOUR
of the
14TH (Service) BATTALION
ROYAL WARWICKSHIRE REGIMENT

OFFICERS

Name.	Rank.	Date of Death.
ADDENBROOKE, A.	Captain	5th Oct., 1916.
ALLCHIN, W. J.	Sec. Lieut.	26th Oct., 1917.
ALLEN, N.	Captain	14th April, 1918.
BARROW, E. S. K.	Sec. Lieut.	8th May, 1917.
BRAITHWAITE, E.	Sec. Lieut.	22nd July, 1916.
BRINKWORTH, A. R.	Sec. Lieut.	7th Sept., 1916.
BRYSON, L. W.	Captain	30th July, 1916.
CHEPMELL, J. D.	Lieutenant	10th April, 1918.
CLEMENT, H.	Temp. Lieut. Act. Capt.	10th Oct., 1917.
CURTIS, K. S.	Sec. Lieut.	26th Oct., 1917.
DAVIS, C. E.	Sec. Lieut.	15th Sept., 1918.
DAVIS, P. H.	Sec. Lieut.	26th Oct., 1917.
DOUGLAS, A. W.	Sec. Lieut.	3rd Sept., 1916.
GREENWOOD, H. S.	Sec. Lieut.	22nd July, 1916.
HEWETT, S. H. P.	Sec. Lieut.	22nd July, 1916.
HODES, F. P.	Sec. Lieut.	24th July, 1916.
HUGHES, C. W.	Captain	1st Oct., 1918.
IZON, E. G.	Captain	27th Sept., 1918.
JACOBI, W. T.	Sec. Lieut.	21st Oct., 1916.
JOSEPH, A. E.	Lieutenant	10th May, 1917.
LEITH, J.	Sec. Lieut.	23rd Aug., 1918.
LYTHGOE, J. W.	Sec. Lieut.	22nd July, 1916.
MACINTOSH, J.	Sec. Lieut.	23rd July, 1916.
MATHEWS, H. S.	Captain	22nd July, 1916.
MOORE, G. A.	Sec. Lieut.	2nd May, 1918.
O'DWYER, A. S.	Sec. Lieut.	29th July, 1916.
PAYTON, R. S.	Lieutenant	22nd July, 1916.
PEARSON, C. T.	Sec. Lieut.	29th Aug., 1918.
PLANT, H.	Sec. Lieut.	20th Dec., 1916.
POCOCK, C. A.	Sec. Lieut.	8th May, 1917.
QUARRY, ST. J. S.	Major (R. Berks. R.)	14th April, 1918.
SANSOME, H. V.	Sec. Lieut.	26th Oct., 1917.
SALISBURY, C. R.	Sec. Lieut.	7th May, 1917.
SMITH, E. A.	Sec. Lieut.	22nd July, 1916.
SMITH, J. B.	Sec. Lieut.	19th Aug., 1917.

The First Birmingham Battalion in the Great War

Name.	Rank.	Date of Death.
TOWNLEY, F. L.	Sec. Lieut.	26th Oct., 1917.
TURNER, B.	Lieut. (Act. Capt.)	8th May, 1917.
TURNER, J. P.	Sec. Lieut.	26th Oct., 1917.
VINCE, W. L.	Lieutenant	8th May, 1917.
WHITBREAD, B.	Sec. Lieut.	22nd July, 1916.
WOOD, L. J.	Sec. Lieut.	4th Oct., 1917.

OTHER RANKS

Name.	Rank.	Regimental No.	Date of Death.
ABBOTT, F. C.	L/Corpl.	28388	13th April, 1918.
ABBOTT, P. Z.	Private	25406	15th Sept., 1918.
ACKLAND, G. H.	Private	32610	8th Feb., 1919.
ADAMS, A.	Private	32509	26th Oct., 1917.
ADAMS, A. G.	Sergeant	843	23rd July, 1916.
ADAMS, E. J.	L/Corpl.	19146	4th Oct., 1917.
ADAMS, H. S.	Private	29888	13th April, 1918.
ADAMS, J. B.	Private	1206	23rd July, 1916.
ALDRED, F. W.	Private	28389	23rd May, 1918.
ALDRIDGE, W. G.	Private	28041	27th Sept., 1918.
ALEXANDER, F. H.	Private	1133	23rd July, 1916.
ALLCOCK, L.	Private	27474	7th May, 1917.
ALLEN, A. W.	Private	1168	23rd July, 1916.
ALLEN, C. B.	Private	30	23rd July, 1916.
ALLEN, R.	Private	16633	15th June, 1917.
ALLEN, T. A.	Private	36516	27th Sept., 1918.
ALLEN, W.	Private	11075	4th Oct., 1917.
ALLUM, W.	Private	30201	3rd Sept., 1916.
ANDERTON, S.	Private	565	23rd July, 1916.
ANDREW, G. H.	Private	25234	14th April, 1918.
ANDREWS, J.	Private	34503	29th May, 1918.
ANSTEY, J. D.	Private	28	23rd July, 1916.
ANTHONY, A. J.	Private	35217	19th Sept., 1918.
APPLETON, W. T.	Private	35815	8th July, 1918.
ASBURY, E.	Private	19771	14th April, 1918.
ASBURY, W. J.	Private	503	23rd July, 1916.
ASHFORD, A. G.	Private	28391	23rd March, 1917.
ASHMEAD, T. F.	Private	14–1253	30th July, 1916.
ASHTON, J. E.	Private	19139	4th Oct., 1917.
ASHWELL, W. J.	Private	30219	26th Oct., 1917.
ASKEW, W.	Private	32435	2nd May, 1918.
ASPEY, A.	Private	34195	14th April, 1918.
BADHAM, W. H.	Private	14–1455	23rd July, 1916.
BAILEY, B. T.	Private	48205	27th Sept., 1918.
BAILEY, H. W.	Private	16915	3rd Sept., 1916.

Roll of Honour

Name.	Rank.	Regimental No.	Date of Death.
BAKER, R.	Private	9326	29th March, 1918.
BAKER, W.	L/Corpl.	558	4th Oct., 1917.
BALLARD, G.	Private	1071	5th Oct., 1917.
BARKER, J.	Private	16833	12th Sept., 1916.
BARKER, W.	Private	17753	8th July, 1917.
BARLOW, B. B.	Sergeant	854	23rd Dec., 1915.
BARLOW, M. R.	Private	14-1382	4th June, 1916.
BARLOW, P. C.	Private	30217	3rd Sept., 1916.
BARNACLE, C. W.	Private	14-1701	23rd July, 1916.
BARRETT, A.	Private	358	23rd July, 1916.
BARRETT, J. F.	Private	855	23rd July, 1916.
BARRETT, W. J.	Private	14-1421	23rd May, 1916.
BARROW, C. H. B.	Private	1149	3rd Sept., 1916.
BARTHOLOMEW, W. C.	Private	38895	8th July, 1918.
BAST, E. A.	Private	50576	27th Aug., 1918.
BATES, T. H.	Private	15813	3rd Sept., 1916.
BATES, W.	Private	17376	30th July, 1916.
BAXTER, A. E.	Private	36100	26th Aug., 1918.
BAYLISS, W. H.	Private	17837	3rd Sept., 1916.
BEALE, J. H.	Private	22354	26th Oct., 1917.
BEASLEY, C. F.	Private	23762	26th Oct., 1917.
BEDDARD, A. J.	Private	104	13th April, 1918.
BEDDOES, C. E.	L/Corpl.	50453	17th Oct., 1918.
BEER, F.	Private	1306	4th Oct., 1917.
BEDFORD, C. E.	Private	16822	30th July, 1916.
BELCHER, J.	Private	43425	7th Sept., 1918.
BELLAMY, F. W.	Private	14-1646	23rd July, 1916.
BELLAMY, W. M. C.	Private	1603	23rd July, 1916.
BENCH, F. G.	Private	22675	10th March, 1917.
BENFIELD, B. W.	Private	510	23rd July, 1916.
BENNETT, H.	Private	16-1691	2nd Aug., 1916.
BENNETT, H. J.	Private	48310	23rd Aug., 1918.
BENNETT, J. H.	Private	17829	3rd Sept., 1916.
BENNETT, P.	Private	18076	7th Sept., 1916.
BENNETT, J. W.	Private	14-1334	30th July, 1916.
BENSON, W.	Private	859	23rd July, 1916.
BENWELL, W. F.	Private	14-1649	23rd July, 1916.
BERRY, F. L.	L/Corpl.	1127	11th Sept., 1916.
BERTIN, B. J.	Private	32521	26th Dec., 1917.
BEST, W.	Private	14-1647	20th Aug., 1916.
BILLETT, J. H.	Private	29893	31st Oct., 1917.
BILLINGLEY, C. H.	Private	14-1684	23rd July, 1916.
BIRCH, H.	Private	17021	15th Sept., 1916.
BIRCH, J. C.	Private	14-513	31st July, 1916.
BIRD, A.	Private	14-1584	3rd Sept., 1916.
BISHOP, S. S.	Private	32514	3rd Oct., 1917.

The First Birmingham Battalion in the Great War

Name.	Rank.	Regimental No.	Date of Death.
BLANCH, J.	Private	16-1447	22nd July, 1916.
BLIGHT, C.	Private	35830	28th Sept., 1918.
BLISS, F. H.	Private	156	23rd July, 1916.
BLOOD, J. V.	Private	20510	26th Oct., 1917.
BLOWER, J.	Private	28525	20th Oct., 1917.
BOLTON, R. J.	Private	25269	14th April, 1918.
BOTT, S. G.	Sergeant	14-1516	18th May, 1917.
BOUGH, W.	Private	21096	14th April, 1918.
BOWMER, J.	Private	14-1505	23rd July, 1916.
BOWEN, A. S.	Private	50587	29th May, 1918.
BOYD, C. T.	Private	863	23rd July, 1916.
BOYD, W.	Private	34089	5th June, 1918.
BRACE, A. S.	Private	43658	27th Sept., 1918.
BRAIN, H. J.	Sergeant	9257	8th Oct., 1918.
BRAIN, J. C.	Corporal	7971	13th April, 1918.
BRANCH, W.	Private	28518	24th June, 1917.
BRANDHAM, G.	Private	30171	4th Oct., 1917.
BRETTELL, F. B.	L/Corpl.	362	16th April, 1916.
BRIDGE, V.	Private	30221	3rd Sept., 1916.
BRIDGWATER, F. H.	Private	16-1938	23rd July, 1916.
BRITT, E. G.	Private	14-1434	11th June, 1916.
BRITTAIN, H. A.	Private	16760	3rd June, 1917.
BRODIE, A.	L/Corpl.	16181	30th July, 1916.
BROMLEY, H.	Private	202405	8th July, 1918.
BROMLEY, W.	Private	10914	23rd Oct., 1917.
BROOKS, P. J.	Private	36354	27th Sept., 1918.
BROUGHTON, E. W.	Private	871	23rd July, 1916.
BROUGHTON, H.	Private	30298	24th April, 1917.
BROWN, A.	Private	21261	27th Feb., 1917.
BROWN, E.	Private	15-1325	23rd July, 1916.
BROWN, E.	L/Corpl.	1093	23rd July, 1916.
BROWN, F.	Private	50591	29th June, 1918.
BROWN, F. H.	Sergeant	579	30th July, 1916.
BROWN, G. H.	Private	28448	9th March, 1917.
BROWN, R.	Private	33723	5th May, 1918.
BRUCE, H.	Private	17745	3rd Sept., 1916.
BRUCE, T. H.	Private	29884	26th Oct., 1917.
BUCKLE, C. L.	Private	38600	20th Oct., 1918.
BUCKLEY, C.	Private	14-1399	23rd July, 1916.
BUGBY, W. J.	Private	28458	7th May, 1917.
BULLIVANT, F. R.	Private	32592	10th May, 1918.
BURGESS, F.	Private	28046	26th Oct., 1917.
BURNELL, A. W. A.	Private	35838	30th Aug., 1918.
BURNESS, W. H.	Private	22194	26th Oct., 1917.
BURNSIDE, J. B.	L/Corpl.	356	30th Dec., 1915.
BURNSIDE, W. D.	L/Corpl.	361	23rd July, 1916.

Roll of Honour

Name.	Rank.	Regimental No.	Date of Death.
BURROWS, A. R.	Private	50443	27th Sept., 1918.
BURROWS, J.	Private	1930	20th May, 1918.
BURT, C.	Private	15-1409	23rd July, 1916.
BURTON, J.	Private	330602	15th Sept., 1918.
BURTON, J.	Private	17101	30th July, 1916.
BUSBY, W. J.	Private	34969	26th Oct., 1917.
BUTCHER, E. L.	Private	32518	5th Oct., 1917.
BUTLER, A. C.	Private	21166	26th Oct., 1917.
BUTLER, F. W.	Private	26757	27th Sept., 1918.
BUTLER, L. S. L.	Private	592	21st July, 1916.
BUTLER, R. W.	Private	35839	20th Sept., 1918.
BYRD, F.	Private	17416	30th July, 1916.
CALLIS, J.	Private	32525	4th Oct., 1917.
CANDLER, F. J.	L/Corpl.	50595	27th Sept., 1918.
CARR, R. G.	Private	38775	28th Aug., 1918.
CARTER, E.	Private	14-1303	21st July, 1916.
CARTWRIGHT, H.	Private	23429	5th Oct., 1917.
CASTLE, R. L.	Private	14-59	21st July, 1916.
CHALCROFT, W.	Private	32615	4th Oct., 1917.
CHALLIS, G.	Private	18599	8th July, 1918.
CHAMBERLAIN, J. P.	Private	1187	23rd July, 1916.
CHANDLER, E. R.	Private	585	23rd July, 1916.
CHANEY, W. G.	L/Corpl.	33880	8th July, 1918.
CHARTER, S.	Private	30194	27th Dec., 1916.
CHATWIN, G. F.	Private	678	26th Oct., 1917.
CHECKETTS, H. W.	Corporal	873	3rd Sept., 1916.
CHERRY, W.	Private	14-1403	23rd July, 1916.
CHERRY, W. H.	Private	34957	26th Oct., 1917.
CHILD, W. H.	L/Corpl.	601	23rd July, 1916.
CHONLARTON, J.	Private	16771	3rd Sept., 1916.
CHRISTIE, R. L.	L/Corpl.	604	30th July, 1916.
CHURCHILL, A. E.	Private	14-1336	23rd July, 1916.
CLAPHAM, F. T.	Private	20691	22nd Sept., 1918.
CLARE, F. C.	Private	868	30th July, 1916.
CLARKE, A.	Private	1432	1st Aug., 1916.
CLARKE, H.	Private	16829	3rd Sept., 1916.
CLARKE, P.	Private	17907	10th June, 1917.
CLARKSON, F. R.	Private	34470	29th June, 1918.
CLEAVER, T.	C/S/Major	945	9th May, 1917.
CLEMENTS, C.	Sergeant	102	23rd July, 1916.
CLEMENTS, G.	Private	22421	27th June, 1917.
CLIMER, H.	Private	16989	27th June, 1917.
CLOW, B. T.	Private	17806	30th July, 1916.
CLOW, F.	Private	32523	26th Oct., 1917.
COCKERILL, H.	Private	15-1582	23rd July, 1916.
CODLING, R.	Private	27706	14th April, 1918.

The First Birmingham Battalion in the Great War

Name.	Rank.	Regimental No.	Date of Death.
COFFEN, N. R.	Private	50603	5th Oct., 1918.
COGBILL, E.	Private	16–1679	23rd July, 1916.
COLE, H. S.	Private	141300	30th July, 1916.
COLEMAN, F. G.	Private	151619	25th Dec., 1916.
COLEY, W.	Private	1150	14th April, 1918.
COLLETT, A.	Private	16326	5th Sept., 1916.
COLLINS, F. B.	Private	22001	26th Oct., 1917.
COLLINS, J.	Private	141265	4th June, 1916.
CONNOLLY, J. N.	Private	16–1852	7th May, 1917.
CONSTABLE, G. F.	Private	32601	27th Oct., 1917.
COOK, E.	Private	30245	26th Oct., 1917.
COOKE, F. C.	Private	28530	23rd Aug., 1918.
COOPER, A. S.	L/Corpl.	16–1647	23rd July, 1918.
COOPER, J. H.	Corporal	12140	13th April, 1918.
COOPER, J. W.	Private	30302	9th Oct., 1917.
COOPER, JAS. W.	Private	35846	23rd Aug., 1918.
COOPER, L. S.	L/Corpl.	1241	7th May, 1917.
COPE, E. A. G.	Private	30246	8th May, 1917.
COSLETT, T. C.	Private	50	23rd July, 1916.
COUCH, H. J.	Sergeant	599	30th July, 1916.
COULDWELL, H.	Private	33771	27th Sept., 1918.
COULING, F. J.	Sergeant	543	7th May, 1917.
COULTHARD, H. D.	A/Sergt.	870	3rd Sept., 1916.
COX, A. J.	Private	14–1268	30th July, 1916.
COX, B.	Corporal	28374	27th Oct., 1917.
COX, F. A.	Private	50411	8th July, 1918.
COX, F. W.	L/Sergt.	58	30th July, 1916.
CRAKE, F. W.	Private	32449	3rd Oct., 1917.
CRANE, G.	Private	15–1457	28th July, 1916.
CRATES, H.	Private	16–1509	21st July, 1916.
CRISP, C. H.	Private	8508	3rd Sept., 1916.
CROSS, K. L.	Private	23128	4th Oct., 1917.
CROSS, F. W.	Private	50613	26th June, 1918.
CROSS, H. C.	Private	1220	21st July, 1916.
CROWE, J. J.	Private	34433	14th April, 1918.
CURTIS, W. G.	Private	64	23rd July, 1916.
CUTLER, S.	Private	37878	27th Sept., 1918.
DAIN, J. L.	Private	882	4th July, 1916.
DALE, A. E.	Private	30174	3rd Sept., 1916.
DANIELS, W. E.	L/Corpl.	30248	21st Oct., 1918.
DATSON, C.	Private	21310	9th Feb., 1917.
DAVEY, R.	Private	36104	8th July, 1918.
DAVIES, J. W.	Private	17520	30th July, 1916.
DAVIES, W.	Private	27821	27th Sept., 1918.
DAVIES, W. H.	Corporal	8769	14th April, 1918.
DAVIS, A. T.	Private	14–1599	18th March, 1916.

Roll of Honour

Name.	Rank.	Regimental No.	Date of Death.
DAW, E. W.	Private	24348	26th Oct., 1917.
DAY, T.	Private	17442	26th Oct., 1917.
DEAN, W. J.	Private	16–1705	3rd Sept., 1916.
DELAMY, T.	Private	15–1670	12th June, 1916.
DENT, W. H.	Private	141251	27th Sept., 1918.
DEVEREUX, G. A. F.	Private	17960	3rd Sept., 1916.
DEVEY, T. G.	Private	14–1277	23rd July, 1916.
DEWBURY, J. P.	L/Corpl.	331	21st July, 1916.
DEYKIN, C. J.	Private	328	23rd July, 1916.
DINGLEY, P. G.	Private	1037	23rd July, 1916.
DIPPER, W. A.	Private	34971	26th Oct., 1917.
DOBSON, W.	Private	14–1256	30th July, 1916.
DOCKER, W. E.	Private	14–1639	23rd July, 1916.
DOCKERILL, J.	A/Corpl.	30250	12th Sept, 1916.
DODD, A. H.	Private	27721	1st Dec., 1916.
DOLMAN, P. A.	Private	50623	23rd Aug., 1918.
DOWLER, A. R.	L/Corpl.	876	23rd July, 1916.
DOWLER, F.	Corporal	613	3rd Sept., 1916.
DOWLING, G. A.	Private	34115	31st Oct., 1917.
DOWLING, R.	Private	875	30th July, 1916.
DRAKE, R. J.	L/Corpl.	30307	26th Oct., 1917.
DRAKE, W.	Private	30415	14th April, 1918.
DREYHELLER, W. E.	Private	551	14th April, 1918.
DRINKWATER, W.	Private	14–1468	23rd July, 1916.
DRUCE, H.	Private	18478	4th Oct., 1917.
DUFFILL, F. H.	Private	14–1568	23rd July, 1916.
DUMBELL, W.	Private	36522	28th Sept., 1918.
DUNKLEY, H.	Private	16711	30th July, 1916.
DWANE, J. W.	Private	14–1575	23rd July, 1916.
EACOTT, H. W. T.	Private	34958	26th Oct., 1917.
EBOURNE, L. E.	Private	552	23rd July, 1916.
EDEN, G.	Private	17802	30th July, 1916.
EDMONDS, J. H. (M.M.)	Private	15151	8th Jan., 1918.
EDWARDS, H. L.	Private	17694	3rd Sept., 1916.
ELDRIDGE, C.	Private	35859	31st Aug., 1918.
ELLIOTT, H.	Corporal	223	15th June, 1916.
ELMER, T.	L/Corpl.	30309	17th Oct., 1916.
ELSEY, C.	Private	36544	17th Sept., 1918.
EMERY, W. F.	Private	50626	27th Sept., 1918.
ENGLAND, A. H.	Private	28514	7th May, 1917.
ENGLAND, R. F.	Private	35860	27th Aug., 1918.
EVANS, G. H.	Private	14–1532	30th July, 1916.
EVANS, P. M.	Private	14–222	25th Nov., 1916.
EVANS, W.	Private	16082	10th June, 1916.
EVERILL, J.	Private	28478	8th Nov., 1917.
EYRE, H. P.	L/Corpl.	1157	30th July, 1916.

The First Birmingham Battalion in the Great War

Name.	Rank.	Regimental No.	Date of Death.
FAIR, R.	Private	32532	26th Oct., 1917.
FAIRBAIRN, J.	Private	34119	13th April, 1918.
FAIRCLOUGH, W.	Corporal	46	3rd Sept., 1916.
FARNELL, A. J.	Private	149	23rd July, 1916.
FARNELL, A. C.	L/Corpl.	150	23rd July, 1916.
FARR, F. H.	L/Sergt.	30253	11th Sept., 1916.
FAULKS, J. G.	Private	15-1416	23rd July, 1916.
FELLOWS, H. J.	Private	1117	22nd July, 1916.
FELTON, J. H.	Private	14-1430	26th May, 1916.
FENNELL, J. L.	Private	16347	13th April, 1918.
FERMOR, C.	Private	22387	4th Oct., 1917.
FIELD, A.	Private	147	23rd July, 1916.
FIELD, J.	Private	231	23rd July, 1916.
FINCH, W.	Private	14-1546	23rd July, 1916.
FINDON, R.	Sergeant	233	23rd July, 1916.
FLETCHER, J. W.	Private	16301	24th Oct., 1917.
FLETCHER, R. V.	Private	646	11th June, 1916.
FLYNN, H.	Private	15-1439	5th Aug., 1916.
FORD, A. J.	Private	21336	26th Oct., 1917.
FORD, E.	Private	30166	3rd Sept., 1916.
FOX, A. A.	L/Corpl.	17614	27th Sept., 1918.
FRANKLIN, H. E.	Private	43277	26th Oct., 1917.
FROGATT, G. E.	Private	1441	23rd July, 1916.
FROST, J.	Private	18052	9th May, 1917.
FULFORD, F. H.	Private	14-1602	24th July, 1916.
FULLER, T. G.	Private	43669	17th Sept., 1918.
GABRIEL, H. M.	Private	1155	30th July, 1916.
GALE, V.	Private	28471	8th May, 1917.
GAMBLE, L. E.	Private	34106	26th Oct., 1917.
GARDNER, J.	Private	27691	21st May, 1917.
GARDNER, W.	Private	9656	11th Sept., 1916.
GARNER, E.	Private	16-1496	30th July, 1916.
GARNER, G.	Private	17393	2nd Oct., 1917.
GARNER, P. A.	Private	7	23rd July, 1916.
GARRATT, H. W.	Private	896	23rd July, 1916.
GEORGE, J. J.	Private	18049	11th Nov., 1917.
GEORGE, J. W.	Private	30311	3rd Sept., 1916.
GILKES, F.	Private	31922	13th April, 1918.
GILROY, W. W.	Private	28441	26th Aug., 1918.
GIVEN, S. J.	A/Sergt.	14-906	11th Sept., 1916.
GLOVER, L. F.	Private	615	1st Aug., 1916.
GLYDON, R.	Private	1191	23rd July, 1916.
GOLDSMITH, F. T.	Private	28400	27th June, 1917.
GOODCHILD, W.	Sergeant	402	6th May, 1917.
GOSWELL, T.	Private	32538	26th Oct., 1917.
GRAINGER, W. H.	Private	18045	13th April, 1918.

Roll of Honour

Name.	Rank.	Regimental No.	Date of Death.
GRALEY, J.	Private	18172	3rd Sept., 1916.
GRAY, A. P.	Private	36421	27th Sept., 1918.
GREAVES, E. J.	Private	28473	26th Oct., 1917.
GREEN, A. P.	Private	205	23rd July, 1916.
GREEN, C. W.	Private	34571	30th April, 1918.
GREEN, J.	Private	1165	22nd July, 1916.
GREEN, J.	Private	27983	4th Oct., 1917.
GREEN, N. F.	Private	606	23rd July, 1916.
GREEN, R. C.	Private	32456	26th Oct., 1917.
GREENHOUSE, J.	Private	28062	8th May, 1917.
GREENWOOD, F.	Private	30312	20th May, 1918.
GRIFFITHS, T.	Private	36543	27th Sept., 1918.
GRIMES, L. C.	Private	609	30th July, 1916.
GUNTER, W. E. J.	Private	18298	4th Oct., 1917.
HABGOOD, G.	Sergeant	32429	23rd Aug., 1918.
HACKETT, A.	Private	1202	8th Dec., 1915.
HADEN, W.	Private	14–1541	13th May, 1916.
HAIGH, H.	Private	656	8th May, 1917.
HALFORD, S. A.	Private	16433	3rd Sept., 1916.
HALL, E.	Private	17023	8th May, 1917.
HALL, F. H.	L/Corpl.	907	23rd July, 1916.
HALL, J.	Private	16978	5th Sept., 1916.
HALL, J. W.	Private	43278	25th May, 1918.
HALL, T.	Private	1169	31st Dec., 1915.
HAMLET, J. D.	Private	260357	26th Oct., 1917.
HAMMOND, A. D.	Private	18776	13th April, 1918.
HAMMOND, A. H.	Private	238051	27th Sept., 1918.
HAMMOND, B.	Private	30313	25th Dec., 1916.
HANCOX, J. F.	Private	25543	14th April, 1918.
HAND, H.	Private	16–1928	30th Aug., 1916.
HANDLEY, J.	Private	14–1279	26th July, 1916.
HANNIGAN, T.	Private	34094	28th Oct., 1917.
HANSON, T. R. (M.M.)	L/Corpl.	380	23rd July, 1916.
HARDIMAN, J. B.	Private	50652	8th July, 1916.
HARKER, F.	Private	27360	27th Sept., 1918.
HARLAND, A. E.	Private	6	23rd July, 1916.
HARRIS, F.	Sergeant	32460	15th Sept., 1918.
HARRIS, T. H.	Private	14–1631	23rd July, 1916.
HARRISON, W. E.	Private	15–1637	4th Feb., 1917.
HARTLAND, F. H.	Private	37435	8th July, 1918.
HARTLEY, R.	Private	11585	25th Oct., 1917.
HARTWELL, W.	Private	14–1650	23rd July, 1916.
HARVEY, W. J.	Private	50655	27th Aug., 1918.
HARWOOD, W.	Private	14–1630	23rd July, 1916.
HASTINGS, C. J.	L/Corpl.	917	30th July, 1916.
HAWCROFT, G.	Private	29907	26th Oct., 1917.

The First Birmingham Battalion in the Great War

Name.	Rank.	Regimental No.	Date of Death.
HAWKER, P. C.	Private	15-1636	23rd July, 1916.
HAYNES, C.	L/Corpl.	408	8th Oct., 1916.
HAYNES, E. J.	Private	14-1651	23rd July, 1916.
HAYNES, J. W. (M.M.)	Private	30209	14th April, 1918.
HEAFIELD, H. C.	Private	15-1597	23rd July, 1916.
HEARN, H.	Private	30175	7th May, 1917.
HEATH, A. H.	Corporal	409	23rd July, 1916.
HEATH, A. R.	Sergeant	6843	4th Oct., 1917.
HEATH, J.	Private	15-1594	29th Aug., 1916.
HEATHCOTE, H. H.	Private	30258	24th Sept., 1916.
HEATHFIELD, W.	Private	13406	30th July, 1916.
HEBBERT, J. W.	Corporal	112	20th July, 1916.
HERBERT, R. T.	Private	8013	5th Oct., 1917.
HERRICK, H. D.	Sergeant	635	23rd July, 1916.
HERRIMAN, G.	L/Corpl.	1136	30th July, 1916.
HERRING, J. I.	Private	18073	3rd Sept., 1916.
HEWITT, E. J.	Private	2772	27th Feb., 1917.
HEWITT, W. H.	Corporal	413	30th July, 1916.
HEWSON, E. S.	Private	30344	3rd Sept., 1916.
HIBELL, A. R.	Private	16-1445	6th Aug., 1916.
HILL, E. C.	Corporal	371	23rd July, 1916.
HILL, F. E.	Private	35296	27th Sept., 1918.
HILL, G.	Private	19175	4th Oct., 1917.
HILTON, D. T.	Dr.	9857	3rd Sept., 1916.
HIRONS, W. T.	Private	16763	14th April, 1918.
HOLDEN, S. N.	Private	693	31st Aug., 1916.
HOLMES, J. F. W.	Private	641	31st Aug., 1916.
HOMER, B. H.	Private	417	23rd July, 1916.
HOPKIN, F. H.	Private	30316	13th April, 1918.
HOPKINS, B. P.	A/L/Sergt.	672	11th Sept., 1916.
HOPKINS, J. S.	Sergeant	14-1570	26th Oct., 1917.
HOUGHTON, P.	Private	36536	17th Sept., 1918.
HOULT, D. G.	Private	33704	14th April, 1918.
HOWE, J. (M.M.)	Sergeant	16003	29th June, 1918.
HOWELL, D.	Private	113	25th March, 1916.
HOWELLS, H. H.	Private	32543	5th Oct., 1917.
HUCKER, W. T.	Private	33703	13th April, 1918.
HUDSON, L. C.	Private	912	4th June, 1916.
HUDSON, W.	Private	17729	26th Oct., 1917.
HUGHES, W.	Private	32546	5th Oct., 1917.
HULBERT. H. H. S.	Private	14-1292	13th Jan., 1917.
HUMBER, W. T.	Private	16159	30th July, 1916.
HUNTER, J. F.	Private	29911	6th July, 1918.
HUNTLEY, A. W. E.	Private	330222	3rd May, 1918.
HURLEY, V. H.	Private	15-1609	23rd July, 1916.
HURRELL, S.	Private	14-1350	23rd July, 1916.

Roll of Honour

Name.	Rank.	Regimental No.	Date of Death.
HUTCHINSON, H. J.	Private	682	30th July, 1916.
INGLE, D.	Private	30199	25th June, 1917.
IZARD, F. T.	Private	925	4th Oct., 1917.
JACKMAN, G.	L/Corpl.	17815	13th April, 1918.
JACKSON, A. E.	Private	17668	11th Nov., 1917.
JACKSON, A. E.	A/Sergt.	14–1487	27th Sept., 1918.
JACKSON, C. Y.	L/Corpl.	1034	23rd July, 1916.
JACKSON, P. T.	Private	168	22nd July, 1916.
JAMES, J.	Corporal	17116	7th May, 1917.
JAMES, T.	Private	16251	3rd June, 1917.
JARRATT, C. A.	Private	15–1347	10th June, 1916.
JARRETT, T.	Private	10018	3rd Sept., 1916.
JARVIS, H. J.	Private	50463	28th Aug., 1918.
JARVIS, J. T.	A/Sergt.	16–1688	3rd Sept., 1916.
JEFFERY, F.	Private	9956	30th July, 1916.
JEFFS, G. O.	Private	17095	30th July, 1916.
JENKINS, J. R.	Private	14–631	24th Jan., 1916.
JINKS, J.	Private	16722	13th April, 1918.
JINKS, W. M.	Private	30178	7th May, 1917.
JOHNSON, A. E.	Private	827	30th July, 1916.
JOHNSON, E. E. V.	Private	9137	3rd Sept., 1916.
JOLLIFFE, L. D.	Private	176	24th July, 1916.
JONES, A.	L/Corpl.	174	23rd July, 1916.
JONES, C. J.	L/Corpl.	1134	22nd July, 1916.
JONES, C. V.	L/Corpl.	1135	23rd July, 1916.
JONES, F.	Private	1572	23rd July, 1916.
JONES, F. G. (M.M.)	Private	169	23rd July, 1916.
JONES, G. F.	Private	14–1397	26th April, 1916.
JONES, G. H.	Private	27714	7th Oct., 1917.
JONES, H. W.	Sergeant	342	3rd Sept., 1916.
JONES, L. W.	Private	14–1254	23rd July, 1916.
JONES, N. E.	L/Corpl.	831	22nd July, 1916.
JONES, R.	Private	2281	14th April, 1918.
JONES, T. J.	Private	22805	9th Oct., 1917.
JONES, W.	Private	14–1379	23rd July, 1916.
JONES, W. R.	L/Corpl.	109	23rd July, 1916.
JORDON, L.	Private	16–2084	23rd July, 1916.
JOSEPH, E.	Sergeant	336	23rd July, 1916.
KAY, A. S.	Private	428	23rd July, 1916.
KEFFORD, L.	Private	25399	23rd April, 1918.
KEMP, G.	Private	15281	3rd Sept., 1916.
KENYON, A. A.	Private	17905	30th July, 1916.
KIGHTLEY, S. F.	Private	17427	30th July, 1916.
KILLICK, W.	Private	32549	29th April, 1918.
KIMSEY, W.	Private	34114	24th Oct., 1917.
KING, F.	Private	21154	27th Sept., 1918.

The First Birmingham Battalion in the Great War

Name.	Rank.	Regimental No.	Date of Death.
KINGWELL, W.	Sergeant	931	23rd March, 1916.
KIRBY, G. F.	Private	14-1263	23rd July, 1916.
KIRBY, J. S. W.	Private	24293	27th Sept., 1918.
KIRBY, R. H. E.	Private	1111	23rd July, 1916.
KISBY, C.	Private	30215	24th Oct., 1917.
KITCHEN, J. M.	C/S/Major	1088	16th Dec., 1915.
KNIGHT, W. G.	Private	36107	8th July, 1918.
KNOWLES, W. E.	Private	35307	29th May, 1918.
LAKE, H. C.	Private	1219	23rd July, 1916.
LALBY, G.	L/Corpl.	32500	26th Aug., 1918.
LANGFORD, A.	Private	18426	30th July, 1916.
LAW, A.	Private	15-1378	23rd July, 1916.
LAWSON, G.	Private	32551	26th Oct., 1917.
LAWSON, G. W.	Private	25136	23rd Aug., 1918.
LEDIARD, G. H.	Private	1754	3rd Sept., 1916.
LEE, H.	Sergeant	804	30th April, 1918.
LEEDING, T.	Private	33762	5th May, 1918.
LEESON, E. R.	Private	1109	23rd July, 1916.
LEWIS, A. E.	Private	634	26th Oct., 1917.
LEWIS, E.	Private	186	23rd July, 1916.
LILLEY, F.	Private	30319	24th Sept., 1916.
LILLEY, L.	L/Corpl.	30206	25th June, 1917.
LIMINTON, W. E.	Private	21271	8th May, 1917.
LIMMAGE, G.	Private	30320	14th April, 1918.
LINCOLN, W.	Private	30218	3rd Sept., 1916.
LINES, W.	Private	1289	5th May, 1917.
LISTER, E.	Private	437	23rd July, 1916.
LLOYD, J.	Private	30381	20th April, 1918.
LOCK, S. V.	Private	260358	26th Oct., 1917.
LOCKWOOD, S.	Private	16-1408	23rd July, 1916.
LONGMORE, C. R.	Private	14-1223	30th July, 1916.
LORD, F. W.	Private	1192	30th July, 1916.
LORD, H. C.	Private	16562	3rd Sept., 1916.
LUCAS, A.	Private	16-1413	27th March, 1916.
LUCAS, C. J.	Private	35892	27th Aug., 1918.
MAHADY, F.	Private	14-1461	30th July, 1916.
MALIN, J.	Private	18019	11th Sept., 1916.
MALIN, R.	C/S/Major	1030	23rd July, 1916.
MANNING, J.	L/Corpl.	16481	30th July, 1916.
MANSFIELD, H.	L/Corpl.	16500	3rd Sept., 1916.
MARKS, F. A.	Private	34409	26th Oct., 1917.
MARLOW, A. E.	Private	15-1371	23rd July, 1916.
MARLOW, H.	Private	34471	16th April, 1918.
MARSH, G. W.	Private	17293	26th Oct., 1917.
MARSHALL, J. H.	Private	17740	7th May, 1917.
MARSHALL, W. P.	Private	35311	14th April, 1918.

Roll of Honour

Name.	Rank.	Regimental No.	Date of Death.
MARTIN, A. J. S.	Private	50261	27th Sept., 1918.
MARTIN, J. A.	Private	28408	18th May, 1917.
MARTIN, W. C.	Private	14-1720	23rd July, 1916.
MAY, W. F.	Sergeant	16630	24th May, 1918.
MAYCOCK, W. J.	Private	23905	5th March, 1919.
MAYRICK, T.	Private	17806	28th Sept., 1916.
MCGOWN, H.	Private	34121	11th Nov., 1917.
MCKEY, M. C.	Corporal	948	11th Oct., 1917.
MCQUAY, F.	Private	215	30th July, 1916.
MEDLOCK, E.	Corporal	30170	12th Sept., 1916.
MEESE, W. H.	Private	50467	10th May, 1918.
MENDHAM, P. W.	Private	30172	3rd Sept., 1916.
MERCER, H. N.	Corporal	14-1491	23rd July, 1916.
MERRICK, A. S.	Private	949	23rd July, 1916.
MERRICK, T.	Private	9238	28th Aug., 1916.
MILLAR, D.	Private	16-948	26th Aug., 1918.
MILLS, H.	Private	16-1946	30th Aug., 1916.
MILLS, H. F.	Private	14-1147	23rd July, 1916.
MILLWARD, J. H.	Private	1075	30th July, 1916.
MILTON, C.	Private	30165	7th May, 1917.
MITCHELL, A.	L/Corpl.	16-2042	28th Aug., 1918.
MOMBER, H.	Corporal	16-1500	30th July, 1916.
MONTGOMERY, A.	Private	21139	26th Oct., 1917.
MOON, A.	Private	17033	3rd Sept., 1916.
MOONEY, N.	Private	32474	2nd May, 1918.
MORGAN, W.	Private	17517	13th April, 1918.
MORLEY, E. W.	L/Corpl.	40	23rd July, 1916.
MORRIS, J.	Private	14-1248	3rd Aug., 1916.
MORRIS, S.	Private	34951	27th Sept., 1918.
MOULDING, A.	Private	14-1474	30th July, 1916.
MOULTON, E. J.	Private	34110	11th Nov., 1917.
MOUNTNEY, J.	Private	14-1307	23rd July, 1916.
MOUSLEY, H. G.	Private	16941	3rd Sept., 1916.
MUCKLOW, C. W.	Private	17942	30th July, 1916.
MULLIS, H.	A/Corpl.	7923	3rd Sept., 1916.
MURPHY, A. D.	Private	14-1638	23rd July, 1916.
MURRELL, P. C.	Private	32471	4th Oct., 1917.
NEALE, D.	Private	14-1318	22nd July, 1916.
NEGUS, P. A.	Private	30269	26th Oct., 1917.
NELSON, A.	Private	14-1623	30th July, 1916.
NEWBERRY, F. W.	Private	192	14th April, 1918.
NEWEY, H. (D.C.M.)	A/Sergt.	305886	18th Aug., 1918.
NEWMAN, A.	Private	42137	27th Sept., 1918.
NEWMAN, J. A.	Private	24638	27th Sept., 1918.
NEWTON, C.	Private	34097	27th Jan., 1918.
NEWTON, G.	Private	8748	26th Oct., 1917.

The First Birmingham Battalion in the Great War

Name.	Rank.	Regimental No.	Date of Death.
NIBLETT, A. T.	Private	235170	27th Sept., 1918.
NICKLESS, W. J.	Corporal	953	23rd July, 1916.
NICKSON, S.	Private	44	23rd July, 1916.
NIX, J.	Private	14–1330	23rd July, 1916.
NOAK, A.	Private	17530	27th Sept., 1916.
NODEN, F. W.	L/Corpl.	456	23rd July, 1916.
NORTH, G. H.	Private	25367	13th April, 1918.
NORTH, W. J.	Private	45	23rd July, 1916.
NORTHFIELD, C.	Private	35171	30th Aug., 1918.
NORTON, H. J.	Private	1070	18th May, 1916.
NURSE, J. J.	Private	16–1736	3rd Sept., 1916.
O'DOWD, B.	Private	21141	18th May, 1917.
OGBURN, H.	Private	14967	30th July, 1916.
OLDHAM, H. H.	Private	35904	28th Sept., 1918.
OLIVER, G.	Private	14–1665	28th Aug., 1918.
OLIVER, H. T.	Private	792	3rd Sept., 1916.
OLLEY, W. B.	Private	35797	17th Sept., 1918.
ONIONS, W. L.	Private	816	23rd July, 1916.
ORME, J.	Private	20731	4th June, 1917.
OWEN, W.	Private	28412	20th May, 1917.
OXFORD, A.	Corporal	16045	23rd Aug., 1918.
OXTON, S.	Private	33706	13th April, 1918.
PACKER, E. G.	L/Corpl.	35323	26th Sept., 1918.
PALMER, A.	Private	32562	26th Oct., 1917.
PARKER, C. W.	Private	30224	3rd Sept., 1916.
PARKER, E. H.	Private	17070	28th July, 1916.
PARKES, H. T.	Private	16–1592	13th April, 1918.
PARSONS, C. W.	Private	22497	9th Feb., 1917.
PAYNE, W.	Private	3985	3rd Sept., 1916.
PEACH, H.	Private	470	23rd July, 1916.
PEARCE, G.	Private	330529	24th May, 1918.
PEARCE, H. W.	Private	15–1487	21st July, 1916.
PEARSON, A. W.	Private	904	3rd Sept., 1916.
PEGG, T.	Private	17497	3rd Sept., 1916.
PILLING, W. A.	Private	28463	10th Nov., 1917.
PENN, W. J.	Private	34276	27th Aug., 1918.
PERKS, R.	Private	16785	7th July, 1917.
PERKINS, C. L.	Private	1423	11th Sept., 1916.
PERRY, P. H.	L/Sergt.	15–1401	23rd July, 1916.
PHELPS, A. C.	Private	40700	24th Aug., 1918.
PHELPS, W. H.	Private	17550	30th July, 1916.
PHILLIPS, A. H.	Sergeant	14–1628	3rd Sept., 1916.
PILGRIM, A. C.	Private	18314	4th Oct., 1918.
PINCHIN, W. H.	Private	125	23rd July, 1916.
PITTS, A.	Private	3689	16th Jan., 1919.
PLATT, S. W.	Private	14–126	23rd July, 1916.

Roll of Honour

Name.	Rank.	Regimental No.	Date of Death.
POOLE, F.	Private	20895	24th April, 1917.
POOLE, F. G.	Private	27398	27th Sept., 1918.
POOLE, L. A.	Private	35910	27th Sept., 1918.
POPE, H.	Private	30270	3rd Sept., 1916.
PORTCH, R. D.	Private	32555	13th Oct., 1917.
POWELL, J.	Private	36528	27th Sept., 1918.
POWELL, J.	Corporal	27290	26th Oct., 1917.
POWELL, W.	Private	16–1398	23rd July, 1916.
POWELL, W. A.	Private	1001	23rd July, 1916.
POWER, B. C.	L/Corpl.	296	23rd July, 1916.
PRESCOTT, T. P.	Private	119	23rd July, 1916.
PRESTON, W. A.	L/Corpl.	131	23rd July, 1916.
PRETTY, W. H.	Private	35329	14th April, 1918.
PRICE, J. E. C.	Private	295	23rd July, 1916.
PRICE, J.	A/Sergt.	962	1st Sept., 1916.
PRICE, J. W.	Private	967	3rd Sept., 1916.
PRIDMORE, H. A.	Private	22532	27th Sept., 1918.
PRITCHARD, F.	L/Corpl.	21959	18th May, 1917.
PROUD, A. E.	Private	1201	30th July, 1916.
PRYER, A. O.	Private	23418	6th May, 1917.
QUARTON, P. B. D.	Private	16819	3rd Sept., 1916.
QUINN, W. E.	Private	25390	28th Aug., 1918.
RAFFERTY, E. P.	Private	38252	27th Sept., 1918.
RANFORD, W. H.	Private	43687	27th Sept., 1918.
RANN, L. C.	Private	35331	13th April, 1918.
RAVENSCROFT, J. S.	Private	36527	27th Sept., 1918.
RAYMOND, A.	Private	30226	3rd Sept., 1916.
READER, C. E.	L/Corpl.	32481	27th Sept., 1918.
REED, F. A.	Private	30227	24th April, 1917.
REID, J.	L/Corpl.	15–1511	11th May, 1917.
REID, J.	Private	34435	1st June, 1918.
RHODES, J. P.	Private	39085	8th July, 1918.
RICHARDS, D.	Private	1218	3rd Sept., 1916.
RICHARDS, T. H.	Private	972	20th Sept., 1918.
RICHARDSON, W. T.	Private	20854	7th May, 1917.
RICKETTS, W.	Private	14–1405	23rd July, 1916.
RIDER, F.	A/Corpl.	833	3rd Sept., 1916.
RIDGWAY, A.	Private	34098	27th Oct., 1917.
RIDLEY, R. G.	Private	35332	13th April, 1918.
RIGG, L.	Corporal	48298	27th Sept., 1918.
RILEY, T.	Private	976	23rd July, 1916.
ROBBINS, T. H.	Private	28477	27th Feb., 1918.
ROBERT, C. T.	Corporal	50423	8th July, 1918.
ROBERTS, G. A.	Private	14–1501	23rd July, 1916.
ROBERTSON, J.	Private	34124	26th Oct., 1917.
ROBINSON, A. J.	Private	17537	30th July, 1916.

The First Birmingham Battalion in the Great War

Name.	Rank.	Regimental No.	Date of Death.
ROBINSON, J.	Corporal	1173	27th Sept., 1916.
ROBINSON, V. A.	Private	34962	26th Oct., 1917.
ROE, F. H.	Private	9	30th July, 1916.
ROGERS, F. R.	L/Corpl.	1203	23rd July, 1916.
ROSE, J. W.	A/Sergt.	483	3rd Sept., 1916.
ROSENTHALL, L. M.	Private	484	23rd July, 1916.
ROWAN, W. J.	Private	14-1414	23rd July, 1916.
ROWCROFT, G. A.	Sergeant	33	23rd July, 1916.
ROWLANDS, T. S.	Private	16-1944	23rd July, 1916.
RUDD, O.	L/Corpl.	486	23rd July, 1916.
RUSHTON, T.	Private	34109	11th Nov., 1917.
RUSSELL, L.	Private	9114	13th April, 1918.
RUSSELL, W. G.	Sergeant	993	26th Oct., 1917.
SABIN, H.	Private	703	4th Aug., 1916.
SABIN, T. E.	Private	36113	27th Sept., 1918.
SACKETT, F. H.	Private	14-1416	20th Sept., 1916.
SALT, G. G.	L-Corpl.	14-1271	3rd Sept., 1916.
SANDERS, F.	Private	20094	26th Oct., 1917.
SANDERS, T. F. P.	Private	272	20th April, 1916.
SAUNDERS, J. E. A. (M.M.)	Private	1446	29th May, 1918.
SAUNTER, H. C.	Private	21149	27th Sept., 1918.
SCARBOROUGH, R. J.	Private	714	24th Sept., 1916.
SCARFF, A. E.	Private	33708	14th April, 1918.
SCOTT, R. W.	Private	274	3rd Sept., 1916.
SEABROOK, F. G.	Private	32490	23rd May, 1918.
SELLARS, F.	L/Corpl.	30228	11th Sept., 1916.
SEVERN, E. C.	Private	14-1614	3rd Sept., 1916.
SEYMOUR, S. H.	Private	35340	14th April, 1918.
SHARPLES, W. A.	Private	18155	3rd Sept., 1916.
SHARPS, E. W. S.	Private	35342	14th April, 1918.
SHATTOCK, G. H.	Private	27356	8th May, 1917.
SHELDON, G. W. A.	Private	141255	23rd July, 1916.
SHENTON, H. E.	L/Sergt.	799	27th Aug., 1916.
SHINTON, G. H.	Corporal	34964	23rd Aug., 1918.
SHORE, J. H.	Private	35343	14th April, 1918.
SHUTT, H.	Private	203792	14th April, 1918.
SICE, W. C.	Private	14-1338	3rd Sept., 1916.
SILK, B. W.	Private	15-1415	23rd July, 1916.
SILK, E. G.	Private	80	20th Sept., 1918.
SIMMONS, E.	Private	14-1527	23rd July, 1916.
SIMMONS, J. A.	Sergeant	214	23rd July, 1916.
SIMPSON, W.	Private	30229	3rd Sept., 1916.
SINCLAIR, W.	Private	30331	3rd Sept., 1916.
SKELSEY, F.	A/Sergt.	289	3rd Sept., 1916.
SKIDMORE, F. A.	L/Corpl.	15-1459	3rd Sept., 1916.

Roll of Honour

Name.	Rank.	Regimental No.	Date of Death.
SLOUGH, P. C.	Sergeant	14–789	23rd July, 1916.
SMALLWOOD, J. W.	Private	712	21st July, 1916.
SMITH, A.	Private	371	9th May, 1917.
SMITH, A.	Private	32568	14th April, 1918.
SMITH, A. B.	Private	17637	3rd Sept., 1916.
SMITH, A. O.	Private	254	23rd July, 1916.
SMITH, A. W.	Private	14–1444	23rd July, 1916.
SMITH, C. E.	Private	708	23rd July, 1916.
SMITH, D.	Private	14–1387	28th July, 1916.
SMITH, G.	Private	18068	3rd Sept., 1916.
SMITH, J. A.	Private	17071	8th May, 1917.
SMITH, J. B.	Private	1764	3rd Sept., 1916.
SMITH, J. B.	Private	21	23rd July, 1916.
SMITH, J. H.	Private	30236	3rd Sept., 1916.
SMITH, J. W.	Private	30288	3rd Sept., 1916.
SMITH, S.	Private	144	17th March, 1916.
SMITH, S. F.	Private	235227	27th Sept., 1918.
SMITH, W.	Private	35351	13th April, 1918.
SMITH, W. G.	Private	987	23rd July, 1916.
SMITH, W. H.	Private	17415	30th July, 1916.
SMITH, W. H.	Private	42742	29th Oct., 1918.
SMITH, W. J.	Sergeant	28048	7th May, 1917.
SOWERBY, W.	Private	25721	5th July, 1918.
SPALL, H.	Private	331334	17th Sept., 1918.
STANLEY, C.	Private	17985	28th Aug., 1916.
STANLEY, J.	Private	11677	23rd Aug., 1918.
STANWORTH, G.	Private	36018	27th Sept., 1918.
STAWFORD, A.	Private	16–1864	23rd July, 1916.
STEVENSON, C.	Private	34411	27th Aug., 1918.
STEVENSON, T. E.	Private	30289	26th Oct., 1917.
STOCKTON, R. H.	L/Corpl.	14818	23rd June, 1917.
STOKES, A.	Private	14471	4th Oct., 1917.
STOKES, A. W.	Private	14–1689	3rd Sept., 1916.
STOKES, J.	Private	15006	3rd Sept., 1916.
STOKES, W. D.	Private	16–1407	23rd July, 1916.
STONE, J.	Private	17700	3rd Sept., 1916.
STORER, E.	Private	28438	7th May, 1917.
STOREY, W. E.	Private	30279	8th May, 1917.
STRATFORD, W. E.	Private	16999	13th Sept., 1916.
STRETTON, C. H.	Private	30335	9th Nov., 1917.
STUBBS, W. E.	Private	996	23rd July, 1916.
STYLES, A. E.	Private	10155	30th July, 1916.
STYLES, E. L.	Private	463	27th July, 1916.
STYLES, F.	Private	14–1756	28th July, 1916.
SUART, R.	Private	29593	27th Aug., 1918.
SUMMERS, W. F.	Private	19	23rd July, 1916.

The First Birmingham Battalion in the Great War

Name.	Rank.	Regimental No.	Date of Death.
SUTER, F. W.	L/Corpl.	10030	26th Oct., 1917.
SUTTON, A. L.	Private	27697	13th Oct., 1916.
SUTTON, A. M.	Private	32486	26th Oct., 1917.
SWEENEY, T.	Private	30476	1st Nov., 1917.
TASKER, E.	Private	16–1405	23rd July, 1916.
TAUNTON, R.	Private	14–1351	23rd July, 1916.
TAYLOR, R. A.	Private	14–1247	24th July, 1916.
TAYLOR, S. A.	L/Corpl.	10395	27th Sept., 1918.
TAYLOR, T. H.	R.S.M.	6317	1st May, 1918.
TAYLOR, W.	Private	15–1291	13th April, 1918.
TAYLOR, W.	Private	14–1606	23rd Aug., 1918.
TAYLOR, W. A.	L/Corpl.	27698	31st March, 1917.
TAYLOR, W. H.	Private	16–1962	30th July, 1916.
TEDMAN, W.	Corporal	32502	10th Nov., 1917.
TEDSTONE, R. R.	L/Corpl.	746	23rd July, 1916.
TENNANT, H.	Private	32491	26th Oct., 1917.
TERRY, H. A.	Private	28459	7th May, 1917.
THACKWELL, F.	Private	21020	26th Oct., 1917.
THOMPSON, A. E.	Private	76	23rd July, 1916.
THOMPSON, H.	Private	797	23rd July, 1916.
THOMPSON, V. H.	Private	311	23rd July, 1916.
THOMPSON, W.	Private	28446	7th May, 1917.
THOMSON, C. M.	Private	34113	26th Oct., 1917.
THORN, F. E.	Private	14–1443	26th Oct., 1917.
THURSTON, A.	Private	17522	30th July, 1916.
TIERNEY, J. T. F.	Private	82	23rd July, 1916.
TILBURY, W. G.	Corporal	30336	26th Oct., 1917.
TINKNELL, F. G.	Private	35358	14th April, 1918.
TONEY, J. S.	Private	15–1544	23rd July, 1916.
TONGE, J. T.	Private	36524	28th Sept., 1918.
TONGUE, F.	Private	14–1551	23rd July, 1916.
TONKS, W. H.	L/Corpl.	4072	20th May, 1917.
TOVEY, P.	Private	28422	27th Sept., 1918.
TOYE, L.	Private	267989	1st Sept., 1918.
TRANTER, A.	Sergeant	312	21st July, 1916.
TRANTER, A. S.	Private	22215	6th May, 1917.
TREBLE, W. H.	Private	27734	3rd Dec., 1916.
TREGLOWN, R. C.	Private	1000	23rd July, 1916.
TRICKETT, A.	Private	26204	28th Aug., 1918.
TRICKETT, C.	Private	17534	8th May, 1917.
TROMAN, C. G.	Private	83	23rd July, 1916.
TROWMAN, A.	Private	14–999	4th Aug., 1916.
TRUEMAN, W.	Private	28450	26th Oct., 1917.
TURLEY, D. E.	Private	14–1459	31st July, 1916.
TURNER, A.	Private	203718	14th April, 1918.
TURNER, A. L. H.	Private	16–1557	28th Nov., 1916.

Roll of Honour

Name.	Rank.	Regimental No.	Date of Death.
Tustin, J.	L/Corpl.	36116	13th Sept., 1918.
Tustin, S. A.	Private	14–313	6th Aug., 1916.
Twittey, G.	Private	14716	24th Jan., 1917.
Tyler, E.	Private	32492	4th Oct., 1917.
Vallis, N. A. J.	Private	28439	28th Oct., 1917.
Verney, T.	Private	21277	26th Oct., 1917.
Vint, S. A.	Private	94	23rd July, 1916.
Virr, S.	Sergeant	1144	8th May, 1917.
Waddup, W.	Private	18467	30th July, 1916.
Wakelin, H. S.	Private	719	19th May, 1915.
Wales, B. W.	L-Corpl.	1025	23rd July, 1916.
Walker, E. A.	L/Corpl.	14–1862	23rd July, 1916.
Walker, E. S.	Private	9507	8th Nov., 1917.
Walker, O. J.	Private	25120	14th April, 1918.
Walker, T.	Private	32586	26th Oct., 1917.
Walkley, V. N.	Private	14–1509	23rd July, 1916.
Wallis, H. J.	Private	32569	26th Oct., 1917.
Wallis, T.	Private	34415	26th Oct., 1917.
Walters, W.	Sergeant	14–1540	3rd Sept., 1916.
Waltho, A.	Private	23161	7th May, 1917.
Ward, W. A.	Private	23495	14th April, 1918.
Warren-Boulton, R.P.	Private	14-496	23rd July, 1916.
Warwood, F. J.	Private	727	30th July, 1916.
Watkins, E. W.	Private	17741	30th July, 1916.
Watson, G.	Corporal	28931	8th July, 1918.
Watson, J. S.	L/Corpl.	259	23rd July, 1916.
Watson, W.	Private	21055	8th May, 1917.
Watts, G. R. E.	A/Corpl.	30233	3rd Sept., 1916.
Watts, M. H.	Private	32548	26th Oct., 1917.
Weatherhead, J.	Sergeant	1086	23rd July, 1916.
Webb, G. A.	Private	17683	30th July, 1916.
Webb, J.	Private	20734	4th June, 1917.
Webb, S. I.	A/Corpl.	15449	3rd Sept., 1916.
Webber, G. L.	Private	260446	17th Sept., 1918.
Wells, J. T.	L/Corpl.	33746	17th Sept., 1918.
Westwood, W. A.	Private	30087	27th Sept., 1918.
Whatley, W.	Private	33720	27th Feb., 1918.
Wheeler, E.	Sergeant	7839	28th Sept., 1918.
Whiley, W.	Private	14–1462	30th July, 1916.
Whitbrook, E. J.	Private	14–1635	23rd July, 1916.
Whitcombe, B.	L/Corpl.	785	3rd Sept., 1916.
White, F.	Private	27194	23rd May, 1918.
White, J. R.	Private	30349	1st Oct., 1917.
White, R. T.	Private	34965	25th Oct., 1917.
Whitehouse, W. T.	Private	665	22nd July, 1916.
Whittaker, N. E.	Private	14–1426	26th July, 1916.

The First Birmingham Battalion in the Great War

Name.	Rank.	Regimental No.	Date of Death.
WHITTET, F.	Private	30337	3rd Sept., 1916.
WICKENS, A. E.	Private	50409	27th Sept., 1918.
WICKS, H. J.	Private	16694	30th July, 1916.
WILCOX, L. C.	Private	15–1367	23rd July, 1916.
WILLCOCK, R. C.	Corporal	285	23rd July, 1916.
WILLETTS, G.	Private	24787	29th Sept., 1918.
WILLETS, G. J.	Private	43703	27th Sept., 1918.
WILLIAMS, A. H.	Private	17730	30th July, 1916.
WILLIAMS, A. J.	Private	1328	23rd July, 1916.
WILLIAMS, C.	Private	21264	7th Nov., 1917.
WILLIAMS, E.	L/Corpl.	9219	26th Oct., 1917.
WILLIAMS, E. W. (M.M.)	Sergeant	281	23rd July, 1916.
WILLIAMS, G. W.	Private	43714	27th Sept., 1918.
WILLIAMS, H. C.	Private	14–1240	20th Jan., 1918.
WILLIAMS, J.	Private	36117	27th Sept., 1918.
WILLIAMS, J. A.	Private	19288	22nd Oct., 1917.
WILLIAMS, T.	Private	14–1402	23rd July, 1916.
WILLIS, P. W.	Private	16–1474	29th May, 1918.
WILSDON, F. G.	Private	17395	3rd Sept., 1916.
WINSBURY, A. C.	Private	15–1662	13th April, 1918.
WINCUP, J.	Private	15956	26th Oct., 1917.
WINDRES, W.	Private	17638	13th April, 1918.
WINDRIDGE, H.	Private	288	23rd July, 1916.
WITCOMBE, R. A.	Private	1020	23rd July, 1916.
WOOD, A. V.	Private	14–1305	23rd July, 1916.
WOOD, G.	Private	16755	8th May, 1917.
WOOD, J. C.	Private	36023	8th July, 1918.
WOOD, S.	Private	30378	3rd Sept., 1916.
WOODSTOCK, F. A.	Private	286	3rd Feb., 1918.
WOODWARD, H.	L/Corpl.	723	6th June, 1917.
WOOKEY, E.	Private	14–1502	23rd July, 1916.
WORTH, C.	Private	28040	26th Oct., 1917.
WRIGHT, A.	Private	288	23rd July, 1916.
WRIGHT, A.	Corporal	32582	4th Oct., 1917.
WRIGHT, E.	Private	17489	3rd Sept., 1916.
WRIGHT, R. A.	Sergeant	662	13th April, 1918.
WYATT, F. J.	Private	14–1693	23rd July, 1916.
WYNESS, J. T. W.	Private	23238	24th Oct., 1917.
YATES, P. W.	L/Corpl.	28052	24th May, 1918.
YEANDLE, H. W.	Corporal	664	20th May, 1917.
YOUNG, H. A.	Private	34416	26th Oct., 1917.
YOUNG, H. L.	Private	34203	26th Oct., 1917.

PERSONAL NOTES.

PERSONAL NOTES.

www.ingramcontent.com/pod-product-compliance
Lightning Source LLC
Chambersburg PA
CBHW070840160426
43192CB00012B/2256